Wildwoods Child

Best Wishes to Beth

Thanks for your
support.

Dianne Gillespie

# Wildwoods Child

## Book One of The Lost Women Series

D.D. Gillespie

# Contents

# Author Information

Cover art by Sherry Andrychuk

**ISBN: 13:978-1522957-45-4**
ISBN: 10: 1522957-45-6

Author Contact:

DDGillespie@thelostwomen.com

www.thelostwomen.com

# Acknowledgements

I would like to thank R. H. (Dick) Waller Supt. Ret., RCMP, for his invaluable assistance in demystifying the everyday running of an RCMP detachment and for being so generous in sharing his ideas for contacts within the law enforcement community.

Linda Breault has generously provided feedback on the role of social workers and public health as well as reading and commenting on the story itself. I must also thank Christine and Andy Bateman whose thoughtful feedback offered valuable advice on improving tension and human interest. Stewart Brady, a knowledgeable outdoorsman who has a thorough knowledge of life in the Skeena watershed, has been a thoughtful and helpful critic of the story.

Finally, I owe more appreciation than I can express to my editor, Luanne Armstrong, whose encouragement prompted me to keep writing, and whose experience and patience helped steer me past many difficulties.

# Dedication

To Stewart who has been so patient as I stumbled towards the completion of this novel.

# Illustrations

*Layout of Bar-T Ranch*

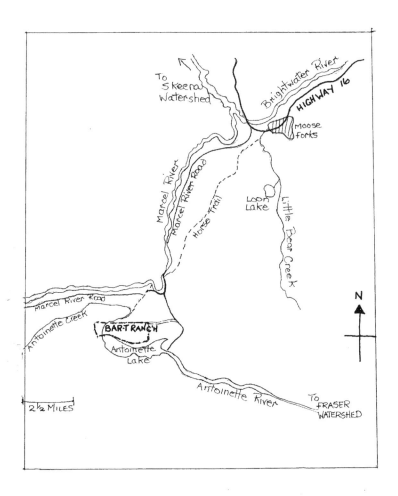

*Setting Of Wildwoods Child*

# 1

## Nora

She settled back into her seat as the Prince George railway station receded into the distance. Constable Nora Macpherson, rattling across the British Columbia Interior riding coach on the "Rupert Rocket", took up the handbook she had just bought from a rack in the station: *Wild BC: The Only Guide You'll Ever Need to the Skeena River Basin.* The cover displayed scenery different from the flatlands she could see from the window. Her imagination focused on visions of the rugged geography to come. She wondered when she would see the mountains again. Determined to spend the time profitably, she opened the guide to see what it offered about the area around her new posting.

"Throughout this country, a network of gravel county roads connects the ranches of the backcountry and the dairy farms of the bottomland. These are also the roads that connect the logging bush camps and mines to the outside world. When the snows come in mid-October, the roads become accessible only to four-wheel drive vehicles that manage well-enough as long as the roads are regularly used by logging semis and ore trucks. Otherwise, they are mostly impassable until April. Spring, the season of mud, lasts well into May.

"The surrounding terrain is rugged, with snow-capped mountains whose lower slopes are covered with a mix of lodge pole pine and spruce. The valley bottoms spread out in narrow swaths along these rivers with a larger expanse of arable land at the confluence of the major streams. The creeks and rivers teem with trout, steelhead and, in the fall, salmon.

"Crossing the area spanning from Edmonton to Prince Rupert is Highway 16, the BC segment of the Yellowhead Highway."

Nora closed the guide book and gazed speculatively at the forested landscape hurtling past her train window. Her first real posting! This wasn't the Prairies anymore, certainly a long way from Winnipeg or Regina. Her mind ranged back to her graduation from the RCMP cadet-training program in Regina and her six months field coaching in Edmonton. Her first real job! She hoped she was ready for it, and they were ready for her.

She flipped open her Advisement of Posting letter. She was ordered to report to Sergeant J. Wasniki, Moose Forks Detachment in the North District of "E" Division – or British Columbia, as most Canadians called it.

Having graduated from the first-ever cohort of female RCMP recruits, Nora was now the first woman Mountie in this part of Canada. She hoped that this Sergeant Wasniki was a flexible, affable type. Surely, the brass wouldn't have placed her there otherwise. Her reverie was broken as a furry brown blur crowned by an impossibly bulky set of antlers whizzed by. A moose stood grazing at the shallow edge of a swamp. Her mind lit up with the possibilities of what else lay in wait – cougars, wolves, bears.

Transfixed by the possibility of more wildlife sightings, Nora kept her eyes glued to the landscape until the train pulled into Moose Forks Station.

# 2

# The Wildwoods Child

"Teresa Talbot?"

A startling pair of China blue eyes riveted first on the exit, and then on Mrs. Clarke's enamel belt buckle.

"Teresa, you haven't finished writing in all the spaces here. Come on. There." Abby pointed to blank spaces on the paper. "Both your parents' names at least. Why don't I write the information for you, just for today, to save time?" Abby Clarke saw the barely decipherable chicken scratches on the page as mute testimony to the effort already expended. Her instincts told her some kindly help was needed.

Tess's response, when it finally came, was surprising in its intensity. Her jaw worked, but she failed to utter a sound; her pinched face contorted as her eyes flew about the room seeking a likely refuge. In the end, her gaze lit on the paper in front of her and rested there, stony and glacial.

For the first time, Abby considered the girl in detail. She was a bit of a beanpole really, at that ungainly thirteen-year-old stage of mostly angles and bony outcroppings. But her skin was alabaster fair, so transparent that the dark tracery of the forehead veins could be easily discerned. Her eyes, fringed by a thick curtain of dark eyelashes, blazed an intense blue-violet and her mouth was a tender pout of coral lipstick, somewhat inexpertly applied. She had the look of a young, fairer Elizabeth Taylor waiting for National Velvet, a fragile, incandescent beauty.

"I done all I could, lady."

"But you must know your mother's name?"

"What do you need her name for? She ain't going to be talking to nobody here."

The girl's voice had the curious quality of rustling leaves drifting off into nothingness; Abby leaned closer to be sure she hadn't misheard. She was aware of the gathering undercurrent of snickers developing amongst the other, suddenly attentive homeroom students.

"Tess, that's what you're usually called isn't it? I'm sure your mom will want to talk to us once she sees how well you do, once you start to feel more comfortable. I know she's not well, but think how she'd enjoy hearing about the things you'll be learning.  I know she's been teaching you herself up until now and will want to know that you're continuing as best you can."

Abby's bag of diplomatic tricks was varied if not terribly original. She was picking her way carefully not only to avoid any mention of Mrs. Talbot's worsening cancer, but also to save herself the embarrassment of arousing the legendary wrath of cranky Hank Talbot, who two years before, had yanked the older daughter, Ellie, out of school permanently, citing "interfering do-gooder teachers" as his unshakable rationale.

This morning, before coming to her first homeroom class, Abby hadn't picked up any new details about Tess. She assumed the thirteen year-old was finally in school now for the first time because her mother was even more ill.  Up until now, she had been kept home even when Ellie and Tim, her older sister and brother, had come in for high school. At elementary school age, Tess had been eligible for homeschooling by her mom, who had done the same for the older siblings, but now, for Grade Eight, Abby guessed Tess was being driven the ten-mile gap from their ranch to a rendezvous with the school bus. Abby thought the dark circles under the girls amazing eyes proved how long a day she had already had. She had likely been up since well before dawn just to get to town. She also radiated a pungent mixed-hay-and-manure odor of horse.

"My mom won't be wondering at all, Mrs. Clarke."  She slumped down in her seat, crossed her arms and proceeded to gnaw away at an already angry-looking hangnail on her grubby thumb.

Before Abby could inquire if the mom had been admitted to a hospital (and not before time, she thought, even given the husband's distrust of most public institutions), Trudy Van Heusen, the most chatty, teacher-pleasing child in the room, raised her hand.

"Ah, Mrs. Clarke, her mom passed away late last spring?" Like many teen-aged girls, Trudy often spoke a sentence curled up at the end in question, even when none was intended. "I mean, she has to come to school now whether she wants to or not, you know?"

A chorus of guffaws erupted from some of the bigger boys. Abby heard disjointed mutters of "cops fined him" and, "he planted the old lady." Tess reacted by collapsing into a bony, shuddering heap, her arms flung over her curly black head to stop her ears, her fingers clutching convulsively at the sleeves of her well-worn jean jacket.

Abby, stunned as much by her own inept handling of the situation as by the tragic content of the girl's loss, cursed under her breath and shook her head, as if to forestall any further unfolding of the drama in her crowded classroom. Dammit! How she disliked the paperwork of the first week of school. Why wasn't the news of the mother's death in that school file, for Pete's sake! She hated being out of the loop. No doubt, if she hadn't been away all summer in Vancouver at UBC, she might have heard the news herself. More than her own ignorance, she regretted that she couldn't bring herself to accept the ignorance – no that wasn't it –the fierce independence of these back-country people who reckoned success in terms of cattle and hay crops and who saw kids as little more than farmhands. She felt real compassion for this delicate sliver of a child, and great frustration at having been the inadvertent cause of her public display of grief. Maybe someday, Abby thought, she'd be able to read the warning signs more clearly, be able to walk on eggs with more dexterity. Just now, all she could manage was to pat the girl's shoulder as she told the rest of the homeroom class to take their break early. She smiled at Trudy and waved her out of the room as well, even though the girl's bright eyes said she had more to offer.

With the room clear, Abby tried to make amends, hauling some tissue out of her purse and remaining quiet as the girl recovered composure. "I don't know what else to say except I'm sorry, Tess. About your mom of course, but also for not realizing just why you were coming to school. We all just assumed your dad had realized it was time to give your mom a break from teaching you at home, because she's been so ill."

Tess raised her head and stared in blatant confusion at the woman sitting in the student's desk beside her. Her astonishing eyes, thickly fringed with black lashes, no longer spoke of clear mountain lakes but of cloudy spring run-off.

"You're telling me you're sorry, Mrs. Clarke? My dad says you teachers never say you're wrong. Fact is, I can't even read any of the stuff on this paper. My mom gave up teaching me a couple of years ago. She said I should tend the horses. That was before she was took real bad." She relapsed into her slouch.

Abby Clarke sighed sympathetically and sought some ground for optimism. "Of course you can read, Tess. We have all your last year's grades from the correspondence courses in the office, and they're pretty good ones too, as I recall."

For the first time, Tess laughed out loud, a hoarse chortling. "Sure, they're good! Ellie ain't dumb like me! Her and Dad fixed it up once Mom got so bad she didn't care what happened. Ellie done all that school stuff, and I done the horses," she summed up proudly.

A public address announcement split the silence. "All grades please report to the gym for a brief assembly that will last about twenty minutes. Dismissal will follow, and regular classes beginning tomorrow."

Dumbfounded, Abby was only dimly aware of the staccato of Teresa's high-heeled cowboy boots exiting the classroom. Damn! Abby had forgotten the assembly was scheduled this morning. She hustled to the women's staff washroom on her way to the gym.

The assembly would be just the usual first-week-of-school reminders and "tone-setters", but the staff would be introduced, and she wanted to see if she looked as frazzled as she felt. The woman in the mirror indeed did look a bit startled: her hazel eyes peered back at her with a quizzical, slightly manic expression; the round, open face framed in curly, light-brown, shoulder-length hair featured a dusting of freckles dotting her slightly snubbed nose. After she lipsticked her generous mouth, Abby fluffed her hair with her fingers and ruefully grinned at the slightly madcap appearance created. That's as good as it gets, folks! She then straightened her turquoise sweater set to minimize her ample bosom before venturing into the throng of students in the hallway.

As she threaded her way towards the gym, she considered her encounter with Tess. She would have to ask around to find out what she could. The girl's lack of hygiene and general air of fatigue were red flags for sure! And her illiteracy! Why hadn't her skill-level been checked out? Squaring her shoulders, Abby determined to follow up.

The hubbub in the gym was the usual chorus of teens greeting each other after a summer apart. They settled onto the bleachers quickly, eager to enjoy their free afternoon as soon as possible. Abby found her seat among the ones set aside for staff in the front row of the bleachers. She waved cheerfully to teachers she hadn't seen all summer and settled in to listen to the principal's welcome.

Tom Cooper, his bald head gleaming in the artificial light, stood behind his podium and waited for their chatter to die down. He hadn't been a principal too long, just three years, so the first school-wide assembly of the year was still a source of some anxiety for him. He grinned at the audience and gave the thumbs up to a few of the taller boys as they appeared. Mr. Cooper was also the basketball coach, and liked everyone to know it.

"Good morning, everyone, students, teachers. Oh, you too, Mr. Lavergne. Glad you could make it!"

The kids all chuckled good-naturedly. They all focused their gaze on Vice Principal Phil Lavergne leaning against the end of the bleachers. He was laughing and red-faced from running in late.

"And while we're at it, let's show our appreciation for our dedicated teachers, back again to help you achieve your best this year. You've just met Mr. Lavergne, our vice-principal. He'll help you get to class on time!" The crowd erupted in good-natured laughter acknowledging the irony of his late arrival at the assembly as well as the disciplinary role for any vice principal. "Next, in alphabetical order, our hardworking teaching staff, first, Mrs. Abby Clarke who will handle English Eight and Learning Assistance, then Mr. Eaton…" The list was two-dozen names long. The announcement of each name was greeted variably but positively, with either polite applause or some appreciative hoots. The atmosphere of the assembly became more and more upbeat and relaxed.

"Anyway," Cooper continued after the last staff member had been introduced, "more seriously, I want to remind you of the important expectations we have here at Moose Forks High School…"

His speech about the usual concerns – attendance, effort, and achievement – was long-winded and clichéd. They had heard it all before, and among the students, a dull undercurrent of boredom was on the verge of bubbling up into open chatter when Mr. Cooper startled everyone with a sharp fist bang on the podium.

"What I am about to say is very serious! There should be no one talking except me!"

When the audience settled into shocked silence, he continued, "I have decided to take this opportunity to remind you about a disappearance that occurred a year ago last spring. The person who went missing was a young woman not much older than any of you. Her name was Monica. Her body was found not too far from here in Terrace, just up Highway 16." He paused for effect. "Now, we know she used to live here and moved away just before this happened. I'm sure some of you knew her. I need to remind you that her death was not an accident. She was murdered."

Cooper stopped for a moment to allow his words to sink in. He knew this wasn't really news, but RCMP Sergeant Wasniki had okayed his idea to remind the students of the crime. The students stared back. His words, unadorned and unpleasant, echoed in the large space of the gymnasium. A few of the girls looked on the verge of tears. A couple of the older boys were smirking.

"The local RCMP has asked me to remind you that the killer has not been caught. We, of course, hope whoever did this terrible crime has left the area, but we can't be sure. So, all of you, boys as well as girls…" He fixed a flinty gaze on the sulky big boys in the back row. "All of you, keep your eyes open and use common sense. Particularly, and I mean this very seriously, don't be caught hitchhiking on the highway." A bubble of objection arose from the older ranks in the back of the bleachers. "I know you all think it's no big deal. All the kids, even some adults do it, but the truth is that it's stupid!" The harsh word echoed in the rafters of the gym, hanging over the assembly like an ugly slur. Somewhere, a nervous kid coughed, and Cooper continued, "You don't know who could be driving through! You can't be sure until it's too late." He raised his voice to signal his final point. "So watch out for each other and don't give some stranger a chance to hurt you.

"Okay, we have an early dismissal, now. See you all bright and early tomorrow!"

The crowd erupted into a cacophony of shrieks and bantering as the kids descended from the bleachers and exited the gym.

Abby herself was in shock. She had also forgotten about that girl. She wondered if such a dire message should be broadcast on the first day of school. It cast a pall over a normally upbeat day. Still, if she had forgotten, the kids would need reminding too. She wandered back to the office area mulling over the best person to ask about Tess Talbot.

# 3

# Nora Settles In

Just a few minutes away across town, the Moose Forks RCMP detachment office was finally quiet. The Labour Day long weekend had been the usual hectic mix of speed traps and crash investigations. Nora had pulled an extra shift right away, with little time for orientation or social chitchat.

Her first impression was that the detachment was a tightly-run outfit, and its sergeant, Jack Wasniki, a tense guy. He had been cordial but distant during her first interactions, a bit uneasy around women. She wondered what his background was. He had an impressive physical presence, a barrel chest, powerful arms and shoulders, and a kind of bulldog aspect to his head. His close-cropped sandy hair was showing grey at the temples. No doubt though, his most remarkable feature was a prominent, misshapen nose whose surface was marred by pockmarks and enlarged blood vessels. Nora had to remind herself not to stare when she spoke to him; privately, she wondered if Wasniki had been a boxer with a drinking problem.

The rest of the staff in the detachment seemed friendly enough. Corporal Jed Fedoruk, her designated mentor and immediate superior, was a bit older, a ten-year veteran. He had lived in Moose Flats for three of those years and was making it home. He had married a local girl, Marnie, and they were the proud parents of a one-year-old boy. Jed and Marnie had helped Nora find her studio apartment above the local real estate office.

At the office, Jed was second-in-command after the sergeant, and to Nora, Jed seemed easygoing but efficient. Nothing seemed to annoy Jed or be too much trouble. Although he was not handsome in the glossy movie star sense, he smiled easily with a disarming lop-sided grin that produced deep dimples in both cheeks. A swatch of soft black hair fell across a broad forehead. He was well-groomed with a baritone so rich that Nora had to resist the urge to immerse herself in the sound. At thirty, Jed could claim physical fitness a younger man would envy.

Wasniki left the general day-to-day running of the office to Jed while he handled official liaison duties with other government agencies. The rest of the detachment consisted of eight patrolmen whose main duty was surveillance in the district. They had a fleet of two squad cars and six four-wheel drive trucks with canopies. Generally, they worked alone on all the shifts with the option of using their CB radios to call in back-up if they needed it.

Wasniki had started Nora at the central office reception desk, since their civilian receptionist, Joanie Grey, was on an indefinite medical leave. Nora had wanted to suggest some other civilian be hired temporarily or a volunteer found to answer the phone. She knew that Depot training required that all members be able to type their own reports, so she knew she wasn't needed for steno work. Still, she hesitated to assert herself as she suspected Wasniki was merely trying to keep tabs on his new rookie.

Nora worked closely with Jed to manage the scheduling for the three shifts of detachment cruiser patrols, to handle incoming calls and to act as office clerk. She felt a bit peeved; after all, she was overqualified to be a secretary, and she bridled at the possibility of the stint lasting for long. Still, Jed had assured her that Sergeant Wasniki would no doubt change her assignment once she had familiarized herself with the community.

Turning to the stacks of paper on her desk, she began to browse through recent alerts and bulletins to acquaint herself with the situation around town. Wasniki had told her that her eventual assignment would be as the detachment Education and Community Liaison Officer. Reading the local weekly bulletin, she noted that the high school assembly had included a reminder about the case of a fifteen year-old who had gone missing the previous year near Terrace, just three hours northwest of Moose Forks on Highway 16. She pondered the implications of this unsolved case. The body had been found not that far from Moose Forks. Monica had been strangled. Given the proximity of the find, the perp could be a local. When Nora felt her gut clench, she realized the depth of her revulsion. She remembered what Jed Fedoruk had repeated to her as a matter of fact: whoever had done this was long gone. She halfway hoped he was right, but also knew in her gut that whoever had done it must be caught.

Nora turned her attention to a map showing the layout of Moose Forks. The detachment building sat on Main Street, a broad road where a variety of the town's amenities and businesses could be found: town hall, health clinic, pool hall, restaurants, post office, federal building, and insurance and real estate offices. The street ran at right angles to Highway 16 and wound its way up the bluff behind the original town site in a general southwest direction to the new subdivision of detached, semi-detached and row houses constructed since the lumber mill had opened several years before. On the other side of the highway ran the Brightwater River, famous worldwide for steelhead trout and salmon runs. It flowed roughly northwest towards the town of Glacier Lake and eventually into the huge Skeena River that emptied into the Pacific. The confluence of the Brightwater and Little Bear Creek had created a marshy bog less than a quarter mile south east of the town site. Jed had told her that before the area had become so populated, the early settlers sitting on their front porches had shot moose grazing on the marsh vegetation. This remarkable convenience had given the town its name of Moose Forks.

As the town grew, peopled largely after the war by immigrants from the Netherlands, Switzerland and Portugal, the settlement's commercial district had expanded north along the highway following the Brightwater River. Here on the southwest side, was an interior mall with a supermarket and sundry small businesses. Next to it sat the best hotel in town, Jed said, the Driftwood Motel with its attached "Dining Lounge for Fine Eating". Behind, backing onto the mall parking lot was the Moose Forks Pub where an assortment of town characters could be found at all hours. After arriving in late August, Nora had spent her first week staying at the Driftwood before she had moved into her apartment. Although the hotel accommodation had been comfortable, the racket drifting up in waves from the pub had been anything but relaxing.

Across the highway next to the river and on the other side of the railway tracks paralleling the highway, a cluster of brightly painted, small frame houses sat above the riverbed. Here, Jed had told her, lived the Portuguese. They had come to build the railroad and had stayed, the men to work in the small sawmills, mines or whatever labour job they could find, the women to raise babies and support the local Our Lady of the Valley Roman Catholic Church. They were a close-knit group who kept to themselves and obeyed the law. Their most serious infractions were related to the occasional sale of homemade wine or hunting moose out of season. Generally, they were homebodies who painted their houses in riotous combinations of purple, lime green and fuchsia, anything cheerful they said, to combat the dreary greens and greys of the northern landscape.

In huge contrast were the meticulous, sober homes of the Dutch and Swiss families. These were the early founders of the town, residents who had established the successful dairy and beef herds so important to the local economy. Their success as pioneers was evident in both the lush bottomland fields of the farms and ranches dotting the valley surrounding the town, and the spacious new homes the retired older generations were building in the new subdivision on the bluff above the original town site. There they mingled with the new elite, the sawmill supervisors and other professionals – teachers, nurses, social workers – come to service the growing community. Also on the bluff was the new high school with its population of 350 students.

Noise coming from the coffee room reminded Nora that her shift was almost over. She popped into the washroom before the men came to use it after shift. There was supposed to be a separate washroom to accommodate women members, but it hadn't materialized yet.

Eyeing herself in the mirror, she again mused that, except for her grey-green eyes, her face, with its broad cheekbones and slightly slanted brows and eyes, was so much like her mother's had been. Her skin was golden with a scatter of chocolate freckles across her nose and upper cheeks. She was a brunette with auburn streaks, her shoulder-length hair pulled into a regulation chignon. Nora tucked her shirt in and straightened her tie before redoing the buttons of her uniform jacket. She knew she looked slim and fit, but was oblivious of how perfectly the flared jacket and straight skirt accentuated the cello perfection of her back and butt. She had the option of wearing the service tunic and straight leg pants and oxfords, but had opted for the skirt and pumps, partly because Sergeant Wasniki had said he expected her to look like a "lady", and partly because the warm weather justified cooler garments.

As she wandered into the detachment coffee room, Nora mused about the best way to connect at the high school. Two young patrolmen, a year or so senior to Nora, hunched over the table with their cups steaming between their hands.

"Hey, Luke? Is it? I know we met at the staff meeting last week, but I didn't catch everybody's name." She looked from one to the other. Both were still in full gear from their day's work, obviously not planning to stay long, maybe just sharing a coffee to catch up after shift.

Luke shifted to face her as she stood next to the door and poured herself a coffee. "Hi, Cora, I think I heard. Is that right? I didn't pick your name up for sure either."

The sudden blush on her lightly tanned face was visible as she corrected him, "No, actually, it's Nora, Nora Macpherson, Luke. I'm the rookie here." She blushed again upon realizing she was stating the obvious. "I just started this week. Mind if I join you?"

The guffaws that erupted as they opened up the space between them provided some assurance of a welcome. The other patrolman, well over six feet tall, was an open-faced, fair-haired, blue-eyed smiling sort. He waved her over. "Hell, no, we're just chewing the fat here after shift. This is Luke Gallagher, and I'm Eddie Braun. I'm the good-looking, smart one around here!"

Luke looked up in wonderment at the brass of his buddy. Luke was the smaller and more compact of the two, a handsome young man with a well-trimmed head of chestnut hair and an athlete's build. His hazel eyes twinkled and laugh lines sprouted as he met Nora's gaze. "Don't mind him. His mom didn't teach him any manners at all. Come and have a seat." He pulled a chair out for her.

"Would you like a smoke?" Eddie shook an Export A out of a package and offered it to her.

"No, thanks. I've been trying to quit ever since Depot." She smiled with some regret, reckoning they, being young officers themselves, would appreciate the reference to the rigours of basic training. Privately, she felt tense enough to appreciate a cigarette, but she just couldn't do it. It had been a tough year since Depot, and she was positive that cutting way back on smoking had made some of that endurance possible. She was a private smoker now, lighting up only when she was home with a cat that didn't seem to care. She smiled her refusal and settled in to drink her coffee.

"Don't mind if I do?" Eddie waved the cigarette in the air in a speculative fashion before lighting up. Luke waved the furling smoke away.

"So do either of you have any connections up at the high school?" Nora was back to her original purpose for taking a break. Maybe these guys would have some idea of community liaison openings for her.

"The high school? I know a teacher at the elementary. She said she'd go out with me if she ever got caught up with her school stuff. How's that for an excuse?" Eddie laughed at the absurdity. "That's as original as turning down a date to shampoo her hair!"

Luke, ignoring Eddie's good-natured grousing, followed up on Nora's question. "I know the principal a bit. Tom Cooper. He's a good guy. I worked with him last winter helping with the senior boys' basketball team. That's a good way in. Offer to volunteer with a girls' sports team, maybe."

Nora flashed him an appreciative grin. "Thanks, Luke. Good idea! The only problem is that my sports were swimming and field hockey. Do they have those teams?" She was realizing that the climate and community probably didn't lend themselves to very much in the way of water sports.

Luke chuckled, "There's no swimming pool in Moose Forks and field hockey, around here, that'd be just weird! Girls' hockey is a possibility. Do you skate? I work with the midget boys' hockey team whenever I can. I know there are girls who want to play, too, but there's no coach. Or do you play volleyball?"

Nora shook her head, "Oh, well. At least I know the high school principal's name. Thanks for your help. I suppose another possibility is to get to know a teacher?" Luke just raised his eyebrows as if to say he wasn't sure.

"You'll figure it out, Nora. Just give it some time." Luke smiled back, and Nora felt the warmth of those hazel eyes.

After she finished her coffee, she left to tidy off her desk. As she was ambling back to the front office, she caught the sound of a low-pitched wolf whistle. She swiveled around in surprise to catch Luke glowing red-faced in an approving grin, and Eddie ostentatiously blowing smoke rings in another direction.

# 4

# Abby Gets a Phone Call

The phone rang just after supper. Abby was watching the evening news but welcomed the interruption because when Matt was on the night shift, the evenings could be tedious. Her face brightened when she heard the voice on the other end.

"Hello, Abigail! How's my very favourite teacher?" Helena Meriwether was a loving, if somewhat over-protective mother, a classic empty-nester. Abby was her only child.

"Hi, Mom."

"Abigail, how are you? Just calling to ask about your first day of school. You know how I love to hear about how my daughter is!"

"It was good, Mom, no problems really. I have a girl in my class who has never been to school, ever. That'll be interesting, I suspect. She was supposed to have been home-schooled because their ranch is so far out, over forty miles out of town and across really rough roads for the last ten miles. Getting to the regular road is impossible, especially in the winter, except by a truck with a plough, but I guess the mom got sick and the girl avoided doing any school stuff. I found out that her older brother and sister used to come to the high school, but they boarded part time with a family out there who lived closer so they could catch the school bus. Since the older girl quit school, she's been doing the younger sister's schoolwork and passing it off as hers."

"Well, what do you expect?" Abby inwardly groaned. Her mom was in one of those moods. She would have to bite her tongue while her mom ranted a bit. "That place is about as far as you can get from civilization! Of course you'll have problems like that…no sense of what's proper or decent! People who choose to live so far out are asking for trouble."

The exasperation in Helena's voice was palpable. Abby knew she wasn't really talking about the Talbots or any of the other residents of the Skeena River Basin. She was talking about her and Matt and about how they insisted they were happy living so far from family. She wanted to remind her mom that they had a perfectly good clinic with qualified nurses and a dedicated ambulance just for the town, but Helena was on a roll.

"Good Lord! You don't even have an airport for emergencies where you are! And how far is the nearest hospital? Forty miles to Glacier Lake? Ridiculous… and on the news tonight, I heard that the body of a young woman who had been murdered was found up near there just last year. Anyway, the news said she had been strangled, and they have no idea by whom. She was found near Terrace. That's not far is it? Just up the highway…" Helena's voice trailed off as if she knew she had said too much.

Abby wondered if the cops had told all the national media outlets to remind people –maybe as a precaution for the opening of school – but she was astonished that the recap had been aired back in Ontario, too.

"Oh, Mom, don't worry so much. People who need help get it here soon enough." As she said it, she thought of Beth Talbot and how she had needed help. Then she continued, "That is, if they need and want the help, they can get it. There is medevac service if someone is hurt in the bush, or even at the mill, and anyway, we're young and healthy. People our age don't need doctors much. And Prince George is just two-and-a-bit hours away. Moose Forks has most of what we need. It's over two thousand people, and more coming all the time to work in one of the biggest, most modern sawmills in the area. Matt is doing so well there, you know?"

"Well, I don't know…" Abby could hear her mom winding up for another fly-past, probably this time an attack on the lack of shopping or museums or other big city attractions, for Pete's sake! Moose Forks was small, no doubt, but it had the basics. It even had a new mall where, if they didn't have it, they'd order it. They didn't lack for much.

"Are you listening, Abigail?" She was swiftly brought back to reality by her mother's biting tone of voice, an echo from her childhood. "I was saying we just got back from a shopping trip to Buffalo. The stores were packed with the Back to School sales. We gassed up over there, too. You wouldn't believe what we paid! Its sixty-seven cents a gallon here and only forty over there, and just a year or so ago it was fifty here! Why do we pay so much when Alberta has oil? Bad enough those Arabs want to make us pay through the nose! And everybody is buying those stupid little VW cars to save gas! Why do we buy from them? We won the war! They should buy from us!"

"Oh, Mom, that's ages ago. Things have changed." Before Helena could launch into another rant about the dangers of German vehicles, Abby interrupted, "I hate to run, Mom, but I need to get some prep done for my classes." She hated to fib, but the drift of the conversation wasn't getting any better. She tried to soften her retreat. "How about I call you for a change, maybe next weekend when the rates are lower? I love you!"

"Oh, all right. It's late here too. I just thought I'd call before I go to bed. You take care of yourself, honey. I love you too."

Putting the phone back onto its cradle, Abby reflected on her mom's motivations. Her mom cared, she knew, but somehow, they just didn't want the same things from life, at least not now. Abby, raised with piano lessons and dance recitals, was now happy to live in blue jeans and lumberjack shirts, at least on the weekends. She loved her job and the sense of accomplishment it brought. In this small town, she was important. Her skills were not commonplace, and she wanted to believe her efforts made a difference.

In the background, the news droned on about more peace talks to sort things out in the Near East. Israel was feeling threatened again.

Abby's mind drifted to her life with Matt. They were secure in their jobs, and they had bought this house. They could even afford the luxury of an occasional weekend flight for a Vancouver concert. Really, what was she missing? Sometimes, she wondered about the drinking and the recklessness, for example, the weed smoking. She shook her head, musing that she sure as hell couldn't ever tell her mom about that stuff!

She thought then about Tess Talbot, and how much of a rough life that girl had seen. Turning off the television, Abby turned her mind to what her after-school chat with the school secretary had revealed about the girl and her home life. Grandmotherly Margaret Vermeer, who ran the school office, was an unabashed but selective gossip. She had been born and raised in Moose Forks. There was nothing she didn't know about life in the small town.

Margaret had described the remoteness of Bar T, the Talbots' ranch. It lay ten miles off Antoinette Lake Road at the end of an isolated gravel lane. The nearest neighbors, the Hitchcocks, had a ranch at the junction of Talbots' road and Antoinette Lake Road. The Talbot place was so far out that it didn't even have a phone. The phone company insisted that the owner pay for every telephone pole needed to hook up the property, and there had never been that kind of spare cash. In winter, the road was impassable unless Hank Talbot took it upon himself to attach the plough to his four-by-four truck, something he did only on days the family had to come to town for supplies. This had presented no problem for the older kids' schooling, because they could ride horses out to the road in summer, and in winter they boarded weekdays with the Hitchcocks, so that they could catch the school bus. Tess had been homeschooled for her elementary school years, as had the older kids.

No one had ever suspected that someone else had done the work Tess was handing in as hers. Margaret added that the older kids had done well enough in high school despite the early homeschooling, so no alarm bells rang when Tess had followed the same path. The public health nurse, Liz Lundstrom, had visited the ranch occasionally to see to Beth Talbot, and had never reported any concerns about the younger daughter. But then, Liz had noticed that Tess was usually out instead of doing schoolwork when she visited, so when the mother began to get very ill during the previous spring, the public health nurse had become concerned and made a note to contact Social Services and get them to assess how well Tess' s schooling was coming along.

What had followed was an explosive visit from Social Services, when Hank confronted the social worker, Mike Horvath, with a loaded rifle, followed by an inquiry into Tess's schooling, and ultimately, an embarrassing investigation by the RCMP into the circumstances of Beth's death and burial without a death certificate. Needless to say, Hank Talbot had griped like a wounded bear dealing with the fall-out of all this bureaucracy. He had had to exhume the body, paying the coroner's expenses, and most distastefully, was made to pay a hefty fine to avoid an indictment on the charge of improper interference with human remains. Then to make matters even worse, there was a rumour that he might be charged with failing to provide the necessities of life because Beth had not had proper medical attention. Given his distaste for any bureaucracy, Margaret figured he was likely still in a foul mood. All this had happened the previous May and June when the school year was almost over. Likely, Hank had made sure Tess showed up at school this September in hopes that her attendance would satisfy the powers that be.

Margaret had also said that there was even more of a mystery concerning why Hank was so leery about any interference from the authorities. Hank had been a rancher's son in Wyoming and had gone to war in Korea. Then, like a few others, he had come up from the States after the war. No one knew much about his war record, only that he kept it to himself. Maybe the few guys he drank with, George Warren or Frank Hughes, might know why Hank Talbot was so anti-government. If so, they weren't saying much either.

Abby sat and pondered her conversation with Margaret. What was there to do next? She had to find out how to get Tess feeling comfortable enough at school to make her want to come.

# 5

# Abby in Trouble

"What in hell happened in there, Abby?" Tom punctuated his question with the slam of his office door. "Hank Talbot's as wound up as a choker cable, saying that yesterday you put his kid on the spot the first day of school. He says the story's out that he's too cheap to give his wife a decent burial, and that Tess's nothing but a scrappy, foul-mouthed…"

He broke off in exasperation and regarded his junior staff member with fatherly concern. After he motioned Abby to sit, he began again, his tone reduced in volume, if not in intensity. It was the end of the school day, so they had some time to sort things out.

Tom continued, "Well, we both know what the kids will say, given the chance. The point is, I had him in here for over an hour earlier today trying to cool him down. He says social services be damned, he'll withdraw Teresa if she comes home riled like that again."

Abby's weak smile and the shake of her head disarmed Tom Cooper. He knew she was kind-hearted, if somewhat naive as a teacher. Keeping decent personnel in the outlying districts of the province was tough, particularly when they showed as much promise as Abby had. He rephrased the comment, lapsing into the professional jargon that he typically used to defuse hot tempers.

"What I mean to say is that he's a concerned parent with a legitimate complaint. He says you embarrassed Teresa purposely and demands a written apology, not that he'd likely read it, mind you." Tom's quick smile and wink seemed to relax him as much as it reassured Abby that he, as principal, understood some of the family history that had really motivated Tess's painful introduction to public school.

"Of course I didn't do it on purpose! What an idiotic thing for him to say!" Abby was beginning to feel anger as opposed to embarrassment where Hank Talbot was concerned.

"Well, he's no idiot for all his lack of formal schooling, Abby. Although it's a small one, that Aberdeen Angus herd he has is one of the best in the valley, even doctors them himself."

"Did the same for his wife, too, no doubt! That's why she's so healthy! Oh, I'm sorry, Tom. That probably was uncalled for, but the fact remains. The man has sacrificed the life of his wife, or at least a decent chance for her recovery, because he's too stubborn! Call it independent if you will, but he's too proud to admit that properly trained people could and should help."

Abby groped for a rationale to offset her cruel opening remark. "And now, he's looking for any excuse to pull Tess out of here, a thirteen year-old who, with her mom's help, is supposed to have been home-schooled on correspondence! Now there's a tragic situation. Do you know where that kid's at, in terms of basic math and reading, I mean?"

Abby paused to catch her breath. The memory of Tess's first two days at school flashed by in poignant detail, and only served to fuel her indignation further.

"Never mind her complete lack of social skills, the fact that she hides in the washroom cubicles or hightails it for the slash pile outback every lunch hour. Never mind that nobody wants to sit near her because she reeks of horses and body odor!"

Tom, nodding, displayed his palms in a gesture that acknowledged the truth of Abby's observations. "Look, Abby, all I'm saying is this family has already had its problems with Liz at Public Health and that new bunch at The Community Resource Board – or whatever that social work bunch calls itself these days – and it didn't go down well with Hank Talbot. He'll be thanking the powers that be for the NDP losing that election last spring."

Abby knew that British Columbia's first ever left-leaning provincial government, led by the New Democratic Party, had lasted a mere three years, and had frightened many conservatives with the pace of change it had introduced. There was tremendous opposition in town to any overt evidence of socialist influence. Teachers, in particular, were suspect because of their overwhelming support for the NDP during the 1972 election. "I don't think I said anything that could be construed as political, Tom."

"But Abby, you need to remember, he's an independent, self-made man who came up from the States almost twenty years ago and built that spread out in the Antoinette Valley out of nothing but a few abandoned out-buildings. He's damned proud of his place, the Bar T, and well he should be. He doesn't like government interference, probably had enough of that with the army. You know he's a Korean vet and none too happy about how he was treated afterwards? Left the States to get away from whatever it was. So I'm guessing that what's been going on in this province the last few years has him spooked. He hates NDP'ers, Socialists, whatever. He calls them Commies, and sees them as little different than what he fought in Korea, so I suspect he's pretty right-wing. Whatever the case, we have to soft pedal here because Tess needs to keep coming to school, and that means doing whatever we must to keep the dad happy.

Tom continued, "So how about inviting him in and talking to him yourself? Tess will be spending most of her time in your learning assistance class, or at least you'll have the most contact with her, so you are the logical one to reassure him that we're not trying to make a public spectacle of her or her family."

"Thanks a bunch, buddy. Guess you've already had your go-round, eh? Do you think he'd even show? The last time he showed up to pull Ellie out, he let everyone within three miles know that neither he nor his kids would ever set foot here again. It was enough of a show that the staffroom still buzzes with the details."

Tom's quick snort confirmed that he, too, recalled the episode. "We all better hope he opts for that instead of bending the ears of the Big Cheese at the board office," groused Tom good-naturedly. The reputation of George Warren, chairman of the school board, as a champion of the local cattlemen was well deserved. Those hoping for financial backing for any school endeavour were well advised not to cross him.

"Okay, Chief. I guess I'm elected. Could I at least have some moral support? Maybe one of the other counselors on hand in case he gets excited?"

"For crying out loud, Abby, he's not an ogre, you know! The man's just lost his wife. All he wants is someone to hear him out, to tell him his daughter won't get centered out as if she were some kind of freak. You and I both know the kid has unique problems, but just focus on the positive. Tell him we're happy to have her and think she'll do fine, given time, and support from home. You know the school policy well enough to handle this one yourself."

Privately, Abby was fuming. Lofty stuff! That's exactly the kind of crap that turns people like Talbot right off. "School policy" my hind end! Abby seethed quietly all the way down the hall, brightening up only when she stopped at Margaret Vermeer's desk to ask her to get a message to Talbot. She was grateful the school secretary would be making this next contact, and not herself.

Abby pondered Tom's strange deflection of the problem onto her. Normally, Tom was the kind of guy who preferred dealing with the big-wigs in town. And Hank Talbot, while not exactly an upstanding model citizen, for some reason was in pretty thick with George Warren, who was indisputably the most successful rancher in the valley as well as chairman of the school board.

Abby reflected on Tom's motives. Why is he passing up a chance to sort out this little skirmish? Maybe he already has all the sports equipment he needs for his precious basketball team and doesn't need another soft touch with Warren! Embarrassed by her own cynicism, Abby shook herself off and wandered to the staffroom to check her mail drawer for messages, musing as she mechanically followed her feet down the hall. She was wondering how long it would be before she was as jaded as the rest of them when the vice-principal's voice interrupted her thoughts.

"Did you do the Lavatory Lil check earlier today, Abby?"

"No. Why?" She regarded Phil Lavergne. The V.P. was a laidback guy, not usually the type to niggle about the neglect of minor duties such as the girls' washroom supervision routine.

"What is it with girls, anyway? I'm getting really peeved with the constant mess in there. Someone's gone and smeared God-knows-what all over the walls and mirrors. Andy's fit to be tied and says he's had enough! Do you know how hard it is to get custodians around here? The mill pays much better than the school board, so we better keep that in mind too!" The growl in Phil's voice revealed he was warming up to a royal snit, but seeing her expression, he waited for Abby to respond.

"Well Phil, I'll see what I can find out."

Abby dumped her load of papers on the staffroom table and slumped over in exasperation. What next? It must be her day to screw up.

# 6

# At Home with the Clarkes

Matt was still bleary-eyed when Abby collapsed on the couch after getting back from weekend shopping on the first Saturday morning of September. She couldn't help but wonder what life was like in a house where nobody worked the night shift.

He sat there in his jeans and off-shift clothes, a threadbare, grey flannel pullover with "Tuk U" emblazoned across the front. He was a tall, lean twenty-eight-year-old with a full brown beard and a thick head of chestnut hair that curled so nicely that Abby was envious. His face looked older with the beard, but she could see vestiges of the boy he had been in the tender curve of his lips and the downward sweep of dark lashes. Those amber brown eyes had been the arresting feature five years before when she had first met him at a rally to protest the Amchitka nuclear testing near Alaska. Despite his lack of university, they had found they shared much in common: an adventurous spirit, a belief in the underdog and a distrust of extreme right-wing thinking. They had clicked over beer and politics.

As he lounged on the couch recovering from a long two-week run of night shifts, she felt once again that silly melting in the pit of her stomach. He was a sweet man, and trying so hard to make their lifestyle work. It hadn't been easy for him to move up from mill hand to shift foreman. It had taken real grit, the sacrifice of the carefree, youthful life they had known during their first years together in Vancouver. Back then, she had waitressed part-time as she finished her degree, and he, just back from a hitchhiking tour of the Yukon and Northwest Territories, had got a job long-shoring at the docks on Burrard Inlet. She saw him as sexually exciting, physically strong, active and affectionate. Perhaps he was a risk-taker who didn't always gauge the impact his actions would have, but without him, Abby thought she would still be stuck back East with her over-protective family. Overall, she felt she had chosen well.

"So what's new up at the dumb-dumb factory?" Matt's opinion of the quality of graduate from the local high school was anything but complimentary. He delighted in regaling her with stories of kids fresh out of school, who were too stupid to read the warning signs posted along the length of the green chain, and who lost fingers or toes through cockiness or sheer ignorance. He meant these stories as cautionary tales, she knew. He couldn't understand how anyone could graduate from high school and be so clueless.

Too depressed and tired to take the bait, she kicked her shoes off and wandered over to the fridge. Damn, all the beer was gone again.

"Matt, honey, were the guys here after shift this morning?"

"Yeah, a few. Why?"

"Oh, nothing. I just thought they were going to go someplace else next time."

"Give it up, Abby. Where the hell they going to go at three in the morning? The bar doesn't open 'til eleven. Besides, they all kick in to pay for whatever they drink. They're not freeloaders."

"Well, there's always the novel concept of checking someone else's fridge out after shift on Fridays, you know, or even passing on booze altogether?" The look he gave her suggested she really didn't understand the loneliness of shift work, and she backed down, "Okay, okay. Forget I said it."

As she had so many times before, Abby pondered the shape of her future in this town. It was so easy to tip back a few beers with the boys every other day, for sure every weekend, to roar with laughter over the antics of grown men and women gone haywire or vacantly desperate in their social and geographical isolation. Most of their friends, like Matt and herself, were from some other place, drawn to the valley by the prospect of steady jobs and cheap land not available in the South. Cut off from family and roots, they found some sense of belonging in each others' company. As a group, they were gregarious and high-spirited, always ready for a back-of-the-pickup party on the local ski hill or on some remote logging road after a day's trout fishing. Most had come to the valley for the work; some like themselves had even bought houses at rock bottom prices. It was a good place to get a start.

But it was a curiously restricted existence they all led, somehow at odds with the vast expanses of mountain and bush they used both as playground and pantry. Somehow, they were like hybrid saplings grafted on to the gnarled trunk of this prehistoric landscape, and not all of them were taking well. Try as she might, Abby still didn't feel as if she really belonged there, at least not in the way people like the Talbots and Warrens did. They, she mused, must be really tough stock, adapted to survive the isolation and uncompromising climate. They probably didn't need to seek oblivion in the bottom of a bottle to forget where they were, or to brazen out the cold.

Thinking of the Talbots reminded Abby that young Tim, Hank Talbot's middle child and only son, worked on Matt's shift at the sawmill.

"Matt, is Tim Talbot still on your crew?"

"Tin-ear Tim? Yeah. Why?" One of the crowd's less endearing habits was attaching nicknames to everybody.

"I was just curious about why he worked at the mill instead of on his dad's ranch."

"Maybe his humming drives the stock as loco as it does everybody else!" Matt hooted, shifting his six-foot frame to make room for her on the couch.

"Is that why you call him 'Tin-ear', because he hums all the time?"

"Yeah, I guess that's it, and the fact that nothing sinks in too quick when you talk to him. I swear, the guy's a few bricks short of a load. Sure as hell he'll never last anywhere with people hearing him humming all the time. He's always humming in the coffee room while everybody's there taking their break, so I guess he hums everywhere else too. Good thing everybody wears ear protection." Matt suddenly warmed to the potential of his topic. "Now there's a prime example of one of your high school graduates. That kid did finish school, didn't he?"

Abby nodded vaguely, casting her eyes upward to picture Tim as a student. That had been her first year at the school, and Tim had spent more time in the halls than in class as she recalled. She couldn't be too sure of his "credentials". He wouldn't have been the first young lad to be "cut a deal" just to quit coming to class. Her uncertainty merely served to fuel Matt's argument.

"Well, he sure as shit can't read, I'll tell you. Held us up for half an hour one night arguing with the lead hand about his pay stub. It's a good thing we'd already met our quota, or I'd have canned him. Would have had to, even if he is a hard worker. The other guys wouldn't have taken too kindly to losing their bonus because of some green kid with a burr in his gaunch. God, that pissed me off."

"But he fits in otherwise? I mean does he hang out after shift with the others?" Abby was trying to get some reading on the boy's sociability. Maybe being loners was a Talbot family trait. She didn't think so somehow. The older sister, Ellie, had been outgoing enough, as she had been told, even a little brash.

"Who? Tim? Hell, yeah! That boy can guzzle brewski with the best of them. Nothing wrong with his hormones, either. Ah, the kid's okay, real hard working, just not too mature. I wouldn't have fired him. What's all the interest in him anyway? Thinking about recruiting him for private lessons? Lordy darling! You gotta leave that stuff at school. Hey, Mrs. School Teacher. I haven't seen you for a week. How about paying some attention to your lover for a change?"

"All right, big guy. Just let me get cleared up in the kitchen."

Clattering at the sink, she speculated about the rest of the weekend. They were slated for a staff party at Tom's, but she knew Matt would rather get into the bush for some quiet time together. She was suddenly grateful for his penchant for the outdoors. Another evening of teacher shoptalk wasn't her idea of a good time either.

The previous week had about done her in, what with coping with Tess as well as the mess in the girls' washroom. Andy, the custodian, was clearly justified in his disgust. Somebody had sprung open the sanitary napkin dispenser and stuffed them down the toilets, then scrawled crudely drawn male genitalia in lipstick all over the walls and mirrors. Odd. As a rule, girls had personal targets when they lashed out inside the stalls. Typically, the theme ran to the dire consequences that "so and so bitch" could expect if some guy weren't acknowledged as off-limits. Today's situation was a curious aberration. The graphics were huge and very public, not the usual private bobby-pin scratchings of adolescent angst. Whoever had done them had gone through a hell of a lot of lipstick.

Matt, rumbling his impatience in the living room, snapped her back to the present. "Babe, how long are you going to be?"

"Where are we going fishing this weekend, Matt? Back up behind the burn again?" She chuckled and flushed, warming to the memory of their last excursion when he had deliberately dumped the canoe so she would have to undress to dry out over a fire hastily built in an abandoned sawmill chip burner. Matt was impetuous all right! His favourite trick was deliberately getting the four-wheel stuck so they'd have to rough it "for fun". The canoe caper was definitely a new twist on an old theme. Wouldn't be so bad, she decided, if the damned sawdust didn't itch so bad next to the skin.

"Thought this afternoon we'd check out the headwaters of the Antoinette Creek. Old Pete told me last night the trout fishing is dynamite in that little lake down there."

"Isn't that back beyond the Marcel?"

"Yeah, just past your buddy Tin-ear's ranch. Why? Want to stop in and give him a hearing test?"

"It's okay, love. I promise to take the whole weekend off, honest."

"That's my girl. Hey, get over here. I gotta present for you."

"Matt, for crying out loud! It's the middle of the day!"

"So? I haven't seen you awake all week!"

# 7

# The Bar T

"Look at that stand of poplar against the spruce, Babe!" Matt down-shifted the four-wheel around another abrupt curve on their climb sky-ward.  He negotiated the road like a kid looking for a crack-up, but he was right: the lemon yellow of the poplar leaves silhouetted against the dark forest green was dazzling.

"Land" or "country" or "bush" – none of those words quite captured the enormity of what all this was; even "wilderness" was somehow too humanized. Abby reflected on her place amidst it all as they rattled onto the plateau above the valley where the town nestled.  She was transfixed, as always, by the sheer volume of rugged landscape confronting her. Here, in the bush, she shivered with the unyielding reality of her insignif-icance, of her mortality.

They were heading roughly south along the Marcel River Road in their pick-up. Altogether, the trip would take them almost thirty miles along gravel logging roads through dense stands of partially logged lodge pole pine and white spruce. Twenty-five miles along, at the point where the Marcel veered due west, they would continue another five miles south over a small mountain pass to Antoinette Lake, teeming with rainbow trout. They would need forty-five or fifty minutes to reach the lake if the roads were good.

Why was it she couldn't center herself here?  What kept her from putting down roots, from accepting and submitting to the enormity of the land that had challenged so many others and made them buckle under until all they really cared about was surviving?  Why did she care about "making a difference"? Was she essentially a flake?  A city-slicker with pretensions?  No, they weren't even pretensions; they were naïve illu-sions she had about making some kind of impact on this isolated community. She shook herself, unwilling to admit the essential accuracy of her insight. She wanted to matter somewhere. Arrogance. Arrogance. The tiers of trees seemed to echo at her as they passed.

"Christamighty! Where'd he come from?" Matt seesawed the wheel frantically to avoid a blur of shaggy brown that seemed to arc diagonally from nowhere. The truck lunged in shuddering assaults on the curves and ruts of the road as it careened past the bull moose frozen on the shoulder.

"Look out! Here we go! We just missed that swamp donkey!" Matt's voice rejoiced with the adrenalin rush of combat, man and machine against whatever the bush chucked out. Abby paled with incomprehension that he could be enjoying such a brush with calamity.

But there was no denying that he was. His face was ruddy with exhilaration, his eyes sparkling and darting to gauge road angle, his ear cocked and attuned to engine tolerance. The bush flashed by in a haze of early autumn colour, tawny brown and sage green. Matt's need to connect with the primeval was real for him as no other fact of their existence in the north country was. When Matt was out driving the truck in the bush, he seemed to live mostly for a chance to flaunt his will to survive. Funny kind of death wish, really. Abby felt her stomach convulse a little at the thought. Nonsense! She shook the thought off. All the guys have big trucks. No other kind of rig was practical.

A half hour later, they were past the Marcel fork and heading south onto the flat stretching for miles below the pass into the Antoinette Creek valley. Here, the trees thinned to rangeland, with only occasional copses left standing near the sparsely graveled roadbed. Encroaching at intervals on the roadside were massive, jagged outcroppings of flinty-grey rock. Matt accelerated, maneuvering the truck to minimize the shock of washboard and pothole. The sky opened up ahead, cloudless and azure.

Then, around a sharp V turn, a blur of black movement obscured by dust arose on the road ahead. Matt hit the brakes, but not soon enough to avoid startling the herd of Aberdeen Angus cattle trundling towards them. The bawling and snorting of the frightened animals as they lunged and stumbled their way around the skidding truck deafened them to the shouts of a rider at the rear of the herd.

The next few minutes hung suspended in Abby's memory for weeks afterward. The horse erupted across their path, and the rider plunged, hugging the arched neck of the huge chestnut mount, pebbles and dust spraying into the windshield. The horse brayed in terror, and then Abby heard the heart-stopping thud of bodies against metal side panels. Matt reacted with almost inhuman self-control, wheeling the rig around so that he managed to orchestrate a glancing collision where a head-on impact had seemed unavoidable only seconds before. The truck veered off to the right, jolting down into the ditch and up the far embankment until it stalled out and settled, shuddering and askew, in the run-off gully.

"Fuck! I just got this bucket fixed from the last time! Just replaced the shocks! Who the hell *was* that?" The animation of his face betrayed his real feelings. The near catastrophe would be catalogued in with all the other "adventures", harmless escapades mostly, that entertained the troops on fishing expeditions and road trips.

"You sons-a-bitches!" The voice seemed muffled and distant, thick and pain-ridden as if strangled by tears.

"Oh my God!" Abby had jumped down from the cab and scrambled across the ditch long before the next sound punctured the stillness of the wilderness road. Matt, with a rueful shake of his head, followed.

"Jesus H. Mahogany Christ! You bastards! You didn't see the cattle guard? You spooked my horse, and she threw me!"

The source of the invective was a rumpled figure on its knees in the ditch opposite. Arms akimbo, chin thrust out punctuating each accusation, the rider seemed too small to be making so much noise. She, for the rider was a young woman in her late teens or early twenties, was flailing her arms in the direction of a chestnut mare already well on its way hobbling south along the road.

Abby, reaching down to offer the young woman some help up, met immediate resistance as she impatiently shrugged Abby off. Still on her knees, the young woman struggled to rise, her face flushed and contorted. Once up, she moved to balance herself on the uneven ground, then lost control as a leg collapsed from under her. Abby sprang in with her shoulder only to be again rebuffed. The young woman's anger this time seemed dulled, perhaps by the sincere smiles of the young couple as they hovered, waiting to be helpful.

"And don't give me some crap about being sorry, either! You obviously don't know bugger-all about what to be sorry for, or you wouldn't have been going so fast to begin with."

The words rushed out one after another, as if they were well-rehearsed, more the grousing of someone tired of cleaning up other people's messes than the abuse of someone suffering acutely. The leg cannot be too bad, thought Abby, probably a bruised ankle or pulled tendon. Damn Matt! Maybe now he'd slow down out here. She eyed him reproachfully, her lips pursed to stem the inevitable "I-told-you-so" before it blurted out to embarrass him further.

"That's my fault." Matt's face was now grim with concern, his eyes scanning to estimate the extent of shock and possible sources of injury. "I did notice the cattle guard, and you're right, I was going too fast. Guess that's the city-slicker-in-the-bush mentality working."

He left the bait just long enough to see that she would be tempted to bite if not diverted. "Hey, what do I know about cattle. I gotta wear this one, no excuses." He then floated the boyish smile with which he was accustomed to disarming all female hostility and waited for some evidence of melting.

The sound of girl's wincing as she shifted her weight to Abby's shoulder broke the awkward pause. Matt, totally practical, led with the obvious. "I suppose we should get you someplace to get your leg looked at. We'll drive you into the clinic and see you get back home after, if that'll help any."

"Hell, no, I don't need them messing with it. I'll be okay if you just get me home. My dad's as good a medic any day. Besides, I want to see if Blaze went home. She's just been broke a year and still spooks pretty easy."

"I've a first aid ticket so, one way or another, we'll get you fixed up. But at least, we've got to get you off that foot. Abby, let's get her home. I'll go get the truck back on the road, and you try to get her boots off. We'll carry her in a hand basket, you know?" His right hand clasped his left wrist quickly to indicate the handhold he meant, and then he was gone, sprinting towards the truck a hundred meters down the road.

"Abby who?" The girl picked up when Matt had left. "You from around here? You look a little familiar."

"Abby Clarke. That's Matt, my husband. We live in town. You're right; I'm sure we've met. What's your name?"

"Eleanor Talbot, but most folks call me Ellie. Only my mom used to call me Eleanor. You teach in town, at the high school, right? You weren't there when I was, but I remember hearing about you later." Her words drifted into a groan as she worked to release her rapidly swelling left foot from a well-worn cowboy boot. "Don't want to cut these suckers off," she panted. "Only pair I got."

"Let me do that, Ellie." Abby wanted to feel useful. The girl's choked voice hinted at the onset of the real discomfort that would follow, now that shock and indignation were wearing off. Ellie sat with her stocky jean-covered legs crooked at the knee. Her round dimpled face, surrounded by cascading waves of dark brown hair, was flushed with the effort of tugging at her left boot from the wrong angle.

"I can't reach good enough to get a haul on them. Shit, I hate being helpless. Dad will be choked about this mess if I can't ride range." She glanced up at Abby's face as if suddenly aware she had said too much. "Oh, don't mind me. Dad's, well, Dad's who he is. He just likes his own space and his own kind of company." Her voice trailed off, shutting Abby out as she muttered about "holes in socks" and "damned cowboy heels". She had an appealing "country girl" kind of look, Abby reflected. She was healthy and solidly built with a no-nonsense air about her. Her denim jeans and jacket were well worn, but clean. She had clear skin, rosy cheeks and the same startling violet-blue eyes as her sister, Tess.

Matt, when he came back a moment later after backing the truck onto the road next to them, found Abby looking concerned, and Ellie, stoic, as impassive as the rocky outcropping behind her.

"That's the turnoff on the right, next to that stand of poplar." They were Ellie's first words during the ten-minute trip south down the Antoinette Valley. Now that they were nearing her dad's place, she seemed to be coming out of herself, shrugging off the silence that had enveloped her ever since they had maneuvered her onto the bench seat of the truck cab.

They were rattling down the ruts of a driveway winding its way toward Antoinette Creek. Travelling through the moss green and gold fringe of poplar skirting the driveway on both sides, Abby could see the value of the spread. In a country dominated by narrow, glaciated valleys, this was prime bottomland. Meadows opened up on both left and right; hayfields, shorn of their crop in July, had been turned over to grazing. Here and there, she could make out the black bulk of the cattle, lazily twitching their tails in the early afternoon sun.

Opening up to the east and south beyond the range was a vista of evergreen-fringed hills and farther back a mountaintop, its craggy heights showing the delicate tracery of the autumn's first dusting of snow.

As they neared the house, Abby was struck by the idea that this wasn't exactly the parent-teacher meeting scenario she had in mind. She hoped Hank Talbot would be too concerned about Ellie to get into a snarl over Tess. She decided she would just say she couldn't really deal with it here. She sighed. If he wanted to tear a strip off her there, she realized she would just have to take it. The prospect made her very uneasy.

"How far to go, Ellie?" Abby gauged the pinched look on the girl's face, and saw real pain etched there. Maybe the injury was more serious.

"Not too much. The place is mostly on this side of the creek but we have some acreage over on the east bank. We can ford the creek most of the year so there's no bridge over there." She pointed ahead to the hills in the distance, and through breaks in the forest cover, Abby could just make out some acreage of higher rangeland dotted with more cattle.

"So where we almost hit you isn't part of your ranch?" Abby was curious about why Ellie had strayed so far off the ranch land itself.

"Oh no, that's open range back there. I was just trying to move that small herd further along to better feed. Now, we'll have to round them up again."

Abby felt even worse when she heard that they'd made even more work for the Talbots.

After about five miles, the road veered to the left and right in an S curve and, clearing a slight rise, they came to the first building, a ramshackle weather-beaten structure that seemed to lean precariously towards the road. She glanced at Ellie, who gestured ahead further, past a cattle guard meant to keep the yard clear of livestock.

'Yard' wasn't quite adequate to describe the open space that next surrounded them. For at least fifty yards, they bumped across a terrain littered with rusty pieces of farm machinery, blown tires and piles of refuse. A stray chicken perched atop the open door of an outbuilding to the right, a toolshed or henhouse, Abby assumed. A large hay barn, equally weather-beaten, but of a sturdier construction, and several corral enclosures were on the left further toward the south. Next to the barn was a newer-looking stable. Then, on the right, the road ended abruptly in a woodpile at the southernmost extension of the fence enclosing the ranch house.

Even before Matt had the truck stopped, Ellie was scrambling to get over Abby's lap and out the door.

"Wait, Ellie, we'd like at least to let your dad know what happened and offer to help get you looked after." And face the music, she added silently, as she climbed down from the cab to let Ellie by.

"I told you he don't…" She corrected herself, "He doesn't like doctors or hospitals or town people, or anyone else, messing in his business. Leave me be, lady. He's a damn good medic, and he'll see to my foot. Sure now, I can get into the house without him being any the wiser. See, that's my bedroom window." She pointed toward the farthest window on the south wall of the house that lay twenty feet beyond the fence gate where they had stopped.

Matt moved to shift the truck into gear again, his patience starting to wear thin. "Come on, Abby. We've done what we could here. We can always check with Tin-ear, um, Tim, to see how Ellie made out. He'll be in touch with his sister."

Ellie froze, and turning around, for the first time cast an interested glance at Matt. "You know my brother?"

"Yeah, he works on my shift at the mill."

Ellie erupted in a hoot that shrilled across the yard. "You're the sonovabitch he's always grousing about! That's freaking hilarious! I always pictured you as a sour old coot with a broomstick shoved up your…"

"Ellie!! Shut your hole!"

The voice slashed across the yard from beside the barn. It was a deep bass, hoarse and grating in its anger. It galvanized Matt out of the truck to meet the man as he sauntered diagonally toward the driver's side of the truck.

Abby, hanging on the open door, caught her first look at Hank Talbot across the bed of the truck. Ellie, standing with her foot dangling next to the fence, breathed an almost silent prayer, "Dear God, we're in for it now."

She called out to her father as he was approaching. "Dad, this is Matt and Abby. They're just giving me a ride home. We had a little run-in up the road a ways. Did Blaze come back? She might be lame. My foot needs cold water, soaking is all, maybe. We'll have to round up the twenty odd cattle I left down near the cattle guard…" Her voice faded as the man came closer, as if her energy were being sapped by his looming presence.

The first visual impression Abby had of Hank Talbot was one of feline grace, a pent-up wellspring of energy waiting to uncoil. He loped across the distance between them with a fluid, motion, a rope twitching in his right hand idly whipping the side seam of his pant leg. Beneath a scrunched straw Stetson, she saw first a long, strong jaw, a salt-and-pepper handlebar moustache and a broad brow furrowed with creases. His was a tall, lean build. Beneath the blue and black lumberjack shirt, the dusty T-shirt betrayed no sign of a gut distending, and the frayed Indian beaded belt that looped through his black denims rested easily above a slim set of haunches. At his belt, a clutch of keys jangled, the only sound to be heard until he flung one word in Ellie's direction.

"Git."

Abby, on principle, had been all set to dislike him on sight. That one syllable seemed to crystallize all her objections in one clear focal point. With the callous flinging of that command, as if the girl were a dog underfoot, Abby bristled in indignation.

But something stopped her from protesting. Hank Talbot smiled. Even from a distance, she saw the grim and resolute character of his face over-washed by a disarming, cock-eyed grin, and a lop-sided, boyish display of white teeth that lifted years from his face. The effect was that of ripples disturbing the dark underlying image on an expanse of pond water. Somehow, she knew a different Hank Talbot was there, resident beneath the ripples, but she was mesmerized by the smile, as if she were a mouse played by a cat. For a moment, the light in that smile blinded her reasoning self. Her woman's intuition understood why Mrs. Talbot had lingered at home instead of insisting on a hospital: Hank Talbot could be damnably charming.

She was taken from her absorption by the sound of a door slamming. Ellie had made her way into the house, hobbling as she opened the gate, fleeing any further involvement with the father approaching across the dusty driveway clearing. The girl's hasty retreat reminded Abby that here was a man with little regard for social nicety or convention, a man with a temper, a law unto himself. Looking up into Hank's face, Abby saw that his smile did not extend to his eyes. They were slate gray and unfathomable.

"Ellie don't have no call to talk to you like that. You're Tim's boss, eh? He says you're okay. He ain't one to judge anyways. He's still trying to figure out for hisself what an honest day's work is. He's just a young'un still, kind of lackadaisical. Not really lazy, but he's gotta have rules 'n such. He's kinda hopeless out here. Maybe a bit like his mom that way, at least kind of like she was." An uncomfortable silence interrupted his gruff rambling for a moment, and then he continued, extending his hand to shake Matt's. "Sure hope you can make a mill hand out of him. Christ knows he'll never make a rancher."

Abby restrained herself to keep from blurting out her first reaction. Miserable old bastard! Which one was "hopeless", the dead wife or the son? Who would want to live out here with him anyway? Then, when she half heard Matt extending their condolences on the loss of Mrs. Talbot, Abby felt chastened, realizing such a gesture should have been her first instinct as well. She suddenly blushed to think she hadn't expressed any sympathy to Ellie either. They had driven in silence all that way in the truck. The girl's reticence seemed even more painful in retrospect. How long since the mom had died? Last spring – a few months?

In her embarrassed confusion, Abby missed the invitation to stop in for a quick drink. All of a sudden, there was Hank opening the wooden gate of the fence surrounding the house and garden, and guiding them ahead onto a wraparound wooden deck. He held a screen door ajar and gestured them inside, saying, "Probably the only kind of brew I got is tea. The wife always had lot of that around anyways. But there might be a beer or two."

Abby's objections were lost in Matt's interest in something wet, whether beer or not. Her next words seemed flung at the men's backs as, hanging behind in the dark entryway, she asked, "Mr. Talbot, I'm wondering about Ellie and her horse. Is it okay? We're really sorry. The cattle appeared in front of us so fast we…"

His reply seemed nonchalant, "Don't worry none about the horse. She came back just a while back, all lathered up and excited, but not hurt bad, far as I can tell, leastways. Not lame, for sure. You came the long way by the road? Yeah, the horse, she knows the trails. If you come on foot or ride the trails, the trip from town goes cross-country cutting off a good bit. As for the cattle, they'll keep 'til tomorrow. They ain't going anywhere. Come on in now. Don't know what's what in the house. The girls are tending to it mostly."

Standing confined in the entryway, Abby surveyed the dim interior of the large kitchen and sitting room that ran the length of the log-building east to west. Ahead, threading his way diagonally towards the right, Hank cleared a path and led Matt around a giant kitchen table, past the cook stove, sink and water pump to a large, overstuffed couch which sat at right angles to a massive fireplace in an alcove on the back west wall. On either side of the fireplace were windows that looked out into a greenhouse built onto the west wall. Three other doors interrupted the length of the south wall to the left of the fireplace, bedroom entrances, probably. Abby guessed Ellie sat listening behind the one farthest to the rear.

Hank scooped lithely, retrieving cast-aside garments and scattered cat dishes. Gesturing with a wave of his arm, he pointed them to the couch. Then he backtracked toward the large table that occupied the center of the room, and was veering over toward the stove when his foot connected, banging into the side of a five-gallon milk pail overflowing with what looked like table leavings. Abby judged that the bucket was the origin of the sour reek that pervaded the space. Hank's quick eye caught her line of sight, and reddening visibly, he flung the pail up and was out the kitchen door in the middle of the north wall, to the left of the stove. The next sound they heard was a distant squeal of hogs being fed.

Sitting on the couch, Abby nudged Matt to note the fluff balls of kittens curled up in the overstuffed armchair that dominated the corner on the right side of the fireplace. Her eyes now adjusting to the interior light, Abby could make out the cups and cereal bowls scattered across the oilcloth expanse of the massive kitchen table. Two more adventure-some calico kittens crouched atop there, lapping a late lunch from the milk remains in one bowl. A swarm of flies buzzed, fitfully lighting from one dish to another. Over the sink, the casement window stood ajar, its pale yellow gingham curtains lifting and falling in the gentle September breeze. The scene had the quality of a sepia print, antiquated and faded, an image preserved as if press-dried from some long past time.

Abruptly, the impression exploded with Hank's re-entry. His slam of the kitchen door rattled the windows, momentarily dissipating the swarm of flies, and sent the calico kitten skittering under the couch where Matt and Abby sat. He dropped the now empty slops pail by the sink and sloshed a quantity of water from the pump into the teakettle to set on the stove.

Hank's domestic efforts were awkward. Inside the house, the cougar grace was gone. He was all knees and elbows as he tried to negotiate the kitchen. His disjointed effort to clear the table of crockery and crumbs was interrupted by the realization that the kindling box was empty and the cook stove water reservoir dry. Banging about the cook stove, lifting first one wrought iron plate, then another, he seemed to be accomplishing nothing more than the sifting of yet another layer of grit onto the many that already clothed the objects in the room.

The door behind the right end of the couch opened, and Ellie hobbled out. She crossed in front of Matt and Abby, barely acknowledging their presence, and seemed to be angling for the kitchen door when she paused well back of where her father stood at the stove, orchestrating his symphony of soot and dust. Her eyes glittered at his shoulder blades. She seemed uncommitted to moving until she saw where he was headed.

Something told him she as there, and he whirled around, lunging across the space towards her. Something in his eyes suggested that the urgency arose more from embarrassment than from rage. Nevertheless, his onslaught took Ellie aback briefly as she staggered slightly to one side, re-establishing her balance by leaning on the wood box next to the kitchen door. Hank's hoarse whisper barely reached Matt and Abby on the far side of the room, making an elaborate pretense of roughhousing with the kittens.

"See this mess, girl? Clear it up now. Make some tea. We got company, see?"

Ellie's body was interfering with Abby's line of sight, so she never could be sure of the nature of the gesture that sent Ellie bouncing kangaroo fashion across to the sink. Whatever the cause, whether frustration or irritation, the father effected his exit quickly, leaving the girl hung awkwardly at the counter, her foot suspended in the air behind her.

Taking his straw hat off and vigorously rubbing the back of his neck, Hank wandered across to where they sat and grinned again in welcome. A conversation about guns and hunting regulations quickly ensued, its stimulus a stuffed moose head above the mantle. Abby, disinterested, excused herself to join the girl at the sink.

"Ellie, I'd like to be helpful. What can I do? How about you sitting with your foot up? I guess there's no ice, eh? Come on, sit at the table and I'll do the tea."

The girl's last reserves of pride seemed to crumble as she turned and, smiling shyly, stammered, "Kindling is out the kitchen door. A handful or two's all I need. There's lots of firewood in the box here. Maybe some water from the sink pump put in the stove reservoir. Thanks." Her round cheeks showed streaks where tears had dried, but her eyes were clear and friendly.

The kitchen door led out into a lean-to area dominated by a collection of empty tin cans. By the looks it, they'd been eating a lot of beans. She wondered how long Mrs. Talbot had lingered bed-ridden. Shaking her head, Abby picked her way past the cans. Next to a rain barrel at the end of the lean-to roof, she found the chopping block. A scattering of wood pieces was all there was to be had. She picked up the hatchet and set to work.

As she chopped kindling, Abby wondered why the house and yard were in such disarray. Ellie hadn't been spending much time in the ranch house or surrounding yard tending to the daily chores and garden. She must have been out most of the time riding range. With Tim not around, Ellie was chief ranch hand. Likely, Tess had helped out in the summer, but now that she was at school, too much seemed to be falling on Ellie's shoulders. It suddenly came to Abby just how much this family was missing the mother who had died. The realization steeled her feelings against Hank once again. Serves him right! Let him manage now that the wife's not here to keep things up. Couldn't manage without "rules 'n such" could she? Well at least she'd have known enough to keep the place clean and healthy!

Back in the kitchen, she set the kindling down beside the cook stove and elbowed Ellie gently over to the table. Soon the girl was seated comfortably enough, her foot elevated and wrapped in cool wet cloths. Abby tossed her a dishrag, and the girl took up where her father had stopped, tidying cups and bowls, cleaning away crumbs and scrubbing the oilcloth on the table. Abby tended to the stove, coaxing a flame from the kindling, setting the water to boil for tea and dirty dishes. The companionable silence that enveloped them seemed to help soothe the girl's disquiet.

Once the water was heated, Abby finished wiping the table and set the dishes to soak, then moved back towards the men, now smoking next to the fireplace. They were fiddling with the knobs of a short-wave radio; its static rose and fell in waves. There were several knee-high piles of magazines propped up against the walls to one side and a ragged pile of newspapers close to the hearth, for lighting fires presumably. A pile of National Geographics and loose-leaf paper, spilling off a coffee table next to an unlit kerosene lamp, reminded Abby that Tess should be about somewhere.

Without thinking, Abby pointed at the pile and inquired, "Is Tess doing some school stuff here, Mr. Talbot? She's got an active imagination you know. She just needs to work on those reading skills. National Geographics are great, eh? All those pictures..." She found her own voice faltering in volume, an unconscious response to the astonished expression that had overtaken Talbot's face.

Abby's next thoughts crowded out all thoughts of tea and convivial conversation. She had forgotten that he didn't know she was Tess's teacher. Her impression had been that he was self-contained, detached even. Maybe he didn't really care about what had happened with Tess the first day of school. Now, seeing the wrath gathering, Abby panicked internally. First, Ellie's accident, and now what?

Hank was appraising her clearly, sizing her up as if for the first time. She was the teacher who had embarrassed Tess. If he had been a man who had come into town much, this situation would never have arisen. It doesn't take long to get to recognize most of 2500 faces, and hers would have been one he'd have sent scuttling as soon as it turned up at his door. This embarrassing situation never would have developed.

Her resolve to face the music had been short-lived. She cast about for a means of graceful exit, anywhere to avoid what she now realized could be a blast of rage akin to the explosion she heard had thundered through the school hallways that May morning three years before.

"You're Tess's teacher!" He stiffened visibly next to Matt on the couch and was about to rise when Ellie's clattering at the table reminded him where he was. Leaning back into a seemingly relaxed, cross-legged pose, his tension suddenly dissipated and then, there was that smile again. "I thought I recognized that name! Oh, sorry, Matt. Abby, is it? Your last name's Clarke? Well, what do you know? Another teacher…small world, eh?" He chuckled, his gaze leveling at her briefly and then, "What the hell, that trouble about Ellie's schooling was long ago. Lots of water under the bridge. Now Tess…"

"Mr. Talbot, I don't mean any disrespect, but I'm not just a teacher, but also a counselor. I just don't understand why Ellie had to quit school. It was so close to graduation, May for heaven's sake, only a month to go." She knew her pursuit of the topic was heedless, but something about the man pushed her past the point of politeness.

His voice in response now had an edge to it. "Call me Hank, and I'll call you Abby, okay? It was branding season, you see. A ranch is only as good as its upkeep. Ellie had work to do here. As it is, I got to hire men for branding and round-up. I'm not made of money. Enough now. I don't need to answer to you for that ancient history. She can read and write and do math. Beth, her mom, seen to that before she passed. Hell, Ellie can even type and do dicta…dicta… whatever that claptrap business stuff is. But whatever, she don't need a diploma for ranch work."

"And how," Abby blurted out, realizing that this was much more sensitive territory, "are you going to ensure that Tess can learn those basics? Her mom's not around anymore, and she's far behind where Ellie was at her age, academically, I mean. Tess is the one who needs the guidance and encouragement now." She broke off in the heat of frustration. She didn't feel she was making her case very well. She noted Matt's alert silence. He wasn't much help really, nor could he be, in all fairness. Still, she was glad he was there. Instinctively, she knew her credibility as a human being in Hank Talbot's eyes was tied to her having a man there to back her up, whatever happened next.

As if reading her mind, Hank's gaze briefly swung to her husband sitting in the corner of the couch. Matt's calm exterior betrayed no sign of agitation or discomfort. Abby looked back to Hank.

"What do you say about Tess?" she repeated.

His response, when it came, seemed to filter from far away. His voice drifted across to her in the golden afternoon light. It hung with the dust motes caught in the sunbeams glancing through the window next to the fireplace. It settled around Ellie, trying to make herself as inconspicuous as possible at the dining table.

"Tess's got her head screwed on all right, never you mind. She knows what matters around here. Right now, I'll tell you where she is. She's doing something useful, out tending that horse of hers that Ellie was riding, and hosing down that leg with some cold water. Besides, she don't take to the house much. She's sort of like me that way, I guess. Don't hang around here much except to eat and sleep. She likes it out-side more, okay? Schooling ain't all there is to life, woman."

And then again, there was that smile. Grimly, Abby mused as she turned her back to avoid its seductive play. That ramrod of a bastard, iso-lating these kids out here! What kind of future did they have? Suddenly, she was unutterably depressed and wanted nothing more than to climb in the truck and go.

But there was still the charade of tea to be endured, and besides, she felt wrong about leaving Ellie to cope with a father who hadn't even seemed to wonder about the state of her foot. Calming herself took real effort, but by the time she had washed the breakfast dishes and readied the tea, Abby had regained most of her composure. Once cookies and tea were served, she thought to ask Ellie if Tess would want to come in for some.

"She's probably just as happy to have a mug out there. If you don't mind taking it out to her?"

Abby shook her head in disbelief. Not even coaxed into the house for communal mealtime? The thought of that slip of a girl left so com-pletely to her own devices made her uneasy.

"Sure," she said, heading for the front door with two mugs of tea in hand. "I'll see if I can find her."

"The barn's to your left across the clearing, " Ellie directed. "Remember, we saw it the other side of the corrals coming in?"

"Yeah," Abby grinned and nodded. " I may be a city-slicker, but I think I can find the barn."

# 8

# The Way It Used To Be

Walking across the clearing to the barn and corral, Abby slowed to get her bearings before finding Tess. The afternoon sun, hanging high above the treetops, seemed to wash the scene clear. She could imagine the family as it had once been here, kids hollering in the yard, Hank tinkering in the shed, the mom somewhere in a garden behind the kitchen, coaxing old fashioned city flowers from the wilderness soil. The scene that lay before her now, the space, littered with refuse and old machinery, seemed devoid of life or real promise. Her heart ached for the remnants of the family caught there.

The gabble of a wedge of geese flapping overhead called her back to the present and the warm mugs of tea in her hands. Where was the girl? She wasn't in the first or second corral behind the barn. There was just the horse, Blaze, chewing through a pile of hay heaped in the corner of the enclosure.

Abby edged her way around close to where Blaze stood to inspect her more closely. The mare seemed calm enough, her tail switching rhythmically as she watched Abby's approach. The animal nickered softly and then snorted more assertively, raised her front end up and wheeled off toward the corner opposite to where Abby stood. Funny how animals seem to smell nervousness, she mused. Watching the mare's movement reeling and pawing in the far corner, she thought the gait seemed nimble enough. There was no obvious injury, but then she didn't know much about horses. Just another thing to learn about this country.

In absentminded concentration, Abby backtracked towards the entrance to the barn. Maybe Tess was hiding out from them there, avoiding them as she had done Liz, the public health nurse. The stable seemed empty except for two other horses and a scruffy, brindled cat sunning itself in the doorway. She called out. Nothing. Maybe Tess was out behind in the corrals closer to the creek.

The pathway that skirted the corrals led her to the east, out beyond the house and kitchen garden way off to her right, through a craggy jumble of granite and damp crevasses bristling with clumps of wild rose bushes heavy with scarlet rose hips. Ahead and below, she could hear the barking of a dog and the rush of water. Probably Tess was down at the creek, Abby decided. Getting down there with the mugs in hand would require a balancing act, given the steep incline and the lack of handholds along the path. She grasped both mugs by the handles in one hand and, feeling vaguely silly, slid-eased her way down to where the creek churned along its gravel bed.

A canopy of tawny-leafed cottonwoods made a grotto of the spot where she finally stopped. The banks of the creek were choked with deadfall, timbers fallen victim to windstorms and old age. Some were enormous, waist high when she leaned across one to inspect the bank of the creek, its pale green satin depths erupting over shallows into trailing beards of white froth.

A splash and a yelp abruptly intersected the murmur of the water, and Abby looked up to catch a glimpse of Tess, in sopping T-shirt and panties, thigh deep in the center of the stream, wrestling a stick from the mouth of an excited black Labrador immersed up to its neck in mid-channel. The two had not noticed her, Abby guessed. Their position downstream and around a bend had concealed her approach. Now their boisterous play absorbed them as she leaned out across the giant cottonwood trunk, craning to keep them in her sights.

The wood was smooth and warm in the dappled sun, its bark long since worn off. Having perched Tess's tea mug on a flat expanse of rock near the flowing water, Abby stretched out to drink and watch as the girl repeatedly flung the stick, and the dog lunged splashing after it.

She was really just a baby, a six-year-old at best, caught in a young woman's body. Here in this setting, Tess seemed almost elfin, not of this world, a spirit from some other time. Her slim limbs flashed like wings in the sun, her giggles all but merging with the chuckling of the creek. Her lithe bending and swooping in the water created arcs of crystal drops that sparkled in the sun spilling down from amongst the cottonwood canopy far overhead. Suddenly, clearly, Abby understood the enormity of Tess's challenge to fit in anywhere else.

The insight brought sudden abashment. She felt like an interloper, sneaking into Tess's private refuge. She gulped the last of her tea and shimmied backwards soundlessly, leaving the girl there with her dog.

Partway up the bank, Abby, remembering the mug left on the rock, wheeled about to retrieve it. Thrashing clumsily downward in her haste, she stumbled out of the bush onto the clearing at the bank. There stood Tess, dripping wet and holding the mug, staring agape at the flustered intruder.

"What's this?" Tess meant the mug, but Abby sensed she wasn't pondering its contents as much as its reason for being there.

"Ellie said you'd likely drink some tea. It's probably pretty cold by now. You could use some warming up I expect. You're pretty wet." The words trailed off as Abby became aware of the tension in the other's stance. "I didn't mean to sneak up on you, Tess. I just wanted to touch base, you know, see how you are. We stopped in with Ellie. We had a little accident on the road."

"You shouldn't be here, lady." The statement hung like a warning. Then, as if just connecting with Abby's last words, Tess rushed on, "An accident? We figured she'd been dumped somewhere when Blaze came back all covered in lather. Pa was madder than fired up hornets so I took off. He's a sight tough to take when he's pissed off, I mean, when he's riled."

"Well, Ellie has hurt her foot in the fall, and it was our fault. We were going too fast. Anyway, we brought her home. She didn't want to get it checked out in town, but I don't know if Blaze is all right. Your dad says he thinks she is."

"Oh, Blaze, yeah, I guess she'll be okay. Her haunch looks a mite bruised and she'll probably run chicken for a bit. We always tend to our own out here, so don't you worry none about Ellie." The embarrassed pause that ensued lingered long enough that they both rushed to fill the awkward silence.

"Thanks for the tea. I gotta find my gear."

"You're shivering Tess. Didn't you bring a towel?"

They both erupted in brittle laughter, the girl's fluting tones an octave higher and quavering with the cold.

"I'll go get my stuff. It's on the other side of the creek. Thanks for the tea." With that she guzzled the drink and held out the cup.

"Aren't you going to come up to the house for something to eat?"

"Yeah, later. I'm not really hungry. Besides, I got some stuff to eat if I want – raisins and peanuts 'n stuff." She looked away to where the dog sat on the bank, as if weighing her next words carefully. Abby got the impression that talk was easier for her when she was on her own turf.

"Mrs. Clarke, is my dad still being ornery? I mean, was he okay to you? Since Mrs. Lundstrom came that day, well, he's just real riled sometimes. I don't know why she said I couldn't keep on here like I was. Schooling by correspondence papers. I even promised I'd really do the stuff myself if she'd leave us be. My dad needs somebody here. Tim don't come by more than once every couple a weeks, and Ellie, well, she won't be here long, not the way her and Dad cuss and sling at each other." Suddenly, the dog's barking interrupted. "Hey! I gotta go. It sounds like Mooch has got wind of something back there." The dog had careened off across the creek, yelping excitedly.

Before Abby could say another word, the girl was gone too, skittering across the gravel into the water, calling to Mooch as she splashed to the other bank. The last Abby saw was a quick dip behind a tree trunk, and then a hurried shrugging of slender white arms into a red-checkered lumberjack shirt. Whooping up the other bank, the girl disappeared into the bush.

"I didn't even get a word in edgewise about the school business, dammit." Abby turned again to heave herself up onto the first dogleg of the corral path. The image of Tess's retreating figure lingered with her, all coltish and wet, her skin white, almost blue in places. Very blue. Abby suddenly recalled seeing dark smudges of bruises on the backs of her upper thighs just below where the upper edge of the T-shirt had clung. Ugly looking bruises, she thought.

The memory of those bruises precipitated a heated scramble up the rocky incline, her breath coming in rasps of invective as she formulated a vision of the old bastard beating the girl. For what? For not wanting to go to school? For wanting to stay home with him? The guy who hadn't wanted to send her in the first place?

By the time Abby had reached the path along the perimeter of the corral, she had cooled down somewhat. She knew some kids might admit to being abused, but she doubted somehow that Tess would, depending as she did on her father's good will to help her stay at home. The irony was tragic. The last place the girl should be was the only place she wanted to be.

Just as Abby was crossing the clearing before the house, she heard the bang of the side door off the kitchen slamming shut, but the angle of the house corner prevented her from seeing who had emerged. Who-ever it was had gone back to the chopping block, for from there could be heard the whack of an axe and grunts of exertion.

For a moment, she hoped it would be Hank Talbot there, and she quickened her pace, images of Tess's thighs freshly spurring her to con-front the father. The old buzzard, beating that waif of a child, and her so accepting and protective of him! Abby had almost worked herself back into a white-hot rage when she finally reached the corner of the house and could see back to where the chopping block stood. There was Ellie, perched on one foot like a stork, heaving about wildly with the axe.

"Ellie! Get off that foot! You can't do that! Why didn't you ask Matt or your dad? You can't chop like that! You'll swing and miss off balance, for crying out loud!"

"I got to do something lady. It isn't my idea of a good time stuck in there with those two."

Oh Lord, Abby thought. What now?

"I found Tess. She was down at the creek with her dog. Sorry I took so long. I didn't expect to have to go so far. She got her tea, though." Lamely she indicated the empty mugs still in hand.

"Yeah. Whatever." Ellie started into another hazardous swing at the chunk of cordwood. In mid-swing, she hesitated, looked at Abby obliquely and lowered the axe.

"Lady, my dad and your old man are into the whisky in there." The statement landed as an accusation. The girl's face was flushed either with anger or effort, maybe both. Her eyes conveyed a frantic mix of pleading and fear. In their depths though, something more ominous was brewing.

Abby expelled her breath in a huff of exasperation. Of course, Matt would share his truck stash with Hank Talbot. Nothing like another drinking buddy! She recalled it would be only a mickey at least, but somehow she sensed the size of the bottle would be small comfort to this girl.

"Ellie, I promise we'll go soon. I didn't think Matt would bring it out. It won't last long, I don't think. There isn't really very much, after all."

At this, Ellie exploded. "You can't go now!! Once he's been drinking, he's an asshole! I mean, Lady, don't you know nothing? Men are freaking animals! I don't care if he is my dad! I won't stay here with him like that!! Geez, my foot! Arghhh!"

An inadvertent touchdown with her sore foot as she seesawed around the chopping stump had left Ellie momentarily speechless. Abby rushed in to steady her by the elbow.

"Leave me be! Haven't you done enough as it is? Bugger up my foot, lame my horse, get my dink of a father drunk! You're some piece of work for a teacher! Maybe my dad's right about some stuff anyway. Teachers are either useless assholes or interfering twits!" Her head dropped as if only in that second had she grasped how heedless her words had been. "Oh, I'm sorry, that was uncalled for, really. I'm just so mad!"

Abby shook off the insults. "Ellie! Be sensible. There's only a mickey. Matt never has any more in the truck. That's not enough to..." Her words died there. A mickey was all Matt had, but there was no telling what Hank kept around.

"It doesn't take much Mrs. Clarke. You don't know my dad. Besides, he's got his own stash. I've never been able to find it. It's out in the shed somewhere, probably. All he needs is an excuse. Guess you folks are it this time. Sorry I lost it just now. My foot hurt some bad there for a minute."

"Oh Ellie! I'm so sorry for..." Abby groped for the words to express the depths of her regret, "...your foot, and your horse and the whisky." The constriction of Abby's breathing loosened; she saw that the girl was no longer furious with her. For a moment, she had felt paralyzed by guilt.

Seeing Ellie wince again, Abby steered her by the elbow to hobble across the back of the yard to a bench outside the greenhouse door at the back of the house. The greenhouse extended across the back behind the massive fireplace and around of the corner to the front of the house.

At once, Abby could see the ingenuity of the arrangement. The greenhouse faced south and west to maximize its exposure to the sun, and the heat of the rock chimney provided a reasonable amount of warmth for spring bedding plants, maybe even offset the fierceness of the winter for some hardy perennials. Clearly, the designer of this house had put some thought into it.

Once settled on the bench, Ellie regarded Abby curiously. "Actually Mrs. Clarke, it's none of it your fault, come to think on it. Mr. Clarke was driving when we got hit, and he's the one what brought in the whisky, though my dad did have to ask if he had any. So I was dead wrong to blame you. Once again, it's a bloody man that's done wrong."

"You know, Ellie, not all men are mean when they drink. Some people just don't have any other way of handling their anger than taking it out on the ones closest. But not every man is like that."

Ellie's resulting snort of derisive laughter chopped Abby off in mid-spiel.

"Dad isn't just mean when he's drunk, Lady. Shit, I wish that's all he was. You know, he's rough on Tim too, but with me and Tess, well, he's different." Then the girl groaned again, cast a wary glance at Abby and continued, her voice low and confidential. "Look, Mrs. Clarke, my dad's okay. He doesn't mean any harm, really. He's just missing Mom bad."

"You mean because she was so ill at the end. Of course, your dad wouldn't be the best one to handle somebody who's sick I guess, so they didn't spend much time together alone?"

"Yeah, something like that. Me and Tess did the nursing for Mom. She didn't want Dad touching her nice sleep clothes." Ellie's eyes sought Abby's. "She said he smelled too bad of cattle and engine grease, and it made her queasy to have him near too much. Anyway, that's what she told me. Him? He just thought she was losing it because of the pain. And it was woman trouble she had too, eh? So they didn't talk much about her actual condition, you see? Mom was private that way."

Abby sensed Ellie preferred not to talk about her father. "Tell me about your mom, Ellie. Where did she come from? What was she like? What was important to her?"

"You're sitting in it. This garden was Mom's favourite place. In spring, summer and fall, she spent more time here than anywhere else.

Dad made her the greenhouse when they first homesteaded, but she did almost all the rest, burned the stumps, pulled the roots, carted in bottom soil from the gully, fenced it to keep out the moose. She did it all. When we were kids, we got hung on the clothesline papoose style. Then we all picked stones for her as soon as we could walk. She did most of the hard stuff herself until Rosie came along.

"Rosie?"

"Rosemary Joseph, a native woman from the Babine. Rosie helped her a lot in those days. She showed Mom all kinds of stuff. Roots and bark medicine, wild rose hips for jelly, canning fish. They were busy ladies. I remember Rosie pretty well, but the others were too young. She was gone when I was seven. Tim was just five, and Tess just born when Rosie quit coming round.

"Rosie was midwife to Mom and helped out some in branding and haying time. Mostly, she just came to visit with Mom, canned and made herb concoctions with her. Rosie was forever bringing by stuff she'd found in the bush, balsam fir gum for insect bites, or the bark to make tea for pain, yarrow for bruises or swelling. She was a walking drugstore! She had a cabin somewhere down by the lake, kept a trap line hereabouts and did a little fishing and hunting."

Sensing Ellie would rather talk about Rosie than the more painful topic of her mom, Abby asked, "Was Rosie similar to your mom, in personality, I mean? You know, independent and private?"

"She was one tough woman who didn't take no guff from anyone. She was strong as stink, and pretty smart. Her mom was Dene, but she didn't know who her dad was. Mom said she was pretty much her own boss, I guess. She had family up north, but for some reason, she didn't want to spend time there. Mom said Rosemary started coming by just before Tim was born. She thought she was a gift from heaven sent to help with the birthing. Must have taken a load off Dad to have her around, the way he is about town and all."

"So where did Beth, your mom, meet your dad then? Not in town, I guess."

"She never talked much about her days before. I know she came from back east and met Dad at a rodeo in Colorado. He used to ride broncos, and she was selling something, handmade jewelry probably. She showed me some she made once when I was real little, pretty shell beads and stones worked with silver wire. Later, I asked for some to wear to school, and she said she had sold it all at the local fair with Rosemary. It was all gone, and she had no stuff to make more. Anyways, they met down there, and he brought her here. They bought this place free and clear with his rodeo winnings. They had enough to get the breeding stock, repair the sheds and barn, and build a new house. He's had a tough life, my dad, but he was born to it. Somehow, I don't think Mom fit in so well. She sure tried hard though. I have to give her that."

"I can tell the house must have been nice and homey. I'll bet there were lots of flowers, and homemade touches. You can still sense that comfy feeling even now." Abby stretched out on the bench, luxuriating in the late afternoon sun.

"Mom was artistic, I think. She had this place looking like it was off the cover of a glossy house magazine. You know, all cheery and clean, fresh curtains, good smells in the kitchen. That's what I remember from when she wasn't sick, but she started spending much of the time in bed starting quite a while ago, so mostly to me, my mom was a sick lady. Poor soul, she suffered some before the end. After that, well you can see, the house hasn't had much attention. It takes all three of us to do the ranch stuff, and Dad doesn't want to spend money he doesn't have to hire year-round ranch hands if we can do it." Ellie shrugged, exhaustion written deep on her young face.

"Anyway, the last stuff Mom did was to plant some kitchen herbs and bulbs in the greenhouse. Some amaryllis I think. She wanted some for Christmas. I've been tending to them a bit. They don't need much except watering. Do you want to see?"

The greenhouse door was wedged shut, but Ellie shouldered it open and held it for Abby. Inside on the potting bench were a variety of trays containing tobacco cans full of soil. No growth was yet apparent. Ellie poked the soil in several of the containers, then grabbing a watering can, she was gone and next could be heard splashing in the rain barrel.

Abby perched on a seat projecting from the rock wall that backed the greenhouse. On shelves above the potting bench were jars of seeds and mesh bags full of bulbs. Bunches of dried herbs, pungently aromatic, hung from the rafters. Beth's presence was almost close enough to touch. To Abby, she seemed to have been a whimsical creature of tattered elegance, pinned like a butterfly not yet etherized.

On the floor at her feet lay a straw sun hat, its ribbons frayed, dried sprigs of cornflowers tucked about its brim. She held it, imagining Beth laying it there, overcome with pain or exhaustion. Putting it on, Abby felt suddenly silly, and was just about to remove the hat when Ellie arrived back with her full watering can.

"That's my mom's. She liked pretty things. She was one for dressing up sometimes, a bit anyhow, as much as she could out here. She finally quit trying to get us to, though. Then after she was gone, the day we buried her, I got some of Mom's make-up stuff out, mostly some powder and cologne and some lipstick, and Tess and I dolled each other up, put on dresses even, so we could look ladylike for her, at least at the end. It wasn't such a good idea though. Dad just about blew a gasket when he saw us. I gave Tess the stuff and told her to hide it somewhere. I don't know what she did with it."

Abby wondered whether the lipstick had ended up on the school washroom mirrors.

"Abby!!! Babe, where you at? We gotta blow this popsicle stand, darlin'!" Matt was feeling the whisky. He reeled around the corner and was well past the outside bench and the greenhouse before he spotted them.

"Come on! If we go now we can catch the evening rise on the lake. I got trout to catch! Can't waste this whole damn day! Besides, Hank is outta whisky, and mine's gone too. Come on! It's almost five o'clock. We only got an hour of good light left."

"Matt Clarke, you aren't driving anywhere!" Abby could see another all-nighter coming up, and she just didn't have the reserves to handle it. They could just damn well go home now!

"Oh, Abby, loverlips. Gimme a kiss. You want some nice rainbow trout for panfry, I know you do. I don't care about driving. But I got to go fishing! It's just the perfect time. Those little suckers just about jump into the boat this time of day! Okay? You can drive, and I'll do all the paddling, see? How's that for a deal? You don't even have to help unload the canoe. When you ever have it so good? Jeez darlin', come on!"

Abby turned to Ellie, the girl's face an inscrutable mask in the shade of the eaves. "Will you be all right, Ellie? Is Tess back, Matt? If Tess's here, won't she help you so you can stay off your foot, Ellie? I'll talk to her. I'm sure she would. You said your dad would look at it. Has he yet?"

"Tess ain't back." Hank's deep bass boomed from the region of the chopping block where he stood wavering.

"Where could she be? I left her ages ago down at the creek, over an hour anyway, if not more. She was wet and cold! Where would she go?"

Hank's response was chilling in its detachment. "She'll be fine. The dog with her? Yeah? Oh hell, she's better off with him than anybody. They was raised up together. He'll protect her against anything out there." With a wave of his hand to dismiss any concern about Tess's welfare, he leaned down and dislodged the axe from the chopping block stump, and with another smooth motion, swooped a round of cordwood from the pile under the eaves.

Just as he raised it to swing, Abby had a sudden horrific vision of truncated limbs and flesh laid open to the bone. The man was crazy to chop wood in his condition! But who else could? Sure enough, Matt was in no better shape. Ellie mustn't, and herself, well, she was useless. She couldn't do it decently, try as she might.

Petrified, she watched as he swung and cleaved the round expertly in two, the panther grace of his movement seemingly unhampered by an afternoon of alcohol. Matt always said some people's coordination was improved by a bit of booze. What could she say? The man could neglect his wife, abuse his kids, and chop wood, drunk or sober. Who was she to criticize?

Motioning her to come along behind, Matt ambled off, lending an arm to help Ellie negotiate the path back to the kitchen entrance. Abby was left to bypass Hank as he was about to take another swing. Just as she came abreast of him on the path, he rested the axe on his shoulder and considered her up and down appraisingly.

"I told you before Miz-Abby-Teacher-Woman, I tend to my own. I don't need no one for nothing, not chopping wood, not raising my kids."

Abby's next impulse was to retreat before she succumbed to the gut instinct to claw that drunken, charming grin off the man's face. The urgency of her need to leave delighted Matt, of course. But she couldn't abide the look of abandonment on Ellie's face.

As she hesitated to leave, Abby juggled possibilities, suggesting maybe they could stop by on the way back into town if it wasn't too late, but Ellie just shook her head, mumbling about going to bed and putting her foot up. As they made to go, she did in fact hobble off to her room, and with a last glance back, shut her door with a deliberate thud. Then Abby thought she heard a bolt slide home.

Abby felt uneasy. If Matt hadn't been drinking, she would have suggested he leave her there and take Hank Talbot instead, then pick her up on the way back. But there was no way either one should be driving, even if the lake was just a few miles off. She would have to drive on the badly rutted ranch road all the way back to the turnoff, and then manage the last leg down to the lake on Antoinette Lake Road. Besides, the thought of having to contend any more with Hank was more than she could stomach. To ease her anxiety, she got Matt to belt himself in even though there was no law yet to require it. He was still grumbling amiably.

As they rounded the corner out of sight of the house clearing, Abby banged the dash in exasperation. She hadn't got a promise from Tess to come back to school. Damn!

At least she would follow up somehow. Maybe she'd give Liz Lundstrom or the social worker a visit, get the lowdown on the family history. Thinking of the public health nurse, Abby remembered Tess's bruises. Yeah, get the old man checked out for abuse. She fumed silently all along the winding, pot-hole filled road to Antoinette Lake.

# 9

# Nora Steps Up

The next day, Constable Nora Macpherson sat at the reception desk of the Moose Forks RCMP Detachment behind the glass partition separating it from the front foyer. She was seething. Here she was, almost two weeks on the job as a full-fledged constable, not a recruit anymore, and still stuck behind the front desk, answering telephone calls!

Again, she reflected on her luck in being one of those thirty-two women who had been selected nationwide as recruits for "Troop 17" at Depot in Regina. She remembered all the sweat and grunt work she had done to get through Depot, the "boot camp" for Mounties. Now, here in Moose Forks (population 2500), her luck seemed to have run out. Here she was window-dressing with a difference. As in so many small communities where the office budget was scant, she was the fill-in "girl Friday", little more that the sergeant's secretary, because the regular civilian receptionist was, she now knew, recovering from being thrown by her horse. She was in traction in the hospital in Prince George, and unlikely to be back for months. Nora groaned inwardly to think of herself still answering the phone come spring!

"Macpherson!" She flung an oblique glance in the direction of the summons, and restrained the impulse to jump to attention at the sound of Sergeant Jack Wasniki's baritone bark. She pushed her office chair back carefully, untangled her long legs and stood up, straightening her navy-blue skirt and tie as she moved towards his office door ten feet behind the reception desk.

"Yes, Sergeant," she smiled to acknowledge she had heard him and was ready to be oh-so helpful. God help me if he wants coffee again, she thought.

But he had official business of a sort. "You're a photographer, Constable?"

"Yes, Sergeant. It's a hobby, but I have Depot training in crime scene photography, the requirements for forensic testimony, chain of custody, all of that. Is that what you mean, Sergeant?"

"Yeah, yeah." He waved his hand dismissively as if listening to her qualifications had been some kind of imposition. "We are lucky to have one of the few dark rooms in the area, and we need more supplies, Constable, so please make sure they are kept stocked up. Add that to your list of duties."

Just then, she heard the reception desk phone ring so, bobbing her head in acknowledgement, she hurried back to answer.

Watching her leave his office provided Wasniki with some enjoyment. She was a tall, well-built girl with a fine rhythmic sway to her ass. Nice package altogether, he mused, especially in that slim skirt that accentuated her curves just so. But his pleasure was cut short by the irritation her presence inevitably aroused.

Why did his detachment have to be the one selected for the "honour" of hosting one of the first official female members in the Force? He was only four or five years from retirement. Was this Division's idea to make him quit early? Did those numbskulls have any idea how having a woman in the squad room hampered the full and free airing of opinion?

He had to admit, however, that he hadn't heard any specific complaints from Jed Fedoruk, who, as detachment corporal, was his second-in-command. Nor for that matter, had any of the others voiced any concern. But he was pretty sure they all must see it the way he did. The Force was a man's business, always was, and always would be. This pandering to the Women's Libbers was not going to get the RCMP anywhere.

Back at her desk, Nora was taking notes as she spoke with Liz Lundstrom. The Public Health Nurse was following up on a complaint her office had lodged at the end of May.

"Constable... Macpherson, is it?" Mrs. Lundstrom conveyed an affable but nonetheless commanding presence over the phone. "My office lodged a complaint against Henry Martin Talbot, DOB November 16, 1931, on May 30, 1976 this past spring, for failure to provide the necessities of life to Elizabeth (Beth) Mary Talbot – DOB March 10,

1932 Deceased May 17, 1976. We expected some follow-up by now. Prior to this, we made a complaint about the inappropriate disposition of the late Mrs. Talbot's body. That was in conjunction with Mike Horvath at the Community Resources Board, who also has some concerns arising from an incident that happened when he tried to ensure that Teresa Talbot, DOB February 2, 1963, was enrolled in school. I was wondering if you could tell me what is the current disposition of the case."

"I will have to look into this for you, Mrs. Lundstrom. I do recall that there was a mention of that file, but I have not been here very long and am still finding my way around." Nora realized her explanation sounded like gutless stonewalling, but she had no alternative.

She knew for a fact that Sergeant Wasniki had the Talbot file buried on his desk and was letting it stay buried because, as she had overheard him say to Fedoruk, "There's no point in ruffling Talbot's feathers. Not only is the guy considered a trailblazer among the other ranchers, but he's also got powerful friends in town. We don't need the hassle. Besides, the wife is dead. A bunch of useless paperwork won't bring her back, and he needs the girl for ranching."

Nora had internalized the absolute imperative of the chain-of-command discipline as well as anyone, but she was still uncomfortable protecting Wasniki, so she decided to do a little discreet probing. "Can you tell me anything about the condition of the family while the mother was ill?" With this angle, she could at least justify her involvement as within her "community liaison" duties as the husband's treatment of the wife could be construed to predict how he might treat the daughter. "Was there home support for Mrs. Talbot or regular therapy?"

Nora was unprepared for the firestorm of scorn in Liz Lundstrom's voice as she answered these questions: "Hank Talbot refused treatment for the wife, no doctor allowed. It was sheer neglect, pure and simple. Thinking about that woman's suffering at the end still makes my blood boil. I want the police to bring charges of failing to provide the necessities of life. I know Talbot has already paid a fine for the death certificate charge, but really, is that enough?"

Nora was stunned into silence, wondering how such a man could be so influential in the valley. Yet, she knew from gossip that he was a friend, and occasional drinking buddy, of both George Warren, and Frank Hughes who was the superintendent of the sawmill.

Liz Lundstrom's voice continued, "Now the younger daughter Teresa is at the high school, and Mike Horvath and I worry that she's living with him out there, so if you could check into this file and get back to me, I'd be very grateful, Constable Macpherson."

Nora, catching the comment about the daughter, suddenly realized how she could respond. "I'll follow this up, Mrs. Lundstrom, and relay your concern to Sergeant Wasniki. He's the one who makes the decisions about which cases will proceed."

She wrote Liz's contact information and Teresa's name and age on a pink memo slip, but instead of popping it into Wasniki's mail slot on the wall behind her, tucked it into her large regulation shoulder bag. She would check up on the Talbot girl, and, when she got the chance, she would find the Talbot file to have a look herself. If Sergeant Wasniki wanted the file "temporarily lost", she'd be happy to oblige!

The rest of the morning was quiet, leaving Nora time to reflect on her decision to investigate the Talbot case. As she completed the typing of routine reports, she thought back to her childhood. As a kid growing up in Winnipeg, she had dreamed of being an RCMP officer and had been overjoyed when she could apply for the Mounties. Now, she wanted some real police work out in the field. She knew there were problems with theft out at the mill for instance, and rumours of marijuana use on the job, too, as well as the usual number of workplace accidents. Maybe the accidents were a Workmen's Compensation Board issue, but the theft and drug problem were police concerns. But she had never been given those cases, supposedly because Wasniki felt the mill environment was too risky. A sensible senior officer would accept her suitability for any assignment, regardless of risk. She would be safe and effective enough wearing her oxfords and trousers, but Wasniki was anything but sensible! He was image-conscious to a fault, a hidebound stickler for detail. He would never let her off the leash. To him she was "just a woman", not a real RCMP officer. Now, she would show him what she could do.

She was pretty sure the problem wasn't with Jed Fedoruk, who struck her as a decent man and a good cop. No, Wasniki was the snag. Jed had confided to her that the sergeant hadn't been keen on her being assigned to his detachment in the first place, but didn't want to look like the chauvinist he really was. Luckily, Wasniki was due to retire in a couple of years, and then who knew? Besides, young officers didn't stay long in any one detachment. She, herself, could be anywhere in two years.

For now, she knew she needed to get some honest-to-god field experience, and the Talbot family case was a reasonable place to start. Besides, if this wasn't in the realm of domestic disputes, she didn't know what was. Wasnsiki couldn't say she was outside her allocated duties. Still, just to be safe, she would cover her tracks by putting with the Talbot file, when she located it, in her bag so Sergeant Wasniki didn't get into a huge nasty man-snit she would end up paying for with even more office duty, or even worse, a letter of reprimand on her file.

# 10

## Abby in a Fix

At the end of a busy school day in mid-September, Abby ran into the small multi-purpose municipal office where the town hall, the health clinic, and the School District Superintendent's satellite office were located. Theirs was a far-flung district, and the school super as a rule was in town only a couple of days a week.

She was hustling past a couple of older men just emerging into the main hallway, when she recognized them as School Superintendent George Warren and Mill Manager Frank Hughes, and smiled briefly without stopping. However, Warren put out his hand to stop her rush past and beaming a grin, asked, "How are your classes this year, Abby?"

Surprised that he even knew her name, Abby paused. How curious! She reflected that she had encountered both of them before and had never got more than a nod of acknowledgement. Now, she felt as if she were being appraised like a prize heifer!

Then she remembered that both men were friends with Hank Talbot. Oh, God, is what happened on Saturday already town gossip?

She answered George Warren's inquiry with a clichéd "Everything's good!" and, after apologizing that she was late for an appointment and couldn't stop, kept on her path towards the health clinic wing.

Liz Lundstrom was just wrapping up and, after nodding Abby towards a chair, closed the open file on the desk in front of her. "Hi! How's it going?" Abby and Matt had met Liz when they first came to town and had maintained a friendly professional acquaintanceship ever since. She was a brisk, tidy woman in her fifties who wore her silver grey hair in a fashionable, short pixie cut.

"I hear you and Matt were out to Bar T this weekend."

Abby groaned, "Does everybody know? Mr. Warren just stopped me in the hallway, and I'm sure he never would have if…"

"Abby, Moose Forks is a small town. Get used to it! Anyway, what can I do for you?" Her smile assured Abby that she wasn't interested in gossip.

"Liz, I need to know what can be done to help Tess Talbot. I feel a bit to blame here, especially after I upset her so badly last week. You know how, the first day of school, she walked out of my class?" Abby knew Liz had been into the school talking to Margaret.

Liz took a deep breath and then let it all out slowly as she seemed to speculate about what to say. She took off her glasses as if to have something to look at while she spoke. "Abby, I wouldn't get myself too invested in trying to change the situation in that family. I mean, Hank Talbot is a force onto himself and not one to ignore interference.

"Off the record, I'll give you the background so you can understand why I say this. Beth Talbot came in first to see me one time when she was in town for the fall fair. I guess it must have been about eleven or twelve years ago. She had the three kids and was feeling "drained" she said. She was still nursing the little one, Tess, at that point. She said she had had some help with the delivery from her friend Rosemary, and that Hank was managing the ranch with the hired hand, Casey Somebody or Other. I can't remember his last name.

So I checked her over a bit, but said she really needed to see a doctor to get a complete physical, you know, to make sure she hadn't done some damage to herself delivering Tess."

"Did she do that, go to the clinic, I mean? Ellie indicated to us that Hank isn't fond of using the clinic."

"No, I never saw her again until a couple of years later, and as far as I know, Doc McCullough never did either. Then I saw her again when she was at the fair with all the kids, and we smiled at each other, and I was about to stop and chat when Hank suddenly turned up. Something – I'd call it sheer terror – in Beth's face told me I shouldn't let on we had ever spoken, and so I just kept going. But I remember thinking she looked pale and underweight even then.

"The next time I saw her was about a year ago. She said Ellie had convinced her to come in and see Dr. McCullough about some swelling she had in her abdomen. She had been afraid to come because of Hank, but she had also been losing weight, and she was afraid it might be something serious. She couldn't get in to the doctor because he was out on a call, so I found some time to talk to her. I was hoping I could persuade her to wait until the doctor got back. Anyway, we chatted. She never said the word 'cancer', but we both knew she was thinking it. I couldn't get her to wait and see the doctor though. She said she wasn't even supposed to be in town."

"So she never even got a diagnosis?"

"Oh, I don't doubt it was some kind of gynecological cancer. She was having irregular periods and pain with intercourse – all the usual symptoms – and there was the weight loss and the abdominal swelling too. I'm sure Beth Talbot was already seriously ill that last time she came into town, but no, she never did get an actual diagnosis. I gave her some painkillers, some samples we had in the clinic, and pleaded with her to come back to see Doc for treatment, but she just shook her head and left. Ellie had driven her in with the family truck, I guess.

"After that, I went out a few times to the ranch to visit Beth, but mostly to take her something for the pain. It felt like the least I could do. I was okay there as long as Hank wasn't around, so last winter, when I thought he was in town so that I could be sure the road would have been cleared, I drove my Jeep out on my own time to see her. But he was there, and just as nasty as he could be, calling me names I won't repeat, and threatening to set the dog on me, yelling that I was interfering in private family business. I left pretty shaken and didn't go back, you understand."

Liz breathed a sigh of exasperation and put her glasses back on as if, in so doing, she could now deal with present needs instead of past discomforts. "So that is all I know about how Hank Talbot deals with official intervention. Just between you, me, and the gatepost, I wouldn't put it past him to have hurried her along a little, if you know what I mean. She smiled ruefully and cocked her head at Abby as if to say 'over to you!'

Abby took a moment to digest the sheer horror of what Liz had just intimated. Murder, that would be. He could be a child-beater and murderer! How narrow a gap there could be between the two!

"Liz, what if I told you that I think he's beating those girls? Would that make a difference in how he's dealt with?"

"Well, that's a horse of an entirely different colour. If you can prove physical abuse, there are laws to protect them, or at least Tess, because she's under-age. Ellie could file her own charge."

"So I would have to get Tess to you and show you?"

"That would be best, but it doesn't have to be me. Any reputable witness, another teacher would do, and you draw a sketch of her body and where the bruises are, how big and what colour, you know? Then you should follow it up with Mike Horvath. He's the one who handles the child welfare cases. If he thinks there is some proof of abuse, he'll arrange for Tess to be taken into protective custody."

Abby made a mental note. The problem was getting Tess even to come to school. Now she had to keep her there long enough to prove she had been beaten. She remembered what else she needed to ask Liz. "And you are the one who filed the complaint about Beth's being buried without a death certificate?"

"Yes, that was me. I did that after talking to Mike Horvath at the Community Resource Board. He had had a similar run-in with Hank Talbot. I had mentioned to Mike that I hadn't seen much of Tess when I went out to see her mom. He decided if the mom was so sick, the girl should be in regular school. So we collaborated. He went out to confront Hank, and Hank got his rifle out."

"Did he actually shoot it?" Abby was remembering the cat-like grace of the man, and imagining him well and truly angry.

"I don't think any bullets were fired. Regardless, we lodged the complaint about the improper disposal of human remains, and he had to pay a fine. I just wanted that man to face the music somewhere, you know? Seemed like a fair consequence. But I also think he should be charged for failing to provide the necessities of life. So far, it hasn't got me anywhere. I called the RCMP office this morning about that complaint and that new female officer, Constable Macpherson, said she'd look into it."

Abby thought about Matt's comments about Tim Talbot. "Liz, have you had anything to do with the brother, Tim?"

"Oh, Tim's a good guy, not the least bit like his father. He can do the ranch work and has done lots of range riding, but he hates it. He's got no patience with animals, but give him a truck and a machine to fix and he's happy. His father, of course, doesn't understand. All those years of worry and sweat, and there's no one but Tess who seems interested in taking over. It must be driving Hank nearly frantic." She snorted as if to say, "Ask me if I care!"

"Your best bet, Abby, where Tess is concerned, is to see if Ellie might be talked into moving into town so that Tess would have a place to stay while she goes to school during the week. I would say to include Tim in the idea too because he has his job at the mill, but he probably doesn't have much extra money now. He just bought himself a fancy new four-wheel drive truck."

Abby was thinking about how much you could find out in a small town just by visiting the public health nurse when her eye caught the time on her wristwatch. She jumped up, "I need to go if I'm going to make the supermarket before closing! Thanks Liz, I'll think about the Ellie apartment idea!" And she was off.

While she was driving the two short blocks to the mall, Abby pondered whether her friend Laura Mendez, who managed the mill office, might help Ellie out with a job. Might be worth a try, anyway.

Ten minutes later, she was browsing through the limited selection of greens in the produce section at Shop-Easy, and again wondering why the market never seemed to have the stuff she could see growing in the Moose Forks' back yard gardens, when once again, she bumped into Frank Hughes who was picking over the apples.

"We can't keep meeting this way, or someone will get suspicious," he joked.

Abby blushed and laughed. "Well, in this town we can't get away with much!" Then she inwardly groaned, realizing she'd given Frank the perfect opening to pry into their Saturday visit out at the ranch.

But Frank seemed more intent on talking about work. "Hey, you know we have another shift opening at the mill, Abby? This town will be just a-hopping soon with a whole load of new people coming all the way from back east. Some of them have very good experience too. Yeah, all the way from Newfoundland, some of them." Then, he went on to comment almost randomly about how new residents were good for business, how the market looked pretty full, and then how he was looking forward to seeing her and Matt at the Christmas staff party!

Later, on her way out of the market, Abby wondered why Frank had been so friendly. First George Warren and now Frank. What was their agenda? Frank had never been that sociable before, at least not unless she was with Matt. She pondered whether he was checking out how happy she was in Moose Forks. Or maybe it was about not causing trouble. Maybe that talk about experienced new workers was a not-so-subtle reminder that Matt wasn't the only sawmill foreman available anymore! There were now others who could do his job.

Arms full of paper grocery bags, Abby was trudging through the maze of parked cars in the mall parking lot when she caught sight of the tall, athletic figure of Constable Macpherson just emerging from the squad car. They were on a course to pass close enough to greet each other. For a moment, she considered introducing herself and reminding her about the Talbot situation. Then, looking more closely at Nora's facial expression, she thought better of the idea. Maybe not. That look on her face would freeze a pot of red-hot chili! She had certainly looked happier when Abby had seen her at the Labour Day BBQ. She wondered what had happened.

While driving home along the curving poplar-lined residential street to their two year-old, split-level house, Abby considered her impulse to chat with the female constable. In retrospect, she was astonished by the urge. Given their dope-smoking connections, Matt would be more than just a little annoyed if she decided to get cozy with some cop! He was antsy enough about her butting into the Talbot problems! What was she thinking? But still, Nora Macpherson likely could help.

The very act of opening the front door with its lovely oak panels and brass knocker seemed to settle her misgivings. This is what she and Matt had been working for, all those years of schooling for her, and for him, those awful winter night shifts on the green chain before his grit and determination got him the foreman's position. She cherished this lovely new house and their annual holidays south, and maybe soon, there would be a baby. Besides, her folks were already disappointed with her move out here. What would they think if they knew she had to deal with people like Hank Talbot? No. Involving the cops was just plain stupid.

As she moved past the foyer and central hallway, she gazed up to admire the cathedral ceiling finished in cedar, and the dove-grey river stone fireplace in the living room. They had carpeted the main floor, and installed a comfy sectional that faced a whole back wall of glass. They could sit in their home with the fire burning cheerfully and look out and see nothing but the graceful spines of birch trees marching off into the distance.

In her kitchen, as Abby cooked up supper for Matt and herself, she spent a moment appreciating her wall oven and counter top range, the dishwasher and the teak cupboards. No, she did to want to jeopardize all this by involving Nora Macpherson. Instead, as she waited for Matt to come in from his day shift, she began planning what to say to her friend Laura Mendez.

# 11

## Nora at Home

After dropping the squad car at the detachment, Nora dallied on her walk home, wandering over to watch the kids in the park playing some softball. It was a clear, crisp, early autumn day, the air acrid with the tang of burning leaves. Winter was creeping up. The days were getting shorter so that soon the kids wouldn't have enough light to play outside after school. Soon they would be at the rink shooting pucks or in the high school gym playing pick-up basketball.

Thoughts of the school reminded Nora that she had seen that schoolteacher coming out of the mall. What was her name? Mrs. Clarke. That was it. "Abby Clarke, married to Matt Clarke, shift foreman at the mill," Jed had said. She considered the somewhat startled look that had appeared on Abby's face. She had seemed on the verge of saying something, but then hadn't. Nora wondered what had stopped her. Her training at Depot had taught her that if she were to have any social set in a small town, it would be among her brother officers, firemen, or whatever other professionals lived there. Abby Clarke fit the bill. She wondered if she would be open for a coffee sometime.

She began ambling homeward down Main Street, something she liked to do to get a sense of the way people felt about her. Since she came from a big city like Winnipeg, Nora didn't really know much about the dynamic of small towns. She was discovering that they were welcoming to strangers, up to a point, but not generally to police officers. It was hard to make friends here. She wondered if it would be different if she were a man. Then she'd have beer-drinking brother-cop buddies anyway, but then she wasn't much of a drinker. She thought a coffee get-together would work, though. She smiled, remembering how coffee and doughnuts had become a professional joke for police. Still, she knew she needed a social life, and so far she had none. She had seen Luke Gallagher and Eddy Braun separately a few times since that first occasion in the coffee room, but they had just smiled or waved and moved on. Nora wondered if they would be more approachable if she weren't stuck behind a desk with Jack Wasniki glowering in the background. She rather liked the looks of Luke, in fact, but stopped herself, remembering the angst of breaking up with Erik when she had left Winnipeg. Someday she'd have the time and energy for another stab at romance, but not yet.

Erik had been her first and only boyfriend, a shy, blonde giant of a man who was so connected to his Icelandic roots in Gimli, Manitoba that he couldn't conceive of ever leaving the province. It had been bad enough that his family had moved to Winnipeg. No way could he imagine going further afield! So Nora's decision to join the Mounties had been in some ways an anguished one. She knew he would react negatively, but she didn't think he would break it off altogether. Somehow, she had been sure their attraction was strong enough to weather her Depot training in Regina and then, maybe a posting back to Manitoba, maybe even to Gimli. But she had reckoned without the Force's policy of posting new recruits out of their home province. Erik had waited until Depot was done, and she was home on leave to tell her he had moved on. The hole in her heart still needed some mending.

Thoughts about her dormant love life made her reflect on Jed, his wife, Marnie, and their new baby, whom she had met when invited for dinner during her first week. They seemed like a solid young couple who shared real affection and mutual respect. She wanted to invite them back to her place, but then she realized she didn't really have the space in her studio suite to entertain more than one other person.

Damn! Picking her way across the graveled parking lot on the way to her studio suite above and behind the real estate office, she winced as, once again, she almost twisted her ankle when the heel on her regulation pump caught. Stupid shoes! She really should start changing at work before she left, or else she was going to break her frigging ankle! Now wouldn't that just tickle Wasniki! She could hear it now. "Do we have to teach you to walk, too?" he would say with that nasal snort that passed for a laugh.

No, she would have to bite the bullet and wear the regulation yellow-striped trousers and oxfords she had been issued. To hell with what the sergeant wanted!

When she opened the door to her place, McNab, the cat, meowed a greeting from somewhere. The apartment was spotless. Depot training with its ironed sheets and meticulously tidy closets still prevailed. To the left of the door, there was a television, stereo and loveseat, and farther back behind a screen, a single bed and clothes closet. Off to the right was what passed for a kitchen, a little galley affair with a table and two chairs tucked away in the corner. The only clutter in the whole place was a stack of photographic equipment by the bathroom door: a Pentax and tripod, a cardboard box with flash attachments, light meter and four different lens cases. Next to them, an enlarger and stainless steel basins for development solution stood on the floor. Ranks of framed black and white shots hung on the walls of the tiny apartment. Nora's private passion was photography.

Shaking her head, Nora dumped her bag and uniform jacket, kicked off the offending pumps and paddled off to change out of her uniform. The sight of the pile of photographic equipment had reminded Nora that she planned on rigging up a darkroom for herself. There was a closet off the kitchen that could work. It was another reason to get a bigger place, but she suspected she wouldn't be there in that apartment, or perhaps even Moose Flats, for long. She wished she had more time and more energy. Since starting at the new posting, she never seemed to have a minute to herself.

Wasniki's order about the detachment darkroom came to mind as she considered the kind of photography she was reduced to producing lately: evidence of graffiti on the arena outside wall, smashed headlights or dents from fender-benders. No chance for her to do her own stuff there, even though the detachment darkroom was under-used. One rule she had grasped absolutely was the Force's strict injunction against the misappropriation of any official equipment or supplies! She longed for some photographic dabbling.

It felt good to be home. McNab, the grey tabby, threaded himself in furry figure eights around her ankles and purred for attention. Well, at least her cat loved her, but then he just wanted food and a cuddle! As she ruffled McNab's furry ears and felt his round tummy pressing against her, he began to purr. Oh, she could use a cuddle too! Especially a cuddle.

Before long, she was humming along to Abba's "Dancing Queen" in the little kitchenette with McNab following every move as she whipped up a quick stir-fry.

# 12

# A Clash at the Clarkes

Abby was having trouble sleeping as sometimes happened when Matt was on afternoon shift. She would go to bed at the usual 10:30 p.m. and drift off, but then wake up when he came in at 2:30 a.m. or sometimes even before. Tonight she was awake after only an hour. What was bothering her was what Frank Hughes had said, about the people coming all the way from Newfoundland with "very good experience."

Putting that comment together with her seeing him at the board office talking to George Warren, she began to get a hollow feeling in the pit of her stomach. Tom Cooper had called Warren "the Big Cheese" for his clout with the ranching community. He had a huge, prosperous ranch southeast of town past Loon Lake.

Now Hank Talbot had caught Warren's ear, asking about herself no doubt, and then one of them had got onto Frank, Matt's boss, and Frank had passed the unspoken message onto her. She could imagine them saying it, "Lay off the Talbot kid or…" Or what? Matt loses his job? She loses her teaching contract?

She realized she had to tell Matt about what Frank had said, but also she had to tell Matt about her suspicions concerning the Talbots so he understood why she couldn't leave it alone. God, she wished he'd get home!

By the time 2:30 a.m. rolled around, she had watched their one CBC television station sign off, read three more chapters of *Shogun*, drunk three mugs of tea, and was about to raid the fridge when she heard the door open softly. He was always such a sweetheart trying not to wake her. All of a sudden, she felt a huge weight of guilt as if the burden of her fears were a sack of old clothes, damp and moldy. No one needed this!

For a moment she considered letting it ride. She could tell by the droop of his shoulders that he was tired, and wouldn't be very receptive to a problem at two in the morning. But she was too wired up and anxious to leave it. The image of Tess's bruises bloomed purple and blue in her memory. She knew, despite her misgivings, that it couldn't wait. Frank was likely to say something the next time he saw Matt.

"Honey, I stayed up because I need to talk to you." She quickly filled him in on the events of the day, George Warren's sudden unusual interest in herself, her visit to Liz Lundstrom at the Public Health Office, and then the odd conversation with Frank Hughes in the supermarket.

"What the hell you doing going to the Public Health Office, Abby?" Matt's face was livid, his voice constrained as if he were stopping himself from exploding.

"Matt, that man is beating his kids, I'm sure of it! This is not a 'maybe' scenario! I saw big, ugly bruises on Tess. Her lower back and upper thighs are covered! Probably Ellie's too. It's not a question of whether he might hurt them sometime! He is hurting them! I need to get another witness so there's a record of it."

"But you're messing with our future here, Abby! Fuck! I don't want Frank Hughes seeing you as an interfering do-gooder. This is a small town. People talk!"

"Honey, this is about what's *right*. I'm her teacher. I'm supposed to look out for my students!"

She was suddenly appalled that he couldn't see the morality of the situation. When had he become such a suck-up to the boss? Wasn't a child's life worth anything? "Matt, I can't believe I'm hearing you right. Are you saying you are more concerned about your image at the mill than you are about a girl's safety? That shows no guts at all!"

Matt by this point was aiming his chin at her face. "You aren't exactly Miss Perfect either, you know. Remember, you smoke pot along with the rest of us. So I wouldn't be so smug about the moral high ground here. We could just as easily get shit for that stuff, too, you even more than me. How would the board like it if they found out you smoked pot? Good-bye teaching job! So don't be hassling me for my lack of guts! Go and smoke a joint with George Warren, why don't you? Then, see how much you get to protect some kid who has a few bruises!"

Speechless with anger, Abby fled to the bedroom before he could continue. She slammed the door and collapsed on the blankets. Was she just asking for trouble? Her chest felt heavy, her throat raw, and her head ached from the tension. She gave in, sobs wracking her body.

A half an hour later, when the tears finally subsided and she had had time to rerun their argument, she realized he was right about one thing anyway. There was no way she would keep her job if they found out she smoked marijuana. Tess seems happy enough out there with her dog. Maybe it would be better to just let it pass. Thinking of the weed they smoked, she also thought maybe it was time to lay off there, too.

The next morning, bleary-eyed, Abby roused herself early to find she had slept alone. When she wandered into the kitchen, she saw that Matt had eaten half a sandwich that he had made himself after she had stormed off, and had left the other half with her name on it in the fridge. She wondered if it were a peace offering. She felt the prickle in her eyes from unshed tears. Her throat constricting, she carefully avoided waking Matt, who was asleep on the couch, and left for work feeling somewhat chastened and confused.

# 13

# Nora Meets Abby

What in hell??

That Tuesday morning after break, Nora had returned to her desk from the dark room to find a wet condom filled with water and sitting on her desk chair. It was a shock. She had been thinking everything was going so well! She should have known better. When she glanced around to see if her reaction was being watched, she saw only Wasniki in his office with his head bent over some paperwork.

Who would do this, she wondered. Why? Stupid question! Probably Wasniki's payback for her wearing the uniform trousers that day. Friggin' juvenile!!

She tipped the jiggly, bloated thing quickly into her wastepaper basket and headed for the washroom. Shutting the door quietly, she burst the condom and dumped it and the water into the toilet.

Before returning to her front desk, she sat slumped in a cubicle for a few minutes, assessing her last few days. Things had been going well, she thought. She had kept up with Wasniki's demands for typed reports, updated bulletin boards and tidied cupboards. She had got the dark room up and running. She had researched the townspeople and sorted out whom she might approach in the various communities. She had learned the names and read the profiles of all the local officials on the town council, school board and chamber of commerce. What more could he ask? Short of giving her some real work on a case in the community, there was nothing she hadn't done well. Maybe that was the problem. The condom prank was just an effort to unhinge her, put her off balance. Well, screw that! She decided it was time for action.

The lunch bell was just sounding as Nora pulled into the high school parking lot to the left of the sprawling building. Despite the ranks of individual electrical outlets for block heaters in deep winter cold, there was a raw, unfinished look to the parking lot. It seemed to be just an expanse of asphalt intruding into the bush on three sides. Reinforcing the impression was an enormous slash pile off to the south end where Nora could see a flock of ravens picking at paper garbage they had scored from the green school bins ranged along the left wall of the building. The school itself was a modern, one story, beige brick construction with very few windows, a feature probably intended to save on heating bills, she thought. It was a generic design with long corridors of classrooms branching off and connecting in a "T" at the front where administration offices were located. A mansard roof on the gymnasium at the end of the right wing seemed to be its only distinctive architectural feature.

Nora sat for a moment as streams of denim-clad students and one heavy-set male teacher rushed past her car on their way out of the building. A couple of the kids paused to turn a speculative glance at her sitting in the cruiser, but hurried on without saying anything, at least anything she could hear. She checked her image in the rearview mirror before leaving the cruiser. She was still a bit shaken by the condom incident, but knew it really signified nothing more than some childish male ego. Her image would be professional.

She knew she needed to be neat and tidy with not too much lipstick, her hair pinned up in place underneath her peaked cap. This inquiry needed to look as legit as possible. Wasniki had to think, if he heard about it, that it had been done by the book, and that she couldn't be rattled. Besides, this was community liaison, and at least on paper, part of her general detachment assignment.

Liz Lundstrom had given her the lead the other day saying that Teresa Talbot was at the high school. It seemed only reasonable to do a friendly September visit to make sure the admin and teachers knew she was their RCMP liaison officer in the community.

At the front desk, Nora found out that Tom Cooper was out for lunch so she scheduled an appointment with him at 1:00 p.m. and then asked if she could by any chance have a quick chat with any of Teresa Talbot's teachers. Margaret Vermeer, the aged and affable school secretary, led her to the staffroom where a group of teachers were eating lunch.

As she waited at the staffroom door, Nora watched Margaret shuffle across to Abby Clarke and whisper in her ear. When Nora realized that Abby was one of Teresa's teachers, and that they would finally have chance to connect, she tamped down any show of personal interest.

When Abby met her near the door, Nora hastened to apologize, "I'm sorry to interrupt your lunch, Mrs. Clarke. I didn't want to come when there was a chance you might be in class. I won't take much of your time, I promise."

"Hey, no problem, I was about finished lunch anyway." The tension on Abby's face dissipated as she smiled and pointed toward the hallway in an invitation to leave the racket of the staffroom conversation behind.

As she walked beside her to the classroom, Nora noted that Abby's face seemed a bit drained, and that there were dark smudges under her eyes. She wondered if all teachers looked so tired early in the year.

"What can I do for you, Constable? Is this official business?" Abby couldn't help but remember Matt's anger from the night before.

"Oh, not really. There's no problem with you, if that's what you're wondering." Nora could see the relief in Abby's expression as she broke into a grin.

"Sorry, Constable, it's just that I've got a lead foot. It runs in the family, you know?"

Nora chuckled silently. "No problem, Abby, is it? May I call you that? And since it's unofficial business, please call me Nora."

By this point they were in Abby's classroom, the tables and chairs still askew as the kids had left them when they had exited for lunch. As Abby hurried to tidy up a place for them to sit, Nora companionably helped re-position some of the chairs.

"I'm the community liaison officer for the RCMP. I'm here for a meeting with Tom Cooper at 1:00 and thought I'd take the opportunity to connect with anyone who is working with Teresa Talbot. Mrs. Lundstrom at Public Health has alerted me to the possibility of some trouble at home, and I just wanted to do a quick follow-up. At this point, it's nothing official."

Abby, surprised at the swiftness of the RCMP's response to Liz's inquiry and unsure of her footing, asked, "What is your concern? Is there some problem I should know about?"

Out of the blue, she was reliving the row with Matt from the night before. Should she tell Nora about the bruises on Tess's thighs that last

Saturday? Oh Christ! Matt would kill her! But this cop seemed okay, somehow.

"I am just following up on a possibility that Teresa might be involved in some domestic dispute. We have had a complaint about irregularities with the mother's death, and I thought I should just check in to see how the daughter is doing at school."

Abby nodded with a smile into Nora's searching grey-green eyes. She certainly could talk about school performance, and wait to see what questions came up. "I have been very concerned about Tess. Her attendance is very irregular, and she isn't fitting in very well when she is here." Nora's quizzical expression cued Abby to provide more detail. "Oh, Tess's personal hygiene is pretty bad. She doesn't know much about feminine products, or looking after herself, you know? So the other girls center her out, and she opts to hang with the bigger boys out behind the slash pile, where they smoke and…" She paused as if to assess whether she should be telling Nora the details. "Tess smokes too, I think. And she skips class with them out there, too.

"This is not looking good for her making much progress in school, as you can probably tell, and I also worry about what might be happening with those boys. Other than that, I don't know what else I can say. I haven't any evidence that she's been in any physical dispute, but I have seen some bruises. I think she may be involved in some minor vandalism around the school, though. We seem to have a lot more problems with the girls' washroom this year!"

Nora nodded her head and smiled encouragingly, "That's fine, Abby, I appreciate your being frank here. It's a touchy situation and we both want what's best for the girl. We should watch for any more bruising maybe. By the way, is Tess here today? Could you point her out to me?"

Abby laughed aloud, partly in relief that the interview with this cop had gone so easily, and partly because Tess's whereabouts was often a matter of speculation. "You know, that's a good question," she hesitated. "Nora, is it?"

"Nora Macpherson – here's my card."

Idly examining the business card Nora had offered, Abby continued, "I was laughing because in the staffroom they make bets on whether Tess'll show up in the morning, and then if she does, on whether she'll stick around for the whole day." Abby wandered over to look out the classroom single window. It opened onto a view of the still-unfinished games field. She nodded Nora over to have a look. "I think you can just see Tess over to the left there, in behind the slash pile. She's the only short person there."

Nora peered across to where Abby was pointing. She could make out the thin figure of a dark-haired girl in faded blue jeans and a red and black lumberjack shirt. Nora's eyebrows lifted in surprise. "She is the only girl out there? Isn't that unusual?"

Abby nodded in agreement, "The girl smokers tend to hang out together down by the creek. Even if a girl starts going with one of the smoker guys, he never seems to take her there."

Shrugging and lifting her palms, Abby admitted, "As I said before, she has social problems. The other girls say she smells, so she gravitates to the boys, who so far haven't really accepted her, but haven't really cold-shouldered her either. I've asked her to come in and spend lunch hour with me. You know, get some extra help, but she's started hanging with the boys. She probably thinks it's nice to be at least allowed to hang out somewhere."

"She's not supposed to smoke because she's under sixteen, right? I bet that takes some time to enforce?" Nora knew the old, turn- of-the-century Tobacco Restraint Act restricted tobacco sales to young teens, but also that the regulation was notoriously hard to enforce.

Abby smiled. "Yes, we just say none of the junior grades are allowed. For some, it's a bit more incentive to pass Grade 10!"

At this point, Nora realized she had taken up enough of Abby's lunch, and that she should head over to the main office to wait for the appointment with Tom Cooper. As she turned toward the door, she checked her watch and, realizing she had a good half-hour to kill, turned back to Abby who was sorting piles of papers on her desk. "Where should I go to wait? The office?"

Abby for a moment seemed confused. She was already onto her next task. "Oh, of course! You can stay here if you like. I was just going to do some quick marking here, but you're welcome to stay if you want…" Her voice trailed off, as she couldn't see what would interest Nora in her classroom.

"Oh, no! Thanks anyway. I just wondered where would be a good place so the students wouldn't get too curious as I sat there. You know, kids…"

Suddenly taking in the constable's yellow-striped trousers and Sam Browne revolver at her belt, Abby exclaimed, "Oh my gosh! Of course! You can sit in the staffroom and have a coffee. Here, I'll come back and get you one. That machine is touchy."

Nora felt bemused by the teacher's breathless energy. She had the impression it was maybe too soon for a sociable coffee together, but perhaps sometime soon.

# 14

# Abby Asks a Favour

That evening after a quick supper, Abby walked over to visit her best friend, Laura. She and her live-in boyfriend, Matt's best friend Ken Snider, often joined her and Matt on weekend treks into the bush. Now Abby wanted to see about a job for Ellie. Abby thought Laura, who ran the mill office, might give Ellie some casual work.

Laura, in pajama bottoms and big sweatshirt, her long blonde hair in pigtails, welcomed her with a quick hug. "Hey, Ab! Great to see you! Pull up a chair. Wanna toke?" Abby was not taken aback by the offer. As Matt had said, she was a social marijuana smoker. This time, though, she reflected on their recent spat and decided she should refuse. Besides, she was there on business.

"No thanks. I'm just here because I have a favour to ask."

Privately, Abby reflected that Laura smoked far more than most of her other friends. She, herself, was leery of too much weed. It really seemed to sap her ambition in the off-hours. Laura, with a "leave-it-at-the-office" kind of job, didn't have that problem. Abby and Laura's social set had already run the whole gamut of arguments about the stupidity of the marijuana laws. Everybody was convinced that if the big corporate tobacco and liquor lobbies hadn't been so powerful, it would already have been at least decriminalized, if not legalized. Hell, rumour had it that even Prime Minister Pierre Trudeau had toked up in his youth! Shaking her head, Abby reflected that wouldn't help much if Wasniki decided to check out one of their parties! She decided not to tell Laura about her tiff with Matt the night before.

"So ask, girlfriend!" Abby smiled and relaxed. Laura was a good friend. If she could help, she would.

"Remember I mentioned going out to the Talbot place on Antoinette Creek last weekend?"

Quickly she unfolded the whole story of their visit to the ranch, her contact with Liz Lundstrom, and that day's surprise visit from Nora Macpherson. She finished up with how concerned she was for the safety of the two girls, especially Tess, and how she was now wondering if there were any way to get Ellie a job so she could move into town where she would likely be happier away from her dad. Then, maybe Tess could live with her sister during the week and go home on weekends to help on the ranch.

"And I come into this whole Good Samaritan routine…how?" Laura's puzzlement lasted only a moment. "Ah, I see. You want me to find Ellie *a job*? Okay, maybe. The mill's got a whole slew of new guys just arrived from back east, Newfies mostly. I could use some help filing, maybe something more. Can this girl, Ellie, can she type? How's her spoken English?"

Abby, remembering Ellie's colourful vocabulary, winced. "Phone skills may not be the best bet to start, but her school records show she has mostly B's and C+'s in Business Machines 12, and Accounting Basics 11. She wasn't able to stay in school long enough to graduate because her dad needed her out on the ranch, but I think she's pretty sharp."

"Sure, get her to give me a call. Few of the local girls stick around Moose Forks, you know. Once they grad, if they don't get hitched, they're gone. So I have to say – having an office assistant that I can depend on to stay here is worth the effort of training her."

"Laura, you're local yourself, right? You're one of the exceptions – someone who decided to stay here? I wonder, do you remember the Talbots from when you were a kid?  I guess what I really wonder is how the dad treated the mom and kids."

"You know, I only remember seeing those kids in town every October for the Fall Fair and Rodeo, and then the whole family would come in the way most ranching folks do and hang out at the fairgrounds for a couple of days. Tim used to ride broncos. He had a nasty go-round last year with an appaloosa so I wonder if he'll be back this year. Ellie, she's a fair barrel-rider and Tess does some trick riding. But that's all I really remember. Hey! That reminds me, the fair and rodeo are just a few weeks off, you know. That's a good time around here. Did you go last year?"

Abby thought back to the previous fall. It had been her second year at the high school. She had still been up to her ears in prep for school until at least November. She shook her head and sighed, "No I missed it last year. It wasn't even on the radar."

"Well, it'll be a good chance to see the Talbots again, if you want to see how the old man behaves in public. Funny thing is, for all he hates public institutions, he never misses the rodeo."

"I wonder if they will show up this year. You know Hank had that trouble with the cops over how he buried his wife. Could be he'll be too embarrassed and will pass on the rodeo this year to avoid any more talk."

"Abby, you *do* know that George Warren's brother-in-law is the local doctor and district coroner? I doubt there is any real trouble over that burial. Liz Lundstrom is just power-tripping because she's never gotten over her own husband's defeat for the position of School Board Chair. George Warren has that one all sewn up for the foreseeable future, I would say, and what George Warren wants, he usually gets, from Frank Hughes at the mill, from *your* boss, Tom Cooper, and definitely from old Jack, the cop, you know, Wasniki. Those guys are thick as they come. My dad told me how they often drink together Friday night, starting out in the private back room of the Driftwood and then moving on to somebody's place. Wasniki has a basement bar all decorated up with Indian stuff. Dad heard Ted asking Frank about Wasniki's collection one time. Hank hangs with them sometimes. His place is pretty far out though, I guess, so he doesn't drink in town as much as the others."

Abby was mute with astonishment. The Ol Boys' Network was alive and well! She turned her attention to one possibility she had not considered.

"Speaking of Liz, do you think her talking to Nora Macpherson might open things up a bit? You know, maybe Nora will put some pressure on Wasniki to move on the not-providing-the-necessities-of-life charge?"

Laura snorted in derision, "Don't bet on it! Anyone who manages to hack through the Horseman's training program is cut from the same damn cloth! They're all fascist rednecks underneath! I wouldn't count on them or be getting chummy with any of them!"

Abby, startled by Laura's vehement condemnation of the RCMP, changed the topic. "Yeah, I bet Matt would like the fair too. I'll check to see what shift he'll be working. Oh hey, do you ever remember seeing a native woman selling jewelry with Beth Talbot at the fair? Her name was Rosemary Joseph?"

"Not sure…what does she look like?"

Abby recounted the details she recalled from the conversation with Ellie, suggesting a native woman of Beth's age, very self-assured by the sound of Ellie's description, but nothing more concrete.

"Abby, why does she matter? I mean, I get how you're worried about these girls, but really, do you think some native woman from fifteen years ago matters?"

"I can't really say…you know? I guess I think Rosemary was a good friend of Beth's, and she helped her have her babies, so maybe Rosemary will care about what's happening to them now that Beth's gone. I know it's a lame idea…" Her voice drifted off in resignation.

"You know, girlfriend, you're sounding more and more like a wannabe mom, yourself!"

"Yeah, maybe, if Matt ever grows up!"

Mutual chuckling absorbed them until Laura offered a new tack, "You know, my mom might know Rosemary Joseph. She's lived here in town or just outside for over thirty years."

# 15

## Nora Takes a Risk

Nora had been mulling all morning about her next move. Her brief chat with Tom Cooper the day before at the high school had confirmed Abby Clarke's story about the Talbot girl. Tess was definitely acting out in ways that suggested some kind of weirdness at home. She considered what to do next. Wait for Abby to catch Tess in the act of vandalism? Use that pretext for a home visit? What kind of guy was Hank Talbot? Well connected no doubt, but was he really dangerous? Were Tess's bruises the result of carelessness or abuse?

She needed to see that file on Jack's desk.

When the office door slammed as Wasniki and Jed Fedoruk left for lunch, Nora sat transfixed for a full five minutes debating the wisdom of her next move. Then, with brisk determination, she got up and crossed to Jack's office door.  Relieved to find it unlocked, she slipped inside and in seconds, had found the Talbot file buried in a pile on the desk. With her heart hammering, she forced herself to measure her pace as she returned to her desk and hid the file in her shoulder bag.

She knew what she was doing – taking the Talbot file home with her – was wrong, that betrayal of trust and disobedience of the chain of command with the Force were seen as the worst kinds of transgressions. If, or more likely when, she was caught, at the very least she would get a letter of reprimand, a permanent blotch on her record.

But something about Abby's description of Tess at school had made her angry. What was it?  As Nora sat alone in her studio suite at the kitchen table later that evening, she pondered her motives. She cast back to her childhood. She had lost her mom when she was eleven. Images of Nora's spirited but fragile mother flooded back. She had been tall and dark-haired like Nora, but where the daughter's eyes were a grey-green, a heritage from her Scots-Irish father, Emily Macpherson had had the sparkling black eyes of her Ojibwa ancestors. Nothing about her mother's outward appearance or behaviour had ever suggested "Indian" or even "Metis", but Emily had defied the bias of the times and had refused to assimilate totally. Being just one quarter-blood herself, she hadn't dressed the part, or even spoken what she remembered of her grandmother's tongue, but Emily Two Feathers Boisclair Macpherson had made sure her daughter knew about the stories and the struggles, about Riel and Dumont, about Batoche and the Red River Rebellion. She had been non-status, so there was little connection to others from the reserve, especially after she had married Nora's father. Few outside the family even knew. Nora shook her head, remembering the bland, white funeral her dad had arranged for Emily. "I know this country, Nora," he had said. "It's better this way."

Nora knew her dad had done what he thought was right for both her mom and herself. He had been a loving and protective father, so her mom's death from breast cancer had not been a total disaster. Still, Nora knew how it felt to be motherless. That vision of little Tess, unkempt and forlorn, smoking behind the slash pile, had wrenched at her gut and would not leave her. She knew that Tess's behaviour was a clear signal that something was very wrong.

Nora had a woman's sensibility of what it meant to be sexually aroused, but she was relatively inexperienced. Her self-image was focused on the coltish flexibility and health of her athletic body. Losing a childhood sweetheart who had not approved of her joining the RCMP had fired her determination to show him and everyone else that she was strong enough emotionally to cope on her own. She had made a fierce mental determination that sexual involvement could wait. It was safer that way. This attitude influenced her genuine concern that Tess was sexually vulnerable, exploitable in a way that Tess herself didn't fully understand. If she was veering into promiscuity, Nora could perhaps redirect her.

She dragged on her one daily cigarette, musing on the contents of the file laid out on the kitchen table before her. Hank Talbot had the usual few traffic violations going back to the late 50's – citations for speeding and transporting cargo hazardously, stuff commonly found in remote regions – it was such a temptation to speed when you knew there was no one around for miles! Besides, who is usually watching when you use a pickup to carry a barrel of fuel oil from town out to your spread?

But there were more troubling recent incidents, most of which had not resulted in any charges being laid or consequences levied:

October 5, 1973 – driving under the influence (CC 53.1) and causing property damage (CC430)

March 14, 1974 – uttering threats against a public health official in the performance of her duties – CC264.1(1)(a)

January 20, 1976 – pointing a firearm (CC 87.1) Mike Horvath from The Community Resource Board had ventured out to inquire about a complaint regarding Teresa's schooling and Talbot had threatened him with his rifle.

May 30, 1976 – failure to report to a coroner or peace officer the death of a person who died of disease for which the person was not treated by a medical practitioner –indictable offence –CC182(a)

May 30, 1976 – disrespect for human remains and failure to perform duty regarding burial –CC182(a) This charge had resulted in a summary conviction for which a penalty of $5000.00 had been levied.

Nora wondered why nothing had happened with the other more serious offences. She was fairly sure Talbot's "connections" must have leaned on Wasniki. But of course, she was in no position to prove anything. What she needed was to copy the statements of complaint filed by the various witnesses so that no one could ever deny their existence. She needed a back-up.

She sat pondering the time it would take to type everything out. She'd be up all night! She wished she had access to a photocopier, but she couldn't risk using the one at the detachment in case Wasniki caught her with the Talbot file. The only other photocopier in town was in the library, which at this hour would be closed, and she had to return this file tomorrow.

She stubbed out her cigarette in sudden disgust. She was smoking again since coming to Moose Forks, only one or two a day, but she was sickened by her need for any tobacco. She got up to pace and think things through. She knew she was on thin ice, knew the stress was getting to her – the smoking was proof.

If she had any brains, she'd take this file back to where she had got it and forget the whole thing! She couldn't copy it all. She didn't have enough time to get all those pages typed, and she couldn't keep it for another day.

Then, she had an idea.

Nora arrived at the office early the next morning to return the Talbot file before Wasniki could notice it was gone. The sergeant's office was locked. She swore softly to herself, realizing she would have to wait until lunch and hope he left it unlocked again.

Before her regular stint in the detachment dark room, Nora turned her attention to the other officers' reports piled up on her desk for typing. She heaved a sigh of frustration.

# 16

## Tess in Trouble

Normally, staff members didn't use the students' washrooms, but to save time, Abby popped in after class change. There she found Tess, lipstick poised to "decorate" the big mirror.

Tess's expression betrayed nothing, not resentment or anger or even relief. Her face was a mask, her shocking blue eyes with their fringe of black lashes, lifeless and oddly unfocused. Removing the lipstick from the girl's hands, Abby realized just how grimy and smelly she really was. She reeked of body odour, wood smoke and cigarettes with a whiff of horse thrown in.

"Tess, what are you thinking? What is the point of doing something like this?" She tried to keep her voice low, hoping to convey concern rather than condemnation. Still no reaction.

She saw lipstick staining the girl's hands, and, intending to lead her to the staff showers in the PE office, Abby wrapped her arm around the girl's shoulders, and started to walk her towards the hallway.

"Tess, I want to get you a shower, okay? I know you don't have one at home and that's no problem. You can use the one here any time you want. All you have to do is ask, all right? And we'll pop your clothes into the washer in the Home Ec. lab so when you finish you'll have something clean to put on. How's that?"

Tess nodded meekly and allowed Abby to lead her to the staff shower where, hiding behind the white nylon curtain, she handed over her jeans, T-shirt and lumberjack shirt. Abby kept her hand extended inside the cubicle, and Tess eventually passed out some underwear that looked particularly grungy in the bright sunlight streaming in through the frosted glass window.

Abby pulled the curtain so Tess could have some privacy as she showered, but then the outline of Tess's lower back and thigh became plastered to the wet shower curtain, and the black and blue marks tattooing her skin left no doubt. The girl back and upper thighs were covered in recent bruises.

Remembering Liz Lundstrom's advice about getting a witness, Abby cast about to recall who might be the best person to involve. After rejecting most of the women on staff because they would be teaching, she settled on grandmotherly Margaret Vermeer, the school secretary who would be both available, and happy to help with no questions asked.

Outrage fueled her steps as she raced down the hallway to the school office. Something must be done to get that girl out of that house!

Within minutes, she was back with Margaret, and, with Tess still in the shower, Abby had shown Margaret Tess's back without Tess being any the wiser. Abby realized that she should get Tess to talk, but the girl had been so skittish about even taking a shower that Nora had decided to get the evidence while she could, and find less tense circumstances to question her so that they could convince Child Services to act to remove Tess from Hank's custody.

Across town, Nora's morning had flown by with the routine work of the office. She had restocked the dark room as Wasniki had asked and done the special enlargements she herself needed. When Jack and Jed had left for lunch, she had managed to return the Talbot file unnoticed.

Now, as she was finishing the typing and pondering the last time-consuming directive Wasniki had laid on her, the office phone rang. It was Liz Lundstrom, wondering if she could get Nora to drive up to the high school because Abby Clarke had something she wanted Nora to see. Liz said she was tied up with immunizations at the elementary or she would go herself.

"What does Mrs. Clarke want me to see?"

"It's Teresa Talbot, Constable. We have witnesses – Abby, that is Mrs. Clarke, and Mrs. Vermeer, the school secretary – to prove her back is covered in bruises."

"I see. There are two witnesses, you say? Both credible by the sounds of it? In that case, I might be putting the wind up the dad by being a witness too, don't you think? We don't want him hauling Tess out of school because he's spooked. I can't actually get away right this very minute. Can this wait? Until after 4:00, perhaps?"

"Tess will likely be gone by then. Abby said the only reason she's still there at all is that her clothes are still in the dryer. She's wearing stuff from the lost-and-found that Tess said she wouldn't be seen dead in, so she stuck around."

"Could Abby bring her down to the detachment?"

"It doesn't sound like Tess is being very cooperative. I don't think so."

"Maybe it's probably better that Tess doesn't see me involved." Inside, she was seething. Damn Wasniki! Why does he need this detachment inventory done today? It's like he knew she had a line on something, and would do whatever he could to tie her up there, where she couldn't get into any trouble! And damn Talbot too! That bastard! For a moment, Nora's thoughts were as black as tar. She needed a court order to remove Tess from Hank's custody, and for that she needed Wasniki on side.

Coming back to daylight, she said, "Mrs. Lundstrom, I'll head up there around four to talk with Mrs. Clarke and Mrs. Vermeer. They'll still be there then?"

"Maybe you had better phone ahead. Okay, I have to go. Grade Two's are here."

Nora worked steadily two more hours to complete the inventory. By the time she was heading up to the school, she had her game plan in place.

Abby stayed in the staffroom as Nora took Margaret's witness statement; then, when Margaret had left for home, she gave the constable her own statement and the sketches they had made. She felt uneasy making it official, but Nora assured her no action could be taken until there was authorization from Mike Horvath at Child Services.

This was Abby's second interaction with Nora Macpherson, and despite herself, she found the constable even more likeable and down-to-earth. She didn't get the sense that Nora was phony or self-important as some police seemed to be. But – and she could hear Laura's voice saying it – she *was* still a cop.

Abby decided not to tell Matt or Laura that she had just signed a witness statement against Hank Talbot. No point in opening that can of worms yet!

# 17

# Coffee with Ellie

As she was coming out of the mall from shopping on the next Saturday morning, Abby caught a glimpse of Tim Talbot's distinctive new lime-green half-ton truck parked at the medical clinic. It had been a week since they had visited the ranch, and she was curious about who was at the clinic. She drove by and looked to see if there were anyone in the truck. Tim was sitting in the driver's seat, Led Zeppelin blaring out of the windows.

Getting out of her car, Abby ran up to the truck and knocked on the window. He was absorbed by his music, humming along to "Stairway to Heaven" and at first didn't respond, so she ended up shouting, "Hi! Tim Talbot, right? I'm Matt Clarke's wife, Abby. How's Ellie's foot?"

Tim, tongue-tied facing his boss's wife, reduced the volume of his music and rolled down the window. When Abby repeated her question, he nodded towards the clinic, "Ellie's getting it looked at. They think she's broken something 'cause the swelling won't go down."

Abby reflected grimly that Hank's doctoring had its limits, and was about to ask Tim how long Ellie would be, when she realized he was again humming along to the music and quite oblivious to her continued presence. Just as Abby was heading into the clinic front door, she encountered Ellie struggling to manage the exit. She was on crutches, swinging her foot in a cast up to her knee.

"Oh Ellie! I'm *so* sorry!" Once again, her apology for the part their truck and Matt's driving had played in the accident seemed so lame. Yet Ellie seemed welcoming, so she ventured a question, "Where you heading to?"

Ellie shrugged, muttering, "Coffee somewhere."

"Let me buy you one, Ellie…"

"Tim's waiting for me, but…" Here a smile snuck across her face. "He'll likely enjoy a beer somewhere, so why not? Don't much feel like heading home right off anyhow."

Abby followed as Ellie swung on her crutches out to the truck. There a heated brother-sister argument ensued.

"I gotta be back damn quick for round-up, Ellie! You *know* that! I told the old man I'd be back by noon! What you going to do here?"

"Never mind, I don't need to tell you everything I do! You go and help with the cattle. I'm no use anyhow like this. I'll find my own way home or crash here someplace. Go on! I'll be okay."

"All right, but the old man is going to be pissed, and you know it!"

Watching him wheel off, Ellie shrugged and rolled her eyes in mock indifference. Tim sped off, squealing tires as he gained speed at the intersection with Highway 16. Abby pointed to her vehicle, a sunshine-yellow Volkswagen bug. After guiding Ellie across the gravel of the parking lot, Abby stashed the crutches crosswise in the back seat and slid back the front passenger seat to maximize legroom.

"Where to? Do you think the Hideaway?" Abby knew that the Hideaway Motel Coffee Shop was the only one with a booth where they could talk privately.

"Sure, anywhere's good, Mrs. Clarke."

"You're not my student, Ellie. Call me Abby, okay?"

After they had settled in with their coffees at a booth at the back of the cafe, Abby opened with an inquiry about Ellie's foot.

"It's a small bone broke in the ankle area, but will heal fine if I stay off it for two weeks. They won't give me a walking cast until early October, and then another six weeks after that with the walking cast before I can manage normal."

"How's that going to work out at the ranch? Is your dad managing without your help?"

Avoiding Abby's eyes, Elli mumbled something Abby couldn't quite catch.

"Ellie! Please, I feel responsible here. Is everything okay at home?"

"Oh, hell, it'll be okay," her voice was now audible, shaking with emotion.

"Ellie, look me in the eye. No, don't do that." Ellie had tried gently to shrug her off. "Look at me! Listen, would you stay in town if you had a decent job?"

Ellie hesitated a moment. "Sure, but what chance is there of that? My school marks weren't that good. I can't afford any more school, not that my dad would let me go even if I could…"

"What would you say if I said there might be a job at the sawmill for you? In the office? The only thing is you have to try to clear up your spoken English so you can do receptionist work on the phone. Laura Mendez, my friend, is the head secretary at the mill office. She says she can use you to help her with extra filing right now, and if you show improvement with the phone skills, you'll have a good shot at a permanent position."

The look on Ellie's face was hopeful at first and then abashed. "What hope do I have to change how I talk?"

Abby launched into her most recent brainwave, "We have a big house. We can take in a boarder. Then, while you're living with us, I can help you with speaking proper English, but…" Remembering Matt, Abby continued, "I have to clear it with my husband, you know – Matt? The guy who got you into this fix in the first place? He's a decent guy. He'll see this is a good way to make it up to you."

They grinned at each other in complicity.

"So where do we go from here, your place?" Ellie's question caught Abby off-guard. She had been thinking about what she had heard about Beth Talbot, about how she had been a well-educated woman.

"Oh, no, not yet. I have to talk to Matt first, remember?"

She was thinking that she definitely couldn't pull a fast one like this on him. They needed some time to sort it out, especially after that blow-up last Wednesday! If Matt was really worried about his job, she needed to be sure this deal wouldn't be the spark that blew everything to hell.

"Ellie, do you want to spend the night in town? Laura from the sawmill office, the friend I mentioned, might be willing to put you up for the night, if that's okay with your dad."

Ellie's eyes narrowed, and when she spoke, the defiance in her voice was palpable, "I don't care anymore what he thinks. He hasn't lifted a finger to fix my foot, and I can't help with the ranch much anyways if I'm on crutches. Likely, I'd trip and break the other foot if I had to go back. Sure as hell, there won't be anyone to help me out at the house. Tim stays in town all week, and Tess practically lives in the barn."

This mention of Tess reminded Abby that Tess, likely embarrassed after Thursday's lipstick incident, had once again not been in class on Friday.

"You know, Ellie, I'd really like to see Tess coming to school more, whenever possible anyway. I know she does ranch work, but…"

Ellie's scornful laugh cut her off. "Not likely! Unless she can bring the bush with her. Even Mom used to call her our 'wildwoods child' for crying out loud! Tess is a lost cause, honest. " She shook her head, "No, not really a lost cause, it's just that she's the only one who will put up with the old man, and that's only because she can escape into the bush anytime she wants and hide there until he cools off. At least most times she can."

Abby, still a bit taken aback by Ellie's earlier mocking outburst, quickly reran what Ellie had just said. "Ellie, tell me the truth. Does your father beat you and the other two kids?

"I wouldn't normally say so, but I'm tired of the asshole so, yes, he does. With the last phrase, her voice tailed off as a huge sigh seemed to replace the words. She continued, "Not all the time, and usually only after he's had a lot of whisky. We all know that's like the trigger on a shotgun. We know to avoid him when he shows up with a bottle. The reason I don't want to go back now is that I can't run no more for a while. But I *am* worried about how Tess will be."

Abby, remembering Tess on Thursday, answered the unspoken question herself, "Not well…"

After briefly telling Ellie about Tess's lipstick mess and shower, but minus the detail about the bruises and the RCMP involvement, Abby finished with a hopeful thought, "Maybe we can do both of you a favour." Then, "Excuse me a moment, I'll just go call Laura."

As she stood at the payphone waiting for Laura to pick up, Abby pondered how she would present the situation to Matt. So many pieces of this mess had to be handled just right!

Laura listened briefly. "Sure, I've got a couch Ellie can have for a couple of nights, but what then? From what I've heard of the old man, he isn't going to like her taking any handouts! So I get it, you want me to interview her right away for that temp-filing job? I don't have the paperwork done yet, but hell, I'm the only one who reads most of it anyway. Can she start Monday?"

Abby said a silent prayer for this angel of a friend. "I don't know how to thank you, Laura. You've no idea how bad this situation is. I haven't been able to stop thinking…"

"Don't get excited, Abby. This might not work out at all. I said I would see how it goes, okay, nothing more! At this point, there's no way it's a permanent thing, and the deal's off if she can't mind her language in the office. There's to be no cussing!

Somewhat chastened, Abby then phoned Liz Lundstrom at home.

After quickly filling Liz in on what Laura had offered, Abby came to the point, "Is there a way to get some financial support for Ellie to live in town and pay room and board, and maybe even include Tess?"

Like Laura, Liz had her doubts. "There's no way Hank will accept charity for Tess, but if Ellie applied, I don't have much doubt that the Community Resource Board would be sympathetic. They aren't exactly Hank Talbot fans over there! Do you want me to arrange an appointment for Ellie to see Mike Horvath? He would likely be the social worker to take her case, and he's already had a run-in with Hank Talbot, so he knows the situation."

As Abby was thinking that at least Ellie's situation might be sorting out, Liz continued. "So Hank wouldn't get much support if he did raise a ruckus. Ellie isn't a minor anymore. She's twenty-one, and maybe he will just think somebody was being nice to her while her foot's in a cast."

Smiling to herself, Abby contemplated how to tell Ellie she had not one, but two new guardian angels! If the job at the mill office didn't work out, at least there would be some financial support.

Back at the table, Ellie, who had been hoping for a bed for the night, was overwhelmed to hear she had a temporary job as well. Abby decided she didn't have the heart to tell Ellie that she would really need to mind her mouth on the job. They could deal with that later. "You know, Ellie, Laura's doing you a real favour, but she's pretty tired, so maybe try to say as little as possible tonight?"

"That's easy! The doc's given me some pills that'll knock me dead as a drunk!"

Abby paused to consider the challenge ahead of her. Ellie was a smart, motivated girl, but she certainly had some bad habits. How to take the edge off a lifetime of Hank's influence?

# 18

## Abby Goes to Bat

Abby bustled around the kitchen fixing Matt's favourite meal, Beef Bourguignon with lots of steak, mushrooms and crusty bread. He had just come off a two-week stint of afternoon shifts, a long haul with mostly soup and sandwiches for supper.

"Lordy! This looks amazing if I do say so myself! Matt, you ready for dinner?" She loved to indulge him, and he always seemed appreciative. It was fortunate that she found cooking fun, so a gourmet meal on short notice was no big deal, provided she could find the ingredients.

Thinking about the shopping for this meal, she remembered the odd encounter with Frank Hughes the week before at the grocery store and felt again a tightening in her gut. Was she putting everything they had at risk? Matt's job? Her job? This house? Kids someday? God, she hoped he'd see it her way!

While she had been cooking, she had mulled over her approach to asking Matt to let Ellie board with them for a few weeks. She had accepted he would resist in the beginning, first because he was a very private person and liked to have her to himself, and second, because it would be seen as interference into the Talbot family's troubles.

Now, she saw her job was convincing him that Ellie's welfare was at stake. She had been injured partly because of his recklessness, and he should feel ready to bear some responsibility for setting the situation right. Being willing to offer her room and board should be seen only as trying to make amends, not as interference.

"Hon? You okay to have the Eric Clapton blues playing for supper? Come on, it's ready."

"Yeah, I'm hungry as a grizzly. What have you got for us?" His eyes were roaming avidly from the Caesar salad to the Bourguignon to the basket of crusty hot rolls, all of it warmly inviting in the candlelight.

Later, over coffee and Gran Marnier, she broached the topic of Ellie and got the resistance she had expected.

"Matt, Ellie can't work easily at the ranch even if she wanted to, which she doesn't. Besides, she may be able to get a job if she moves into town, something not very realistic if she stays out at the ranch. She's bound to leave sooner or later anyway. Why not now, when medically, and in practical terms, it makes sense?"

"Because it's sticking our noses in where we have no business, Abby!"

"But we had no business spooking her horse so it threw her either!"

A moment's silence settled as she let him recognize that they, themselves, had played a role in creating the problem.

"We are at least partly responsible! Matt, you know I'm crazy about you, and I'd never do anything to jeopardize what we have! I know that you think I work too much, spread myself too thin, and lose sight of 'us'. But all I want to do here is a quick fix. It won't be for long, just a couple of weeks. Doing this is just a kind, caring thing to do, to help her until she gets on her feet. Oh, no pun intended!" She smiled wryly thinking of Ellie wobbling across that parking lot earlier in the day.

She saw when he cracked a smile at her sorry excuse for a joke that she might be getting through. Whatever happened, she did not want him thinking she was manipulating him into doing something that only she saw as fair and reasonable. He had to buy into the rightness of it too. This needed to be a fine balance of logic and persuasion.

"I will tell Ellie up front that she has to start looking for a place for October first. That's not even two weeks away. You know, Laura said she had some work lined up, so Ellie will have some income. We just need to give her a bed for a bit."

"Oh hell, Abby, why can't I ever say 'no' to you?" Matt puffed out his cheeks, then let out a long sigh and groaned in capitulation. "But not a word to anyone, okay? No telling the teachers, and definitely not that weasel, Tom Cooper! Have I told you how there's nothing that guy won't do for Hughes to get stuff for his freaking basketball team?"

Suddenly, the wine, music and candlelight seemed to kick in, and his eyes did a funny dance across her face. "Come on over here. I haven't felt that lovely bum of yours in ages!"

In the background, the blues beat of Clapton's "I Shot the Sheriff" seemed somehow ironic.

# 19

## Ellie's Story

"My mom was from Boston," Ellie volunteered as Abby served her baked beans the following Monday night. "She used to make what she called 'Boston Baked Beans' with molasses, but these are good too."

"Oh, I didn't realize she was from back there," Abby offered conversationally. "Was her family in Boston long?"

"Oh, yeah, Old Boston money. She told me once that she had a very strict upbringing, so when she could, she cut loose and never went back. I guess she had a wild few years in her early twenties before meeting my dad."

There was silence as Matt gestured for the cornbread and salad to be passed.

"I really miss her." Ellie's eyes were focused somewhere else as if visualizing Beth as she had been. "She knew how to talk proper, you know. She was always correcting our grammar and stuff. She told me she had been to a fancy all girls' college in Massachusetts for a term or two. Smith, I think she said."

Abby smiled and nodded. So Ellie actually might know how to speak properly. She could just try to sound like her mom! "Smith College is a well-known liberal arts school, I think."

Matt kept on eating silently. Abby hoped he wasn't just tuning out her conversation with Ellie.

"Funny, eh? Mom got all that fancy schooling and us kids were home schooled, me until Grade 9, and Tim was in Grade 8 when Mom got just too sick. I just feel lucky I managed to get all of Grade 11 and most of Grade 12 at the high school before I had to quit. If it weren't for a couple of picky courses like French, I'd have had enough credits to graduate maybe."

"So how much are you missing? You know, we can work on conversational skills here so you can aim for that switchboard job at the sawmill office. I know Laura isn't worried about you not having grad, but it's a shame to get so close only to give up. Maybe there's a way to get those missing credits."

Abby was on the verge of launching into some version of her "Stay in School" lecture when Ellie shook her head, "I know why Dad did it. He needed me at the ranch that May. Ranching is a family business, Mrs. Clarke, uh, Abby." The warmth in the brief smile accompanying that shift in name assured Abby that Ellie was ready to be friends.

"Your dad and mom built the Bar T on their own, did they?" Matt's interest had revived with mention of the ranch.

"Yeah, pretty much. There was an old homestead there, but there wasn't much left, no house or barn, just some falling down old sheds and some zigzag split rail fencing that had to be replaced anyway. We're still doing that and repairing the barbed wire fencing every fall after the main herd's gone. My hands are wrecked from dealing with that wire." She inspected her calloused fingers and broken nails. "Guess I can clean them up now for office work."

Abby could imagine a young Hank Talbot, a stubborn, powerful character who pulled others along by sheer force of his magnetic personality. "So your mom came from Boston, and your dad…?"

"He told me once that he got back to Montana from the Korean War in one piece and started to feel too crowded by all the cars and houses taking up all the good land. So he went without even tobacco and whisky for a year and saved up enough rodeo prize money to bankroll a nice chunk of land up here in north central BC. He said he wanted some as far back as he could get down a logging road. He had come to dislike life in the States, and thought he'd give Canada a shot.

"Mom said he'd already saved up the money when she met him at a rodeo in Colorado in '54. She was selling her jewelry and he was riding broncos for show money. So they got together, and then I was born in '55 and he brought the family up from the States in '57. I was just a baby so I don't remember anything before the ranch."

"And Tim was born here?" Abby was still curious about the midwife story.

"Yeah, Tim was born soon after they got here. Dad was out most of the time on the range so Mom was alone with me. Mom said Rosemary Joseph just showed up one afternoon a few days before Tim was born."

"And Casey? The hired man?"

"Where did you hear about *him*?" Ellie's astonishment was obvious.

"Someone mentioned to me –I don't remember who exactly," she didn't really want to lie, but didn't want Ellie to know she had been talking so freely to Liz Lundstrom either. "Whoever it was suggested he worked on the ranch a few years ago." Abby somehow felt ashamed, as if she had been prying. Still, she made a mental note to ask more about Rosemary when she next got the chance.

"Oh, hey, no problem, I was just surprised to hear his name. Casey was an old cowhand from around Williams Lake who just needed a bunk and a fire for the winter. He rode out from town one day in the fall. Rosemary was already staying close by us by then. Tim was just a baby. I was about four maybe? At first, I think Dad didn't like Casey, but Casey knew cattle and Dad needed a hand with the stock." She chuckled remembering, "Damn good thing he was there, you know? Tim, as he got older, had no interest in ranching. That pissed Dad off something fierce, but lots seemed to piss him off…especially government stuff."

"Lots of the ranch folk don't like the government getting their noses into the cattle business," Matt interjected, "especially if they don't know boom-all!" Abby was surprised at the vehemence in his voice.

"Yeah, well my dad sure as hell is on side with them! Mom says he got into a snit with the government early on. He argued about his taxes, seeing that he had no services to speak of out on Antoinette Creek, so he couldn't see why he had to pay so much. Antoinette Road was always the last to get plowed in a storm, or graded in the spring, and we had no power. I mean, I can see his point, you know? We lived independent. Between us and the Hitchcocks, we kept our ranch roads open and our fences mended. We didn't interfere with anyone else living out there, and we didn't need much from town."

"Except, now you can see that you could have used help with school? Or your…" she was about to add that Ellie's mom could certainly have used some medical attention when Ellie picked up on the schooling thread.

"So far as school went, Dad figured, when the time came, that Mom could do a good enough job considering. None of what she knew was costing the government any money, so why did he have to pay so much? He thought it was all just a money grab, all that registering for home schooling and buying textbooks. It really made him mad to have to pay for it.

"You know," she continued, "at one time, all that used to really rile Dad was the government, but since Mom died, he's way more hot-headed and downright mean. He used to be more fun even when he was tired. Now he's just an asshole wanting what he has no right to ask."

There was a long pause before Abby asked, "What does that mean, Ellie?"

Ellie, suddenly ashen-faced, avoided her eyes, and looking at Matt, asked, "Hey, do you know a guy they all call Schnauzer? A big tall blonde guy with a funny way of talking and a big nose? He's a friend of Tim's at the mill."

Suddenly, the two were chuckling about sawmill gossip, and Abby got up to clear away the dishes.

Later, alone with Ellie to work on her spoken English, Abby was pleased to see that the girl was a quick study. Still, the girl's odd periods of silence and deep brooding looks continued, and Abby was sure they reflected some inner turmoil.

# 20

# Hank Visits the School

Abby was staying late finishing up some prep at school the next Wednesday when Hank Talbot came sauntering into her classroom unannounced.

Oh my God! What was he doing there? "Mr. Talbot..." Her mind was racing. She was probably the only one there, except maybe for a janitor on the other side of the building who would never hear her if...

Even before Hank spoke a word, Abby was paralyzed by his appearance, and the smell was enough to make her retch. Not only did he smell worse than Tess ever had, but also he was covered head to toe in splotches of deep red.

Noticing her eyes riveted on his clothes, Hank spoke, "Sorry Mrs. Clarke, a rancher has to do his business in town quick, not much time for the social niceties. I just brought all the butchered hogs in to sell them at the Co-op, and didn't think to bring no change of clothes."

Before Abby could say anything, he waved her off as if to say he had no time to listen to whatever she might say, and rushed on, his words spraying like machine gun bullets in her face.

"That stupid bitch, Ellie, drove out to the ranch last night with Tim and tried to talk Tess into moving in with her! It seems somebody has helped Ellie get a job at the mill so she can pay for a place starting October first. Tess hasn't said she wants to go, but she sure as hell seems to be thinking about it! She says she's missing Ellie, and doesn't want to stick around the house all the time. She can't cook worth shit anyway as far as that goes! I can do better myself..."

Something in Abby's face must have been a red flag for Hank; suddenly he was frothing with rage, his index finger first jabbing at her face and then poking towards her chest. In the face of the assault by this blood-splotched madman, Abby's arms flew up across her breasts in self-defense.

"This is all your fault, you stupid cow! Now, I'm going to be left with no one to help on the ranch. You're the one who keeps harassing the kid about missing school. You're the one who says Tess needs more time for homework and fuck the chores!"

Everything now seemed to Abby to flow in slow motion. He was advancing across the classroom towards her, his arms arcing as he flung them in all directions.

"If the little twit leaves, she can forget about coming back on week-ends. I told her she can say good-bye to Blaze and Mooch, too."

Abby stood, astonished by his anger and appalled by his vindictiveness. Why punish Tess by taking away both her horse and dog? That was just emotional blackmail. Maybe the horse couldn't come to town, but sure as hell Mooch wouldn't be a problem!

"I…Mr. Talbot…you…Tess lives for that dog…"

Hank cut her off savagely, "Shut your hole! You ain't making no halfway deal here! Either she stays put, or she goes, you see?" The hysterical edge in his voice betrayed his desperation.

Abby saw that Hank had realized he could be losing even the one child who still seemed loyal to him. He had come to the school to threaten Abby into leaving Tess alone. What would he do if she just said 'so what'? She had to think clearly, and keep her temper.

"You have to stop trying to bend her your way, or maybe I'll talk to someone who'll make you stop. I got friends you know. I may be a just a cowpoke to you, but I know people who can make you squirm!"

Abby swallowed hard and gritted her teeth, "I need to remind you, Mr. Talbot, that by law, Tess must come to school, or you must agree to home school her. You can contact the school board if you don't believe me." There was no reaction, so she hastened to make her case before he stopped her again. "I can also add that she'd have a better chance if she came regularly, and had a home environment where she could do extra study. As it is, her attendance record is so patchy that she isn't making much progress, but with a regular schedule of reading and composition…"

Hank broke in with a hacking snort, "What a pile of horseshit! She don't need much of that stuff to run the ranch! Some simple accounts books to keep, and the odd seed or tackle catalogue to page through is all. Lady, you're wasting her time and mine. This here's round-up time. She's needed at home. Regulations be damned!"

Before Abby could respond, he was sounding off again, "As for Ellie, at least she is working, not sponging off anyone, and her foot is on the mend. Maybe she'll feel better about life at the ranch after a bit of a break. She ain't worth diddly to me with her foot all gimped up, anyways. She better be back by snowfall, though. I ain't trucking all the way to town through snowdrifts to get her."

Abby was quite sure Ellie couldn't care less about living back at the ranch. But she did care about her sister, and wouldn't be happy to hear that Hank would keep her at home where he had total control. Besides, if Tess could live with Ellie, there'd be no issue about coming in to school. But before she could tailor a reply, he had wheeled around and left, slamming the door behind him.

Abby was still shaking when she reached home fifteen minutes later and found Ellie out somewhere, and Matt already sprawled on the couch. Unable to hide her distress, she flung herself down beside him and blurted out the whole story of Hank's classroom visit.

Matt became increasingly livid as each detail unfolded. "What did you expect? You're prying into his family business, interfering where you don't belong! I told you this would happen! Why didn't you listen?"

Abby crumpled in the face of his wrath, unable to defend herself. Somehow, doing "the right thing" seemed impossibly hard. Matt, seeing her so vulnerable, calmed down and enveloped her in his arms, letting her soak his shoulder with her tears.

"Okay, girl, I'm sorry. That was kind of overboard, I just... I mean I can't protect you if you go out on a limb like you do! What I really want is to drive out to the ranch and call the bastard out.... "

"But he won't be there yet..." Abby was right. Hank was unlikely to be all the way out there if he had just been at the school hassling Abby.

Matt thought out loud, "More likely, he'll be at the Driftwood sucking back a few before he heads home. We might as well just eat, and I'll think about what to do."

Abby was unaware that he had already decided.

Just then Ellie arrived from work at the mill office, and they spent the next hour over supper hearing about her day. Then, luckily for Matt,

Laura dropped by with news for Ellie, so Matt was able to slip out with little explanation as the women settled down to chat.

Laura was excited. "I have news about Rosemary Joseph! My mom remembers her. She even has pictures of herself, Rosemary and Beth together from one year at the Fall Fair. It must be from about 1962. A guy at the fair with a Polaroid Land camera was taking pictures for a dollar each, so there's one of the three of them with my mom's garden produce, and another of just Rosemary and Beth with their jewelry.

"I don't have the pictures because Mom has to find them, but I'll bring them over as soon as I can." Glancing at Ellie, Laura added, "Maybe she can get copies so you'll have more photos of your mom."

Ellie smiled her thanks. "We don't have many pictures of Mom, just a few from when they got married and from when her and Dad were working rodeo back in the States. Having more would be great, thanks! And I don't have a real clear picture of Rosemary in my head, but I remember she was a good friend to Mom and a kind lady, especially if somebody was sick."

Abby ventured to ask, "Would she be someone you would like to get in touch with again?"

"Sure, I guess. Why not?"

Laura looked puzzled, "Abby mentioned her once, but I haven't heard much about her. Who was she again?"

Ellie cast her eyes upwards as she recalled, "I told Abby about her a bit. Rosemary stopped coming around when I was about seven, but I remember she was medium height, just a bit shorter than Mom, a dark-haired, brown-skinned woman in a moose hide jacket and denim jeans. She ran a trap line and walked everywhere. There wasn't much to her. I mean, she was real slim and always carried a cool, one-of-a-kind moose hide bag, more of a backpack actually, with a huge bull moose silhouette beaded on the outside of the main compartment. It held her grab bag of herbal stuff, I guess. Anyways, I remember her doling stuff out for us from there."

"She sounds like someone people would remember," Laura ventured.

"Yeah," Ellie sighed. "Funny, how she just disappeared. I heard her folks came looking a while later."

"And?" Abby found the story of Rosemary intriguing.

"And nothing…at least nothing we heard. But Mom was sick by then and we had other worries."

# 21

## Matt Takes on Hank

The Driftwood Motel and Restaurant Lounge for Fine Dining, Moose Forks' only decent eatery, had a private back room. Jimmy Jaworski, the owner, had no trouble letting Matt Clarke in to see who was there. Usually it was just a select group – supervisor types – so Jimmy felt Matt fit in okay. He wasn't a young punk anyway. A sawmill shift foreman had some credibility in Moose Forks.

Tucked into a corner was Hank, and luckily for Matt, he was all by himself at the table. Across the way near the rear exit sign were two men in business suits, likely just strangers passing through.

Matt slid into a seat across the table from Hank, and leaning forward as casually as possible, breathed in a low, even voice, "Hey Hank, just want a quiet word here. You know, between drinking buddies?" There was a pause as Matt sized up Hank's level of sobriety. Hank nodded and gazed into his half-empty glass. Then Matt continued, "Leave my wife alone. She's just doing her job."

An awkward silence reigned as the serving girl came by to take Matt's order. After ordering a glass of draft and waiting for the girl to leave, he sat back and waited for Hank to say something.

"Yeah, Clarke, she's a cutie, your wife."

Matt's shoulders stiffened and he rose in his chair, his clasped hands showing white knuckles where he was clenching the edge of the table to control his temper.

"No, no, don't get excited! I don't mean nothing by that. Just that she has a winning way about her. She's got both my girls thinking she knows better than their dad. I thought I'd give the high school a try, just to see if Tess took to it, but you know what? She *don't*! All the do-gooders in the world are not going to make that girl a scholar. I know it, and she knows it, and your wife should know it too! So how come she don't?"

"Abby just wants Tess to get the basics…"

Hank shook his head, "Ain't right. You know it ain't right that a man should raise them kids, and they just walk out after all those years just when they're getting useful? Where's the justice in that?"

"I don't think that's Abby's problem, Hank. You…"

"Course it's not her problem! It's mine! And I gotta solve it! I got the right to keep Tess at home to help on the ranch. Everybody agrees on that! I did with the older kids and no one complained! What's different now?"

"Maybe that your wife's gone?"

At that Hank exploded, "Fucking hell! She died! I buried her! What did they want? Spending a fortune on some fancy funeral?"

"No, the point is she did the home schooling, Hank, and if you're not going to make sure that Tess can at least read, write and so basic math, then…"

"Actually, to tell the truth, it was Ellie did all that with Tess this last bit, when she could get her to come into the house and sit down anyways. Beth wasn't up to much since a year last August.

"Ah Christ! This is ALL women's business, Matt! You're right about your wife just doing her job. All I want is to get my herd to market. How do I do that with no help? Right now, thanks to that fine I had to pay for burying the wife on my own, I ain't got no ready cash to hire cowhands, and besides, they all want the bigger money at the mill. You should know that! You hire enough of them, including my own son! I came up to this country from the States years ago thinking it was a place a man could get away from interfering pencil pushers! Now, if it isn't fucking unions raisin' pay rates for simple labouring jobs, it's fucking school teachers stealing your own kids just when you need them most! I got a spread to run! I got a fucking hundred head of cattle to get to market in the next month! I'm a widower, man! I got expenses now I didn't figure on! Lawyers, government fines…Christ! Five thousand dollars I had to pay to satisfy that bitch at Public Health! That was the cash I had set aside for hiring help for round up! The bank says they might give me a line o' credit, but I don't want that hassle! Is it any wonder a man drinks?" His explosion of temper ended in a wavering acknowledgement of the empty drink glass in his hand. Without any further regard for Matt, Hank waved to the waitress for a refill, and stood up, hitching up his jeans as he wove his way back to the men's washroom.

Matt nodded silently. Hank might be a callous old coot, and maybe he did beat his kids, but you had to feel for him. He was in a bind. His wife's death had cost him dearly, in more ways than one.

It was only when he was driving home that Matt realized Hank had not been wearing the blood-spattered, pig-killing clothes Abby had described. Matt wondered if Hank had deliberately stayed dressed that way to scare her off and had changed afterwards. If so, his harassment had a darker, calculated edge to it, something not evident just now when he had been talking to Matt. The thought made Matt clench the truck steering wheel and rev the engine even more.

# 22

# A Surprise at the Fairgrounds

It was another Friday nightshift, and Abby was feeling at loose ends. The weather was getting crisper. The poplar leaves that had first bloomed golden were now crinkling bronze against the deep hue of the evergreen backdrop. The previous two weeks since Ellie had moved in had sped by. She had proven to be a considerate houseguest and an apt speech student. Abby felt confident that she was fitting in well at the mill office. In fact, tonight she was out with someone she had met at work. Abby, with Matt on another nightshift, had eaten a solitary supper.

Tess, on the other hand, was still missing almost as much school as she was attending. Abby wondered if that was entirely voluntary. Or was she away because she was too sore and miserable to come?

Abby had just finished eating when she was awakened from her pondering by the phone. It was Laura, like herself, alone on Friday night. "Do you want to check out the fairgrounds? It's just the usual dumb rides for the kids, but we'll just go for an hour and then catch a drink some-where. Bring a coat 'cause it looks like rain, maybe. Can you drive?"

For an hour they wandered around the fairgrounds, the booths all bedecked in garish hot pink and acid green bunting. They were hard-pressed to avoid the come-ons of the sketchy looking carnies and fairway hucksters until Laura noticed a family she hadn't seen in a while. To give Laura time to catch up on the latest gossip, Abby wandered across the parking lot over to the corral fence to check out the livestock waiting for their big day at the rodeo.

She was peering at the cattle bunched in one corner of the corral, trying to see if she could make out any of the brands on their haunches when suddenly, she was aware almost simultaneously, that someone was hovering behind her, and that the sky was about to open up. Just as the downpour released, she whirled in panic to see Hank Talbot looming so close he could almost touch her.

"Oh! Jesus! Wha…..!"

All over the fairground people were rushing for shelter. She couldn't see what had happened to Laura. Hank yelled, "Here, get in my truck!" and grabbed her arm. Too startled to protest, she found herself being dragged into the truck parked right next to where she had been standing. Had he been there the whole time, and she hadn't even realized?

In an awkward silence, they sat and waited for the rain to subside. Abby could smell the mixed scent of horse and tobacco emanating from Hank. But there was a definite tang of whisky as well. He had been drinking again.

After a few minutes, when she realized the tattoo of rain was abating, Abby nodded, "Well, thanks for the shelter, Mr. Talbot," and reached for the door handle.

"Hey, Mrs. Clarke, please wait, so I can say how sorry I am for that scene at the school last week. I shouldn't really take my troubles out on you."

Oh my God! He was sloppy-assed drunk! His speech was rambling and jumbled, the words overriding one another. What had Ellie said about how they avoided him when he was drinking? Not wanting to give him the false impression that she was comfortable, Abby sat stiffly. He seemed oblivious however, and just kept on rambling.

"The ranching business has changed, you know? Nothing's as simple as it used to be. The young fellas are just into big trucks and machines, and they don't have a feel for the earth no more. Time was, people around here lived on the land and knew how to make their living without having to run into town all the time for God knows what…"

Warming to his subject, he stopped to roll a cigarette. "When I first came to this valley, folks was more helpful and understanding. They just pitched in when they seen a man needed a hand…"

"Now Beth…"

Abby perked up. What would he say about his wife?

"Now she was a real sport. In those early years at Bar T, me and her, we had to work like animals to build our house and get that Angus herd going. She would have tried anything I asked her. She even had her babies out at the ranch. We was lucky in having Rosie Joseph and Casey to help there…"

Out from his jean jacket came a mickey, and he took a long slug. Abby shifted uncomfortably and re-examined the door handle.

"Now there was a woman, that Rosie! I got a lot a time for a woman like her! Man, she was a strong one, and a hell of an outdoorswoman. You had to admire how she was with a rifle and knife. She could hunt, fish, trap. Hell, if she hadn't of been an Injun I'd of taken to her myself. She was just a lean one, too, but strong like a bear!"

Abruptly, his tone changed, "What I couldn't stomach was the way she came between me and Beth. One time I just made a little joke or two, and that bitch blew up and ran off to tell Beth what I done."

"What did you do to make her to act like that?"

"Lady, you gotta learn to quit asking questions. What happened in my house ain't nobody's business outside of it."

"That's not technically true, Mr. Talbot. If you hurt Tess, I have a responsibility to report it…"

"Bullshit! You don't need to say nothing. I didn't hurt that girl any, just a swat or two. Christ almighty! I don't remember when I even did that!"

Hank paused, as if trying to recall, and then without preamble, he lunged at her, his left hand clutching her wrists as the fingers of his right thrust beneath, probing amongst the buttons of her blouse. Her shock was even greater when that hand traveled down past her blouse to her jeans zipper and kept searching within to find the soft gash between her thighs and to push insistently inside. Outraged, she gagged from his whisky breath venting full in her face. Her frantic squirming seemed to do nothing to throw him off. His sweating, grimacing face was a monstrous mask of naked hunger.

"You ASSHOLE! Hank, HANK! Get off me!"

Her high keening shriek and energetic resistance stopped him long enough for her to flip the door handle to get halfway out, her feet on the ground. He stared at her stupidly, his mouth slack and moist.

As she was about to slam the door on him, he slurred softly after her, "You asked what I did with Rosie, so I just showed you. You know, a lady sometimes likes a little attention. Rosie sure liked it at first. Maybe she usually only got bucks to fuck her.  Now you, lady, you're a sweeter package altogether! Your husband was right about that last week!"

Furious, she pulled her jeans together where the zipper had been forced down and started to tuck in her shirt. "What about my husband? When the hell did you talk to him last week?"

For an answer, he winked and turned the ignition as she furiously slammed the door.

# 23

# Nora and Abby Have a Chat

As she turned to find her own car in the parking lot, Abby spotted Nora Macpherson heading towards her.

Oh hell! What now? She could report Hank for being drunk and about to drive, but her memory of his threat that day in her classroom to get his big-shot friends involved stopped her. She didn't want to provoke him any more than she had to. She wondered what Constable Macpherson had seen or heard.

Nora approached Abby with her head cocked to one side, her eyes focused on the undone buttons of her blouse.

Shit! Was she going to think Abby had been enjoying some serious sucking face with Hank? As if!! And what was that Hank had said about Matt? But Abby had no time to think because there was the constable, in her yellow-striped regulation trousers, striding across the slick gravel of the parking lot.

"Hey! What's up? I heard a bit of an outburst there. Is there anything the matter?" Nora's semi-casual approach caught Abby totally flustered, gaping in confusion. Swallowing hard, she smiled to stall for time…

"Oh, Constable, hi. Yeah, Hank Talbot was good enough to let me shelter from the rain in his truck…" The ridiculousness of that work 'good ' applied to Hank and the evidence of her undone buttons forced her to a reality check. She decided that surely, this woman couldn't be the hard ass that so many cops were. She needed to know what had been happening with the Talbots.

"Yeah, can we go somewhere to talk? Wait, I need to find someone and let her know." She was thinking that Laura could hitch a ride with those neighbours, and she would fill her in later.

Pointing to her squad car, Nora replied, "I'll meet you there in ten minutes."

When Abby climbed into the front seat of the squad car, Nora asked, "Do you mind if we drive around and talk? I'm supposed to be patrolling until ten."

"Okay, but could we maybe drive out on the highway instead of around town?"

Nora, giving her an appraising look, smiled, "Sure."

A few minutes down the highway, Nora pulled into a roadside picnic spot and, maneuvering the squad car to face the highway, turned off the ignition. The only light was the distant moon, now peeking out from behind the disappearing rainclouds. The air had a fresh astringent smell, newly washed, and the poplars encircling the picnic spot stood sentinel against the sky, bare of leaves.

At first there was an awkward silence as Abby tried to organize her thoughts. She wasn't sure where to start. The only sound in the cruiser was the intermittent squawk of the police radio as calls were sent out and picked up. The moon ducked behind a cloud making the scene darker and somehow safer.

Nora offered, "I wasn't really watching you, you know. I was just hanging out at the fairgrounds to get to know the community. I couldn't help but notice there was bit of commotion coming from the pickup back there and when you got out, you looked a bit, ah, uncomfortable, shall we say? So do you want to tell me about it?"

When Abby failed to respond, Nora prodded again gently, "Who was that in the pickup? How do you know him?"

Abby, who was just a splash of a white face in the semi-darkness, murmured, "You know, he's the father of the girl I pointed out to you a couple of weeks ago."

"He's the father of….?" Nora played dumb to give Abby a chance to explain the situation.

"Tess Talbot. You came around a couple of weeks ago asking about her?"

Nora nodded acknowledgement, and probed further, "How's she been doing since then?"

"As I said that day you came, she's really struggling at school because she stays away so much to help on the ranch, I guess. And I have been trying to get her and her dad to see how important it is that she gets at least the basics. She can't read or write beyond a Grade 3 level, and she's over thirteen. There's no doubt that she's anxious because she's acting out in all kinds of ways. You saw her smoking with the older boys behind the slash pile, and last week I caught her about to smear lipstick all over the girls' washroom mirror. It won't be long before those boys get more interested.

"So Hank and I have had a couple of conversations about Tess's schooling in the last month since school started. I even had a visit from Hank at school one afternoon. He was questioning Tess's need to come to school, saying he was within his rights to homeschool her."

Recalling the scene, Abby suddenly saw red all over again. "I was thinking he might call…" She was about to say that Hank could call in a few favours from all kinds of powerful friends to get her to back off, but she wasn't sure how much she should trust Nora. Some of those "powerful people" might be her friends too. "I told him then he should call the school board to sort it out."

"So how did you end up talking to him here tonight?"

"Tonight? Oh, he was there by the corral when the downpour started, and I jumped in the cab of his truck to stay dry, a dumb move as it turns out." She laughed in embarrassment, grateful to see a sympathetic nod from Nora. Abby continued, "He wasn't really interested in talking about Tess. Oh Lord, I feel like such an idiot!"

Recalling what Liz Lundstrom had said about Hank's treatment of his wife, Nora probed further, "Is there anything else you can tell me that might explain Tess's behaviour?"

"Oh hell, Constable…Nora, what can I say? The man's a beast! He beats his kids. You saw those sketches Margaret and I made. Also, just by the way Ellie acts around him, I don't doubt that she's had the same and …"

"Ellie?"

"Eleanor, the older Talbot daughter. Hank withdrew her from school a couple of years ago to help at home. She was just a couple of months short of graduation. It's a damn shame because she's a quick learner. She just got a job in the sawmill office as a clerk, and is getting her own place too, despite what her father wants. She's been staying with Matt and me for the last couple of weeks." Thoughts of Ellie reminded Abby of the girl's odd silences and her comment about Hank's "wanting what he had no right to ask." It wasn't hard to figure out what she meant by that, especially not after Hank's behaviour in the truck just now. She was certain Ellie hadn't just been warding off her dad's beatings. Hank had been sexually assaulting her. What about Tess?

Nora was waiting for her to continue. What should she say? It came to her suddenly. Somebody, some adult other than herself, had to know what Hank might be up to out there on Antoinette Creek.

"Nora I'm pretty sure he's an abusive father. Ellie might not actually come out and say so, but I don't think we're talking about just beatings here. " She paused, knowing Nora would catch the implication.

"What happened in the truck, Abby?" The abruptness of the question caught Abby off guard.

"I… we… he had been drinking…"

"Yes…and…?"

"He's in a tough spot with his wife gone and the older kids rebelling. They don't want to do ranch work. He's got a business to run."

"Do you feel sorry for him?"

"No, not really, but somehow I felt for Tess's sake I should listen, and all of a sudden, I don't even really know how, he had me pinned down. He's really strong and wiry, you know? Anyway, he was pulling at my blouse buttons and breathing in my face, and I couldn't stop myself from screaming out. I certainly didn't welcome his advances, if that's what you're wondering!"

"What you describe is assault. Do you want to press charges?"

"God, no! I don't really want anyone else, not even my husband, to know…"

"Then you run the risk of it happening again, Abby. That's the message non-action sends. If you want Hank Talbot to get the right message, maybe you need to step up and do something?" Her tone of voice suggested someone who had heard plenty of excuses.

Abby stared at Nora for a full thirty seconds before slowly shaking her head. "I would rather try to protect the girls than target the father. Anyway, what's happening with the witness statements from Margaret and me? How long until we get some action from you and Child Services? What happened tonight is not the real problem. I mean, Constable,

Nora, I'm a teacher. No matter who's at fault here, it will look bad for me. But those girls need protection from their father."

Nora stared at Abby as if trying to read her real motivations, and then nodded. "Okay, if that's how you want it. We can only do what the law allows, and we can't press charges in a case like this without a complainant." She shook her head, frustrated by Abby's lack of grit.

"Now the Talbot girls, that's another story, maybe. You say Eleanor might be willing to talk to us? What about Tess?"

"I really can't say. Ellie is angry with her dad, for sure, but I don't know how angry. Going to the police is a pretty serious step, especially for that family, I'd guess."

"Why so much for that family, pray tell?"

Nora's tone caught Abby by surprise. Up until then, she had seemed so normal, just as if, if she hadn't known she was a cop, she could imagine she was sitting with a girlfriend, even. But suddenly, there was that sharpness in the policewoman's voice, as if she's heard too many excuses, and Abby felt she was face to face with someone like her mother.

Something in Abby's face must have cued Nora to the fact that she had pressed too hard, and she raised her hands in surrender. "Okay, I get it. We're cops, not exactly everybody's favourite social contact, but I'm just trying to get a feel for a family in some kind of trouble. Tell me what you can so I can approach my superiors with a case for investigating Tess's situation. Our recommendation goes a long way with Public Health for instance, and I know that office is also concerned."

Abby felt somehow abashed by Nora's sincerity. The obvious logic of involving the police on some level was undeniable. She remembered the description that her principal, Tom Cooper had given of Hank; the words from that confrontation still echoed: "an independent, self-made man who came up from the States and built that spread out in the Antoinette Valley out of nothing but a few abandoned out-buildings, a man who doesn't like government interference."

"I guess what I would say about Hank is that he doesn't like *any* prying into his family's life. He avoids all government agencies, even doctors – much to the disadvantage of his wife for instance – did you hear that he refused to bring her in to get treatment for cancer? When she died, the Public Nurse guilt-tripped him into sending Tess to school because he had buried his wife without even a death certificate. In fact, he ended up paying a fine for that, I guess. Now, I heard this from Liz Lundstrom, the Public Health Nurse, so please don't quote me! I guess the Community Resource Board – he compares them to Commies, for crying out loud – have also had some attitude from him. That's really all I know."

Nora nodded and was about to speak when Abby added, " …and he has powerful friends in this town. His drinking buddies are George Warren, the school superintendent, and Frank Hughes, the mill superintendent. You can't get much higher than that around here! One's my boss and the other's my husband's! Now do you see why I don't want to press charges?"

Nora raised her hands again and smiled her most reassuring grin. "I get it, Mrs. Clarke, ma'am, I really do. You're a teacher here, and you're not the problem. Abby, I understand, and I want you to know I am going to do whatever I can to get those girls, especially Tess, some protection, if it turns out that's what they need. The law's pretty clear about the obligations of parents where minor children are concerned. But that man is a problem for women in general, in my opinion. Let's not lose sight of the obvious."

With that, she turned the ignition and they were off back into town. She swung round to drop Abby by her Volkswagen bug.

As Abby was getting out, Nora suddenly blurted out, "Hey, can we do an unofficial coffee sometime? You know, when I'm not on duty, and you call me 'Nora' instead of 'Constable'?"

Then there was that wonderful girlish grin again, and Abby couldn't help but say, "Sure, I guess. Why not! Okay, Nora, you take care!" And as soon as she slammed her own car door shut, the squad car was off across the parking lot.

Nora felt lucky that Matt was still at work when she got home, so there was no immediate need to reveal either her embarrassing encounter with Hank or her subsequent conversation with Nora.

Even so, she knew she couldn't keep him in the dark forever.

# 24

# An Old Photograph

The next morning, Abby phoned Laura to fill her in on her conversation with Constable Macpherson.

"I'm not going to tell Matt about it just yet, either."

"I wonder why! Bet you he'd be choked if he thought you were hanging out with a cop in your spare time! But you said she seemed okay? That's a switch! You mean because she's a chick?"

"You know, Laura, she's not hard to talk to. She doesn't seem like any of the cops we've had to deal with."

"Certainly not like that jerk, Wasniki, eh? Good thing! Man, that guy gives me the creeps! Whenever I'm near him, I feel as if he's sniffing around me, if you know what I mean. He's a bloodhound with that nose."

Abby avoided mention of Nora's overture of friendship. It was a slippery slope she would have to negotiate to befriend Nora and not compromise her weed-smoking friends.

"Oh wow! I almost forgot! I have that Polaroid of Rosemary Joseph and Beth Talbot that Mom found. You can check it out when we see each other at the rodeo. What time?"

When Laura hung up, Abby took a moment to reflect on how thankful Ellie would be that there were packrats like Nell Mendez, Laura's mom.

When Ellie was up and breakfasted, and Matt had rolled out of bed after his late nightshift, Abby and Matt drove with her to the rodeo grounds. On the way, Ellie pointed to a house down the street from Matt and Abby's place. "I've got the furnished basement suite there starting tomorrow. Now that I have a walking cast, I can manage a place on my own."

The tremor in her voice betrayed just how important this move was.

In the last two weeks, Abby had seen real growth in Ellie. Once on her own, she had emerged as a person full of determination. She had worked hard to clean up her language and was even feeling confident of keeping her job at the mill office. In the meantime, Liz Lundstrom had contacted Mike Horvath at Social Services who had arranged money for living expenses for the next month.

"Yeah, I told Tim I'd come home with him today, just for the night, and come back tomorrow – Sunday. Then I can move my stuff out of your place."

"Hey, that's great news, Ellie! I didn't realize you had things organized already. Isn't that cool, Matt?"

The huge grin on Matt's face on hearing Ellie's news confirmed something for Abby. Hank was not the only man who saw his home as his castle.

The main attraction that day was the rodeo events themselves. Matt hurried ahead to examine the line-up of bronco riders, leaving the women to wander through the carny stalls where some new jewelry booths invited attention.

Seeing the jewelry reminded Abby that Laura had checked with her mom about Rosemary Joseph. Something about Hank's comments the night before was niggling away at her. Why was Hank still so animated about Rosemary Joseph, a woman who had been out of the picture for so long?

About the photo, Laura responded, "Oh yeah, I got it here…in my purse. It's just a black and white Polaroid, and not a close-up, but you can see the two of them by their jewelry stand, right on these grounds. Must have been taken about October 1962, my mom figures."

Ellie, crowding in to take a look, exclaimed suddenly, "Yeah! That's her, that's Rosie, and Mom. Oh my God, look how young she is! And she must have been expecting Tess in this picture. You can't tell, though, she's so slim She was the sweetest lady, my mom. God, I miss her."

Looking more closely, she burst out again, "See, Abby? There's that backpack I was telling you about, the one with the moose silhouette beaded on the back. She always had that with her wherever she went. She kept medicinal herbs and stuff in it. Wow! This is so cool! Thanks Laura, I will treasure this!"

They all looked closely at the photo, and sure enough, there hanging over Rosemary's arm was the moose hide bag with its distinctive design just recognizable. Everyone could see how close Rosemary and Beth must have been, for they were standing not just next to each other, but with their arms intertwined. Both were smiling broadly, caught in the radiance of the sun's glow.

The memory of Hank's comments about Rosemary from the night before, prompted Abby to ask, "Does anyone know what happened to her, Ellie? I mean, you say she just stopped coming around?"

Ellie shrugged and shook her head, "Yeah, I don't know, I was so young then, you know? Just seven or so. I don't even remember what the time of year was when she went away. Let me think, maybe around Easter? I vaguely remember she was supposed to help us with an egg hunt but she wasn't around anymore. She shrugged again. "Too bad, Mom would have appreciated having her around when she got sick this last time."

Abby pondered the image of Rosemary from the Polaroid, her imagination captivated by the pretty woman with the laughing face and deep dimples that even the smallness of the photo couldn't obscure. Beaming a dazzling smile, she stood proudly beside her friend, Beth, whose jewelry she was helping to sell. By contrast, Beth seemed almost otherworldly and frail in her beauty, as if a good wind would blow her away. Beth was fair where Rosemary was brunette, and pale where Rosemary was darker, but in the photo they stood shoulder to shoulder.

Looking around, Abby gauged the height of the canopy support for a nearby booth and comparing it to the image in the photo, approximated the women's height at about five foot six or so. So they weren't tiny women. In her mind's eye, she was imagining Rosie struggling against Hank. She might have given him a run for his money.

Funny, how few Indians there were in Moose Forks. There was only one family that she knew of, and they were newcomers, so she didn't think there were many people she could even ask about Rosemary.

Ellie interrupted her thoughts, "I should find Tim to key up my ride back to the ranch. If I don't see you later today, I'll see you for dinner tomorrow." With that, she headed into the crowd, the lop-sided gait from the walking cast causing others to make way for her as she passed.

"And if we don't head over soon, we won't get any seats in the stands." Laura had already told Abby that the Saturday afternoon events were the premiere attraction of the rodeo. They hustled along and just managed to squeeze in beside Matt and Dan who had saved a bit of space on the sunny end of the tiers of wooden benches.

At first, there was no sign of Tim or Tess. Abby wondered if Tess might have been too sore from her bruises to ride, or maybe she hadn't wanted to spend any more time with Hank than she had to. And Tim? Hadn't Liz said he had had a bad fall last year? Still, something didn't seem right. Hank was there. He ought to have had at least one of the kids with him.

Then, at the far end of the rodeo oval, she saw them, all three Talbot kids, seated slouched down in a row at the top of the tier. Somehow, they were a pathetic little clutch of denim, all hunched together with their cowboy hats pulled down. Abby remembered that they were all going out to help Hank at the ranch as soon as the events were done. She hoped that asshole appreciated the gesture! It would be just like him to take it for granted, she thought.

# 25

# Blow-up at Bar T

The next day, on Sunday, just as it was getting dark, Tim dropped Ellie off at Abby and Matt's to move her stuff out. Unexpectedly, she had Tess and Mooch, her dog, in tow. Picking away at her plate of meatloaf, Ellie filled them in.

The weekend had not gone well. Hank, who was already home when Tim and Ellie arrived around four, had been surly when he had seen that Tim had driven Ellie out to the ranch in his pickup. Ellie had said she had a walking cast and could drive the truck if Hank needed her help. She said she knew it was round–up time, and there was beef to get to market.

Somewhat mollified by Ellie's offer, Hank growled that he had done most of it himself already, and then harrumphed off to spent the rest of the afternoon in the high range with Tim and a couple of the Hitchcock neighbor boys who had offered to help. In the last few days with the Hitchcocks, Hank had separated out the steers, the cows, the dry cows without calves, and the calves all into separate corrals. Then with Tim's help on the Saturday, Hank had decided which animals to load into trucks to take to the railroad for shipping and which to keep over the winter. These last would be left in the upper range to feed as long as they could before the snows came towards the end of October.

Ellie had been happy to be able to avoid her dad by staying in the truck, tending to the fence gates and running sandwiches and coffee out from the house. Tess had spent the day in the barn and around the corrals, feeding and watering the pent-up, restless herd of animals. About an hour after dark, the family had all fallen exhausted into bed after a hasty meal of pork and beans and toast.

That day, Sunday, they had been up at dawn and working. Tim,

Hank and the Hitchcock brothers had checked the calves separated from their mothers and branded, inoculated and castrated any that had been missed in the spring. The long day of riding range, lassoing and wrangling cattle had exhausted all of them. For some reason, they had had an unusually hard time managing the herd. The cattle had been more edgy than usual, and Hank's temper had been particularly foul. Tim, not a fan of ranch work at the best of times, could hardly wait to leave. They were all happy that the cattle trucks had arrived on time, and there had been no trouble loading the steers and getting them to the rail yard. The mopping up had been all done when a huge blow-up with Hank resulted in all three kids driving off abruptly around suppertime.

"What was the blow-up about?" Abby hadn't much doubt that Hank was at the bottom of it, but neither Ellie nor Tess wanted to elaborate.

"Tess just decided to come into town with me for the week," Ellie offered. "She asked to bring Mooch with her, and I couldn't find a good enough reason to say no. My new place has a back yard, and I'll square it up with the owners. Likely it's temporary anyway. I mean about the dog staying there too."

Tess's eyes during this exchange were riveted on Ellie's face, and she seemed ready to object when Ellie said the arrangement with Mooch was temporary, but for no apparent reason, she then slumped back in her seat and continued to pick at her meal. Mooch, who had been given an old coat to lie on in the front hallway, was also restless, seeming unable to settle down, several times during the meal wandering from the front door into the living room and back again to the table and to his bed.

Abby was puzzled. Tess's eyes had a queer, cloudy look, and the dog seemed spooked too. At one point, when the girl leaned down to pet him, she winced from the effort, and Abby could see once again that her lower back was a study in black and blue. God damn him! How much of this did Tess have to put up with? At least with Ellie, she was safe.

# 26

# Bruises and Red Tape

The next day, Tess was back at school and struggling with reading and writing. She preferred to lean against the wall to read, and Abby, knowing she had painful bruises, put her to work writing out some vocabulary exercises on the chalkboard, something Tess found novel and therefore entertaining for a while. However, when lunchtime came, she continued to hide out behind the slash pile, and once again was caught smoking. Not for the first time, Abby wondered whether Ellie could manage her rebellious little sister. She was relieved to see that Tess showed up for her afternoon classes.

Once again, she had called Margaret in while Tess had been absorbed at the chalkboard and had her witness the state of Tess's lower back where the bruises showed when her T-shirt lifted with her raised arm.

Abby was becoming more irritated with Nora. When would something be done? All she, as a teacher, could do was deal with the situation one day at a time. She was getting tired of just recording the abuse. When would Hank face the music?

She had called Nora at the detachment office, but the constable hadn't had any time yet to follow up on the suggestion that Ellie or Tess might be willing to talk to the police about Hank. The detachment had been absorbed that morning with a fatal crash on Highway 16; a heavily loaded semi-transport on its way to Prince Rupert had lost its brakes on Hungry Hill, a long, straight, treacherous slope on the way to Glacier Lake. It had careened down the hill and thundered over a family sedan trying to make a left turn. The sedan had been so badly crushed that the police still weren't sure about the number of fatalities. They'd be busy for at least the next day or so determining identities and notifying next-of-kin.

"Be patient, Abby. I'll do what I can as soon as this fatality case is cleared. I haven't got the paperwork yet anyway."

"Can you at least give me an estimate?"

"Listen, this fatal accident takes priority. Deal with it." The memory of crushed limbs and torsos in purpling bags of greyish skin still made her stomach churn. Dealing with Tess was way down her list. She hastened to justify her position. "Besides, taking custody of a minor does require a court order, and that has to be initiated by Social Services. I have Mike Horvath working on it. If there are charges to be laid for assault or failure to provide the necessities for Tess, then that's our area. Social Services deal with custody of a minor."

"I understand." Abby, hearing the curtness in Nora's voice, continued, "I'll tell Ellie that Mike is involved. Oh, you haven't heard the latest. Tess is staying in town this week with her sister, so at least she's safe for now. I guess they had a blow-up with their dad last night, and Ellie decided to bring Tess into town to stay with her at the new apartment."

Nora seemed surprised at the news. "That's some progress, anyway! So there's less urgency until she decides to move back home. That should give us time to get the paperwork done."

Abby signed off feeling frustrated. Why did it seem that when you didn't want interference from the authorities, they were everywhere, and when you did, it was so hard to get them to do something?

Late in the day, just as the school buses were loading, news came of a bush fire, beyond Antoinette Lake several miles south from the Bar T. Abby thought little of it. Bush fires were common in the fall. Both ranchers and farmers tended to burn slash before the wood got too damp. They depended on the rain or snow in November to keep any wildfires from burning too far. The land past Antoinette Lake was farther east in another fire district. A fire there, even a really bad one, was unlikely to affect people in Moose Forks.

# 27

# Wasnicki Gets Friendly

Later, on that Monday afternoon, Nora was at the front desk of the detachment office catching up on some typing. Everyone else was out on patrol or dealing with the accident, so she was alone. It felt good to have some personal space, something rare whenever Wasniki was in the office.

He was an odd character. He lived alone in a spacious new house on "Hamburger Heights," where most of the newcomers to town had bought in the subdivision built to accommodate the opening of the mill a few years before. Rumour was that there had been a Mrs. Wasniki, but that she had split before the posting to Moose Forks. Wasniki had bought the big house to entice her back, but it hadn't worked.

Nora, considering once again the enigma that was her boss, thought it was small wonder he was single. The man was the most chauvinist, bigoted jerk in God's creation! She marveled that he had ever achieved a leadership position.

Nora had accepted an invitation to Wasniki's place on the weekend. Jed and Angie Fedoruk had been there along with the auxiliary staff, a small party of a dozen or so, including Eddie Braun, who in his usual fashion, had flirted with Nora whenever he got the chance. Nora found herself wishing Eddie had pulled the weekend shift instead of Luke Gallagher, who showed up briefly only as the party was about to break up. Apparently, the detachment got together for a social every few months or so, but the last time, the first that Nora could have attended, she had pulled an afternoon shift. This Saturday night had been her first visit to Jack Wasniki's basement party room.

Nora had felt a bit out of place as an unescorted female, especially since Jack had paid her far more attention than his job as host required. Early in the evening, she had sat on a stool at his well-provisioned bar in the basement and had been captivated by the display of indigenous art and tools hanging from the walls and lining the shelves. Everything from framed collections of Blackfoot and Assiniboine arrowheads to Haida argillite carvings and bone fishhooks from K'san, near Hazelton, was labeled and artfully displayed. He had spent virtually the whole evening plying her with wine and showing off his favourite trophies. He was a genuine collector as opposed to a decorator. He knew the stories behind most of his pieces and regaled her with accounts of how he had outwitted the hapless "squaws and bucks" who had sold to him.

"These are beauts." Wasniki had been extending a pair of moose hide leggings with decorative fringe and geometric beading. "I got them at the Standing Buffalo Reserve just northeast of Regina, when I was at Depot back in '53. That dumb old chief sold them to me for just a couple of bucks. If you see any in your travels, let me know, eh?" Jack had had a few too many, it was obvious. His words were running together like water beads on a glass, and he was leaning far too close.

"Wonder what I could get for them now? You know, if you sell this stuff to museums, you make a nice little bundle. Course, you wouldn't be interested in this old stuff, not a honey like you. You want modern stuff, fancy clothes, expensive jewelry. Am I right? Can I pour you another? No? How about something different? Drambuie? Crème de Menthe? Tia Maria?"

As she marveled at his intense personal interest, she found herself asking what he would say if she told him who her great-grandmother was, if she told him she was Metis. She had chuckled to herself upon realizing he's probably just use the connection to get himself more moccasins! Jack was pretty transparent, she had decided.

She had been very happy to see Luke Gallagher when he arrived at the end of his shift. The party was winding down, people sitting in small groups chatting. He wandered over to where she was sitting at the bar to get himself a beer and hung around, lounging casually up against the corner where the counter met the wall.

"So Nora! How's it going? Have you got that office sorted out yet? We could sure use your help out in the field. Tell that sergeant of yours to quit being such a skinflint and hire a proper temp!" He laughed to see Jack jerk his head around to confront him. "Oh, come on Sarge! It's just a little joke! But sure, I know a girl from the high school who graduated in June. Great little secretary material! Just wants something short term while she decides where to go for school. Want me to give her a call?"

Nora didn't hear Jack's reply as there had been a sudden outburst of laughter immediately behind her, but Wasniki's flushed face gave her the impression that he had not been amused.

Later, as they were all leaving, Luke had flashed a smile at her, and said he hoped he'd see her soon. Something about his tone seemed to suggest more than just office-level contact. She wasn't sure how she felt about that.

Nora snapped back to the present in the detachment office as she remembered Abby Clarke's phone call from earlier in the day. It was time to try to move on that case. She had a background profile of previous illegal activities, and evidence of physical abuse with testimony from credible witnesses. The younger girl was now safe from the father so she wouldn't suffer any reprisals. Nora just needed the older daughter prepared to press charges. She would ask Jed to look at the assembled case first, and get him to be there when she presented it to Wasniki for his approval.

But once again, her best-laid plans had to be set aside. Just as she had decided to arrange an interview with Ellie Talbot, the office phone rang. The bush fire the other side of Antoinette Lake had moved towards the Marcel River area, and for the first time, was threatening the roads and ranches immediately to the southwest of Moose Forks. All personnel from the detachment were needed to establish a security perimeter to keep gawkers from moving in, and to help the ranch residents evacuate. The Talbot case would have to wait. Actually, theirs would be one of the ranches the RCMP would have to contact. Nora realized that she might be able to check out the home situation without anyone being the wiser.

The rest of the afternoon was spent getting fitted out with a uniform suited to rough terrain. Out came her regulation yellow-striped trousers and oxford shoes. She also grabbed the regulation navy parka issued for cold weather, just in case. She hoped Wasniki was going to be too busy to gripe about her not looking "like a lady."

Nora wondered just how much he could dictate personal choices like the uniform she chose for fieldwork. Something told her that he was on thin ice if his dress code fixation interfered with her doing her job.

# 28

# Wasnicki in a Corner

Nora was dog-tired, with a raw throat and eyes swollen from smoke exposure. She had spent virtually all of the last three days on a grueling detail in the backcountry, rattling with Corporal Fedoruk in their four-wheel drive Chevy along washboard roads or bare tire track ruts in the bush. They had a map of the ranches and farms to notify and, if necessary, evacuate in the face of the encroaching fire. The fire crews had been battling non-stop since Monday, the land gangs constructing firebreaks and the water bombers dumping loads of lake water in hopes of slowing the advance. It had been a near thing, but the worst was over thanks to some heavy rain overnight that had subdued the worst of the flames.

She and Jed had worked well as a team. His no-nonsense style calmed nervous residents; his smiles were genuine and frequent, his patience and energy seemingly limitless. Nora felt she had lucked out in getting him as her mentor.

Now she was back at her apartment, collapsed on the couch and wondering how she was supposed to report for duty again in the morning. For just a moment, she contemplated having her daily cigarette, but realized that the last thing she needed was more smoke in her lungs. Stupid habit!

She pondered what she had seen in the last three days of frantic activity. She and Jed had been one unit out of many, mostly volunteers, urging the ranchers and farmers along the fire's perimeter to evacuate north to town for a day or two until there was a clearer sense of the fire's path. Some had cooperated willingly; others had argued and wasted their time. Not until about noon today had they been sure that the worst was over, at least for their district, and that they could open the roads to general traffic.

This afternoon they had been out almost as far as the Talbot Bar T Ranch, but had been forced to turn back when the "stand-down" message had come through saying the detachment could end evacuation duty and move on to traffic control to ensure only residents travelled into the fire zone.

Nora wondered if the Talbot place had come through undamaged. She was hoping the girls had stayed put in town. It would be just like Tess to bolt out there to save her horse. She decided she should call Abby to see how things were with the girls, and maybe set up a time to meet Ellie about pressing charges. But the hour was already late, and all Nora could really contemplate was her bed.

The next day, a Friday, Nora waited calmly outside Wasniki's office for Fedoruk to finish his update on the fire evacuation and stand-down. Still feeling the effects of the smoke exposure, she had to steel herself for what she knew would be a tense interview with Wasniki. She had contacted Ellie who had agreed to come in on Monday to talk about laying charges against her father. Now, she had to show Wasniki that there was enough evidence to approach Talbot about a restraining order to keep Tess safe. She had decided she would face Wasnicki without having Jed there. It was time she stood on her own feet.

Jack's office door opened and Jed was halfway out, when seeing Nora there, he paused, his eyes querying her tense expression.

"You seeing the Sarge about something important, Nora? Everything okay?"

"Hey, Jed. I'm checking into the Talbot girl's situation, but it's all right, I've got it." She sounded more self-assured than she felt.

Jed, sensing that internal hesitation, replied, "Listen, I can sit in if you want. I've had some dealings with old Hank." He glanced over to see Wasniki listening in on their conversation from his desk, and quickly revised his choice of words, "I mean, Mr. Talbot."

Nora blushed with embarrassment that her need for collegial support was so obvious, but she nodded her thanks.

Sitting opposite Wasniki, she realized that, because everybody had been so busy with the emergency, this was their first face-to-face since the get-together the weekend before. She hoped he would be friendlier, or at least less patronizing.

She straightened her shoulders, smoothed down her skirt and began,

"Sergeant, I wanted to let you know that Eleanor Talbot, the older daughter of Henry Talbot, the owner of the Bar T Ranch, has indicated that she wants to come in Monday, and I expect that she may wish to press charges for assault against her father, or at least get a restraining order to keep him away from Teresa, her younger sister."

It had all come out in a rush, and she felt relieved for having said it, and for having Jed there to back her up. She watched Wasniki's face. It was a study in conflict. Without a doubt, he was surprised by what he had heard, but also angry, shocked, and puzzled.

"What do you mean, 'keep him away'?" Wasniki was staring at her in bewilderment, his face all blotchy, his mouth a mere slash across his face. The tendons in his massive neck stood out like heavy-duty cables. "I was under the impression that she lived with her father. Where is she?"

Keeping her voice calm and her gaze level, Nora briefed him on the move the girls had made the previous weekend, filling him in on the involvement of Abby and Matt Clarke and Laura Mendez.

"Oh, that bunch!" He snorted in derision. "Him and his crew are pretty wild, from what I've heard, you know, underage drinking, drugs, that kind of thing. They've got some high school-aged girlfriends, some of those young punks. You think that's a good influence for that young one?"

"I don't think you can paint them all with the same brush, Sergeant. I've talked with Mrs. Clarke a couple of times. She's a teacher at the high school and seems pretty levelheaded, a decent sort. Anyway, it's not about them. The Talbot girls are living in a basement suite on their own now."

"So what's the problem? They're set up in town, the girl's in school, the brother? Is he working?"

"Yes, Tim and Ellie both have jobs at the mill and can support themselves. Ellie wants to have custody of Tess, and in view of the evidence, I have contacted Mike Horvath at Social Services to organize a court order to that effect. Ellie feels that Tess is at risk if Talbot wants to come and take her back to the ranch."

"And why shouldn't he? She's his daughter, isn't she? She's under age isn't she? What in hell is the point of interfering here?"

"Sergeant Was-ni-ki…" She said his name slowly and carefully, as if to emphasize her self-control. "You need to understand. The father had been beating Tess and her sister, not once, but repeatedly. I have testimony from witnesses all lined up. There is no deniability. This is assault."

Suddenly, Wasniki looked like a fish flopping on a riverbank, his mouth gaping open and shut as if in search of water. "You have evidence... witnesses...CHRIST!! Why didn't you let me know you were doing this? Why didn't you clear it with me first before you went ahead harassing one of the town's most prominent citizens!" With each word, the volume of his voice seemed to increase so that by the end, he was standing at his desk and leaning over, screaming in her face, and Jed, who had said nothing all this time, had got out of his chair and was standing with his arm raised between Wasniki and Nora, as if to deflect the sergeant's attention.

"Sergeant, I think Nora, Constable Macpherson, is perfectly within her beat here. This is clearly a domestic problem. There hasn't been any harassment on our part. Evidence has been compiled suggesting that a minor, a thirteen-year-old girl, has been assaulted. Now I know Mr. Talbot is an important man, but that's a good reason not to allow him to get away with something that could come back and look bad for him later on, not to mention look bad for us, if we were told about the physical abuse and did nothing."

Wasniki glowered in mute disbelief. Then he erupted again. "Who called it "abuse"? A man's got a right to discipline his kids, for Christ sake!"

Jed stared back, unflappable, and Nora said quietly, when Wasniki seemed ready to listen again, "We have witness statements from the school detailing several incidents of bruising on Teresa's back and upper thighs. I think Ellie will be happy just to have Talbot keep his distance for now. She may not want to press charges. Maybe the best thing would be for one of his friends to mediate here. You know, to have a quiet chat, and just let him know that it would be in everybody's best interest if he stayed away for the time being. Maybe that way, we can keep it out of court altogether? Or at least protect the girls while their dad gets help on the ranch?"

Jed nodded in agreement, and cocked his head for a moment as if to think. "George Warren might be the logical choice. They're good friends. Do you want to call him? Or should I? What do you think, Jack?"

Wasniki growled," I think you two had this all organized before you ever came in here. Sonuvabitch! All right, get out! Let me think about it!"

# 29

# A Visit to Bar T

Later that evening at Matt and Abby's place, the rocking wail of Steely Dan's "Reelin' in the Years" drowned out some of the chatter of the assembled throng of young women. Ellie, Tess and Laura and a few others with boyfriends on the same shift had dropped over to keep Abby company until the men got home. It had been a weird week, with some of the guys pressed into service fighting the fire and others having to work extra, shortened shifts to ensure there was no lost production. Everyone was relieved the crisis was over; they were keen to party.

With everyone looking forward to the Thanksgiving long weekend, the house was simmering with girlish energy and giggles. For the actual holiday on Monday, Abby had plans to cook a turkey and invite the Talbot kids as well as Ken and Laura.

When she saw Ellie on her own fixing herself a drink, Abby had a minute to touch base. "How's the new place working out? Do you have everything you need? Towels, sheets…?"

"Oh, thanks Abby, you're so nice. No we're good for all that stuff. We're mostly using sleeping bags for now, and Mr. Horvath, you know the Social Services guy, made sure we got some towels and dishes and stuff. He said as long as everything's cool here, we don't need to push right away for a custody order. I'm so grateful for everything you've all done. Even Tess seems settled in for now.

"Oh, I meant to tell you. That lady Mountie called me today. She wants me to go in to the police station on Monday and talk about laying charges against my dad. I have to think about it. You know he'll go ballistic if I do!"

Abby thought for a moment. "I think you need to consider Tess, and whether she will be able to go back home safely. You need to be able to leave her there and know he won't hurt her. At least that's how I see it. Your dad needs to understand that beating her, even if she is his daughter, is not okay, and that…" she searched for the right words to frame her concern about the sexual molestation, "…that any touching is just *wrong*!"

She watched Ellie's face to see her reaction. The girl was steely-eyed. Then, Ellie shook herself as if to clear her memory of unpleasant images, and did a "thumb's up" sign to Abby before turning back to join the others in the living room.

Now, Thin Lizzie's "The Boys Are Back in Town" was thundering through the house, and everyone got up to work off some pent-up energy. Partying while waiting for the guys to come off shift was their routine every fortnight. The room was warm with sisterhood.

Conversation drifted off to plans for skiing that winter and the new snowmobile trails being built in the backcountry. "The Wesleys are buying a Bombardier Ski-doo this year," Laura offered. "They say the cost of keeping it running will work out to way less than what they have to pay to buy feed for their horses, not to mention saving time on grooming and exercising them."

Tess who had been quiet, stirred at this topic, "Horses don't like the noise those things make, you know. I hope nobody buys any!" There was a general chuckle as they humoured Tess, glad to see her participating.

When the men showed up, the party got lively. Somewhere after midnight, with The Rolling Stones' "Brown Sugar" throbbing through the main floor, Abby realized she hadn't seen Tess for a while, and thinking the girl might want to crash in the guest room upstairs away from the music, went looking. Abby found her sitting on the floor in tears on the bottom level of the house, an unfinished basement room.

"What's wrong, Tess?"

"Aw, that talk about snowmobiles reminded me of Blaze." Her eyes welled up again, and she stopped speaking as she wrapped her arms around herself and clawed at the sleeves of her denim jacket, great sobs shaking her thin frame.

"Oh, Tess, you're just homesick. You know, the fire being under control means you and Ellie can go home for the weekend. Maybe Tim will drive you?"

Tess peered out from behind her crossed arms. "I was planning to go anyway, but forgot about you having a big dinner for us Monday."

"Oh, you know, I'll understand if you want to stay longer to help your dad over the long weekend. There's no school on Monday, and turkey leftovers are always better anyway! You just need to keep in mind that you must stay safe and not be alone with your dad."

Tess's amazing china blue eyes clouded slightly then cleared. The last Abby saw of her, she was chatting happily with her sister.

The next morning, Matt and Abby had woken up late from the Friday nightshift party, and were having a leisurely late breakfast when the Talbot kids all appeared on their doorstep at about eleven.

Tim, hesitant as ever, started to explain, " We went out real early, about seven, to the ranch because Tess had promised Dad to help out this weekend, and when we got there, it was all gone. I mean, the fire got it! It's all burnt!"

Ellie took over, "The house is gone, and some of the out-buildings close by, they're burned to the ground! Even Dad's truck, next to the house, got burnt. The barn is okay, the stock, Blaze and the pack ponies; they're all okay, because they were out in the pasture. There was a small herd of cattle, yearlings, this year's calves and their mothers, wintering in a corral behind the barn. Looks like they spooked bad so now they've headed for the hills and will need rounding up all over again.

"But the house, I can't describe it, it's just gone! Nothing left but charred timbers, that tall rock chimneystack and the fireplace. There's no sign of Dad either, and Ebony's gone, maybe one packhorse too."

"Ebony?" Abby vaguely remembered hearing about this horse.

"Yeah, Dad's coal black stallion. You remember, he rode him at the rodeo? Big black stallion with white stockings. He's valuable. I can't imagine Dad leaving him behind."

Matt, coffee mug in hand, waved all three young Talbots into the kitchen. Tim and Ellie seemed to be bearing up stoically, but Abby could see Tess was in shock, and now starting to cry. Pouring cups of hot coffee all round, she tried to imagine the scene.

"So Tim took you and Tess out to help at the ranch? Ellie, you went to…?"

"I didn't want her going out there without me. My foot's okay in this walking cast. I can drive a truck and do coffee at least. Besides, Tim would be busy and who knows what might happen to Tess on her own?" The question hung ominously in the air. Hank's disappearance had not altered Ellie's hostility.

Matt picked up on the crucial detail, "Your dad's not around any-where? Can we assume he headed into town? Nobody's heard from him? How long since the big burn out there? Four, five days?"

All his questions dangled unanswered. Matt heaved a big sigh and shook his head, "That's a long time with no sign of him. I think we have to go to the cops and report him missing. Maybe he was injured in the blaze, and was too confused to find his way to town?" He didn't want to say it in front of the kids, but chances were equally good that Hank was lying burnt to a crisp in the bush somewhere, and that the missing horses had just somehow wandered away.

Tess suddenly came to life, her eyes lighting up with her recollec-tion, "No! We looked everywhere! The barn, the creek, that's where he always told us to go if there was a bush fire, but he wasn't anywhere around. Her words seemed frantic. "We even searched the bottom part of the high range for him. We drove up in the truck and honked the horn and everything." Her voice was high-pitched, choking with pent-up tears.

Tim agreed, "Yeah, we were there until just an hour ago, bush whacking and looking, but nothing, not even horse hoof prints. If he's alive and rode Ebony away, there's no sign…and anyway, it's been almost a week and there's been rain…" He looked exhausted, the strain showing in the dark circles under his eyes.

Tess suddenly wailed, "I shouldn't have moved out! If I hadn't left, if I'd stayed to help…" She collapsed in a bundle of anguish into Ellie's arms.

Tim straightened up and addressed Matt, "Do you think you could give Mr. Hughes a call, and ask him to call around? Somebody might know where he is, George Warren, maybe?"

Matt nodded, "No problem."

Ellie added, "We also need to report the fire and Dad's disappear-ance. I guess I'll see the cops before I expected." She shook her head in disbelief.

At Ellie's words, Tess poked her head up to ask, "What about Blaze and the other stock? Who's going to feed and water them?"

Tim volunteered, "Me, maybe, if I can get some shifts off. Matt, can you get someone to cover for me at the mill? I'll go back to the ranch tonight and come back into town Monday after I get some hired help. Then I'll start back on my regular shift."

Tess once again raised her head in protest, "I can ride too, you know!"

"Hey, Miss Muffin, you know you didn't get any range-riding time in. You can't shoot a rifle for one thing. You're better off here keeping Ellie company. I can camp in the range cabin, as long as it made it through the fire, and get the Hitchcocks to help round up again."

"Where's the range cabin, Tim? This was the first Abby had heard of another building apart from the main ranch site.

"It's about a half hour's horseback ride south towards the lake, up on a bluff on the same level as the upper range. We got couple of hundred acres of hayfields up there that spreads out on the highlands north of the lake. The road's real rough so you need four-wheel drive to get in if you want to drive, and even then you can't drive all the way. The drive takes at least fifteen minutes, if you're lucky, and then there's ten to fifteen minutes walking. I'll maybe leave my truck below and take Blaze up.

"Guess we better be getting over to the cop-shop," Ellie's voice cracked a little as she spoke. She wasn't looking forward to the trip.

"Remember to come back here for turkey, Ellie and Tess, and Tim, too, if you get finished out there." Abby realized the kids could now come to their Thanksgiving dinner. She did wonder, though, whether they'd have any appetite.

# 30

# Up in Smoke

At the detachment office, the Talbot kids found Jed on duty and ready to listen to their story. "You say you went out to the ranch and that the whole house is gone?"

Ellie quickly filled him in on what they had found, and then asked if she could talk to Constable Macpherson. Jed at first hesitated, and then seeing the pinched looks on Tess and Ellie's faces, decided Nora was the sensible choice to handle their statements. "I'll check to see if she is available. Why don't you all sit there in the meantime?" He pointed towards a collection of wooden chairs lined up along the wall in the foyer next to the main entrance.

Within twenty minutes, Nora came rushing into the detachment, her tie flying. She first closeted herself with Jed in his office and then emerged with him behind.

"Hello, Ellie, Tess...and Tim?" Nora had never actually formally met any of them. She had only talked to Ellie on the phone. "What's this I hear about a fire at the ranch?"

Ellie again volunteered to give a recap of where they had been and what they had seen that morning. Nora's eyes watched Ellie's face intently the whole time as if trying to assess her emotional state. Then, with her elbows on the counter, she clasped her hands together as she spoke. "We need statements from each of you, okay? We need to hear as much detail of what you saw or heard when you were there as you can give us. This may take a while, so one of you can go first, and the others can sit there and wait, or come back."

Ellie said, "I'll go first. Tim, why don't you take Tess back to my place, and you can both get some lunch?"

In the interview room, Ellie sat opposite Nora, and Jed signaled Nora to begin. He would just sit by as she handled the questioning.

"Ellie, thanks for coming in today. We understand that you must be pretty upset by what you saw out there, and want to find out what happened as soon as possible. The best way to help us is to take your time to remember as much detail as possible, and tell us where you went at what time and what you saw. Can I get you some water before you start?"

"No, that's okay. We drove out early, about seven this morning to the ranch, because Tess had said she'd help Dad do some work out there. We saw…"

"Just a sec, Ellie. How long did it take you to get there? We need to know the times when things happened. So when you describe some event, please try to give us an estimate of time, okay?"

"Oh, it's a forty to forty-five-minute drive, so about a quarter to eight we got there maybe. The sun was just coming up. And we drove into the yard, and right away, we saw the house was all burnt, nothing left but the chimney sticking up. The greenhouse, the woodshed, it's all gone. But the garden shed is still there somehow. Good thing the barn didn't catch. We had some stock nearby."

"So how long did you spend looking around the house site, Ellie? Did you touch or move anything?"

"No, we didn't go into the house, where it used to be anyway, at all, actually. It looked too messy and dangerous. There were beams fallen in from the roof all burnt…" She stopped briefly in a shudder and then with a deep sigh, continued, "We wondered right off where Dad was, so we split up to look. I checked the barn and saw that the saddle for Ebony, his horse, was gone too, and Tim went with Tess over to the creek."

"How big is your family's ranch, Ellie?"

"We've got more than a section, over seven hundred acres altogether along Antoinette Creek, close to where it flows into the lake. That's just past our place a mile and a bit overland."

"Did you go anywhere else on the ranch?" Nora was wondering about other buildings where Hank could be.

"We drove around behind the barn just to check on the cattle. We had a herd we're keeping over the winter in a corral behind there. They were gone into the farthest fields, over towards the road, probably spooked by the fire. We were afraid they had injured themselves crashing through the corral fencing, but we found some with Blaze and the stock ponies up in the backfield. The rest are probably up in the upper range."

"Wait a minute, Ellie. Wasn't that area behind the barn burnt? Didn't the fire reach all that area too?"

"No, I know that's weird, but it seems untouched. There was a smell of smoke, but we didn't see much timber or grass burnt! That's funny, eh? The house and yard got hit, maybe because it was closer to the creek where the fire came down through the valley, but not the land even closer to the big burn."

"So is there anywhere else your dad could be on the ranch, anywhere he could stay for a while?"

"There's a cabin up top, the range cabin where Old Casey used to stay when he was with us. He might be there, but I don't think so."

"Why not? And who's Old Casey?"

"I think Dad would have come in to find us, if he could have. Going up there doesn't make sense if he was hurt. Casey was a hired hand we used to have working for us years ago. He left several years ago."

"So you're assuming your dad was hurt?"

Ellie stopped dead, suddenly, her eyes locked on her hands in her lap. Jed watched her intently as Nora reread what had already been said.

"Ellie? Why do you think he's hurt?"

"Well it makes sense, don't it? The house all burnt to rat shit. Sorry, Constable. You know what I mean, though. He wouldn't have just run away from that house when it caught fire! He would have stayed and tried to fight it. So he'll have some burns at least."

"But it doesn't seem logical that the house was part of the damage from the forest fire if there's all that untouched area in between, so how did the house catch fire?"

"Jeez, lady! *I* don't know! I wasn't *there*! And it doesn't matter how it started because my dad would have fought it, anyway!"

"Okay, Ellie. Let's go back to the others. Where were they when you were in the barn and corrals? And what time was this?"

Ellie heaved a sigh that seemed to wrack her whole frame and then stared doggedly at Nora's chin. "By the time we checked out the house, it was about fifteen minutes later, about eight o'clock. Then I went to the barn, and Tim and Tess checked out around the creek, probably another half hour. So by the time we headed over to check the field behind the barn, it must have been about eight-thirty. We came back to the yard by nine-fifteen or nine-thirty. Tess had found Blaze and checked her over good. We had trouble getting her to come away." Ellie made a wry face as if all little sisters were a breed apart.

"And then what did you do?"

"Tim wanted to check the barn again to see if he could figure out if Dad had taken any of the other stock animals, or whether he should look for them with the yearlings."

"Did he find anything? How would he know if your father had taken them?"

"He looked to see if all the tack was still there. The stock ponies wouldn't have that on if they were just out to pasture. All that stuff's kept in the barn. Anyway, most of that tack was there when Tim looked. Maybe some is still up top."

"So what time was it by the time you finished there?"

"About ten or ten fifteen I guess. We were back into town by about eleven and it's only a forty-five-minute drive."

"And before this, when was the last time you saw your father, Ellie?"

Ellie's eyes were still riveted on Nora. Now, they seemed to be latched onto her moving lips. When she finally answered, Ellie's voice had a peculiar tone, as if she were speaking from someplace far away. "Last weekend, I went out with Tim and Tess to help with getting the stock ready for market. We came home about suppertime Sunday evening. He was in the house when we left."

"How was he? Did you get any sense he was not himself? You know, was he upset about anything?"

Ellie guffawed out loud, her hoots taking both Jed and Nora aback. "Geez, lady! My dad was almost always 'upset', as you say. That was normal for him! Remember I was coming in to Monday to lay charges against the ass – uh, sorry. But really, Constable, to ask if he was upset is like asking if he was breathing!"

"All right, Ellie. I understand you aren't on very good terms with your dad. All I need to know is what was the gist of your last words with him. You know, what kind of goodbye was it?"

"I don't remember any real goodbye, to tell the truth. We found Tess hurt, and I just got her the hell outta there as fast as I could before he could stop us."

"What was your dad doing when you left?"

"Before we left, he was lying on the couch having a drink."

"Alcohol?"

"Yes, whisky."

"And you don't remember him saying he had plans to go anywhere this week?"

"No, only into town here to go to the bank maybe. He would have had some banking to do when he got the money for the cattle he shipped last weekend, but he might have already done that."

"Okay, Ellie, just one last question. Did you have any sense of a fire when you were out working the range? You know it was spotted out near there the next day…"

"Only afterwards, Tim and I thought about it and realized the animals were more than a little spooked all that Sunday. It must have been they smelled the smoke. But we didn't see any fire, that's for sure."

"Thanks, Ellie. That will help us get started. We'll need to get a search party going. We could use the help of your friends and neighbours. Maybe you could let us know who to contact, please."

Looking at Jed, she raised her eyebrows as if to ask if he had any other questions. Then she slapped her forehead and chuckled briefly, "I guess I need a physical description of your father if we are going to get a Missing Persons Report started. Just a minute, I'll get that form. Jed, can you check to see if Tim and Tess are back yet?"

Ellie left to fill in the form and Ted brought Tim in. They soon saw that he didn't have anything substantive to add to Ellie's statement. In fact, Nora wondered whether he always had trouble stringing more than one or two sentences together. Tess was even more reticent; she would only nod and shake her head.

Nora was struck by the fragility of the two younger siblings. They seemed so young to be on their own, and yet clearly very protective of each other.

Afterwards, Nora compared notes with Jed. "What do you think? Anything jump out at you? I think they're holding back a bit."

Jed scratched his head and poured himself a coffee. "Oh, I don't know. I don't think they acted any different than any other kids their age would have under the same circumstances. Don't forget, their dad is missing, and the only home they've ever known has just burned to ashes.

"Of course, they're in shock," he continued. "We can get Tim and Tess to come in later when they remember more. Right now, the priority is to get a search party to find Hank Talbot, and then to send out an APB to detachments in the rest of the province. He may have ridden his horse out, but if he's hurt his head or something, he could be anywhere."

Nora's thoughts were much darker: what a perfect opportunity to escape consequences! He's a sly one, she thought.

# 31

# Clearing the Air

Later that Saturday afternoon, after they had heard from Ellie that the police were getting a search party together, Matt and Abby chatted with Ken Snider, Laura's boyfriend and Matt's best friend, and they agreed to offer their help. They and the Talbot kids had all got together at the Clarkes for their Thanksgiving turkey dinner anyway, so by suppertime, they had set up a telephone tree to contact as many of the Antoinette Valley ranchers as they could reach to ask them to watch for Hank, and to get their help for the search party starting the next morning.

Later, after the Talbot kids had left, the four friends considered the events of the day over a few beers and an after-dinner smoke.

Abby remembered her impression of Mooch the Sunday night the Talbot kids had come back from the ranch, "Ken, you're a ranching guy. Do you think the animals' behaviour means anything? I mean could that fire get close enough to bother the stock but not be noticeable to humans?" She stopped as the others zeroed in on where she was going with the idea. "I guess, what I really wonder is whether the bushfire was the cause of the Talbot ranch house fire."

Ken stretched back on the couch, his long, lanky legs flung over the back. Laura snuggled alongside. "I don't know for sure. Naturally, none of us can be certain, but I kind of doubt the bushfire could jump all the way across a large field and hit just the house. Isn't that what Tim said, that the area behind the barn over towards Antoinette River Road was clear of burn? But then, if there's wind, sometimes a new fire can spark up from blowing ash."

Laura and Matt nodded in agreement. They were all familiar with basic fire-fighting skills. Anyone who worked in a lumberyard had to be, and they both agreed with Ken.

Matt added, "And smoke in the sky in that general direction might explain why no one further into town on Antoinette Lake Road noticed any smoke from the Talbot ranch. Just bad luck for old Hank. The crazy sonovabitch wasn't even a smoker. Frank told me he chewed snooze some, from being an old mill hand."

"So you're saying the ranch house fire didn't start with a cigarette…" Abby was remembering the litter of garbage in the yard, and the piles of papers and magazines she had seen in the house. The place would have caught fast with all that fuel lying around. She was jerked back to the present by Laura's voice.

"Hey, Ellie told me he could even have had a phone by now but he refused to get one. That might have helped! Every other ranch out on Antoinette Creek has a phone. But he resented the pole charge the telephone company charged for stringing a line all the way along that ten-mile long driveway into the ranch house. It would have been expensive maybe, but, what a dinosaur!"

A general chuckle of agreement sent them off on a tangent about how bush isolation seemed to warp the psyches of some people, especially single men of a certain age. Stories of Yukon sourdoughs abounded in the valley. Almost every family seemed to have an old uncle who had caught gold fever and never been seen again. Hank might not be quite as isolated as some, but he was certainly more of a lone wolf than anyone else in the valley.

Abby broke into the discussion with the question on everybody's mind, "Where is Hank Talbot? Why, if he could get on a horse and ride, didn't he ride into Moose Forks, or at least to a neighbour's?"

Matt picked up the thread, "What if he was injured and headed the wrong way? Maybe he got hit on the head and was disoriented. Maybe he headed into the bush. And with winter coming on, if he's in the bush, how will he survive?"

Ken offered some insight, "If he's with his horse, it will have a better sense than he has for finding its way to water. Once Hank finds a creek, it's easy enough to follow it to something he'll recognize. On the other hand, he might still be bushwhacking his way following some creek that's taken him way the hell and gone into the backcountry. Not much of that area south of Antoinette Lake's ever been settled and it's Fraser watershed so creeks run south or east, the opposite direction from town. Could be all kinds of game trails and waterways we don't know about. Might be a while before he figures out where he is."

"Well, I suppose we'll get some idea tomorrow. The search party starts at eight at the cop shop. Nice way to spend Thanksgiving weekend, eh?"

"Who all's going, Matt?" Abby was wondering about Tess again. She didn't think bouncing around the bush in a four-by-four all the next day was what the girl needed.

"Well, Tim and Ellie need to go and show the cops where their dad might be expected to go. I expect Tim'll take his truck. You and Laura can come with Ken and me if you want…"

"And Tess? Is she going too?"

"I expect so. Why not?" Abby sat and thought while Matt got up to wander over to the fridge.

"More beer, anyone?"

Laura picked up on Abby's silence. "Hey, Abby, why shouldn't Tess go tomorrow? Is she all right?"

Abby hadn't really kept Laura in the loop about how much she had been working with the police and wasn't sure this was the right time, but decided she had to clear the air.

"Well, Tess has had a tough week already, what with getting beaten by her dad and then moving into town and leaving her horse and all. She's probably not happy at having to deal with cops, and she'll have to again tomorrow. She didn't much like talking to the constable today either, you know, when the kids went in to report Hank missing?"

"What do you mean see the cops "again"? She hasn't had any other run-ins has she?"

"I guess she knows that we, I mean, Ellie and she were planning on getting a restraining order, until Hank went missing anyways…" Abby's voice drifted off.

There was a stunned silence as Laura pushed herself up and away from Ken on the couch and leaned towards where Abby was sitting. "You said "we" at first. Abby. Are you helping them get a restraining order against Hank? Are you crazy? Don't you know what kind of shit he can cause for Matt? Or for you for that matter?" Laura then switched from puzzlement to annoyance. She, more than any of the others, had had some heavy-handed encounters with the RCMP over smoking marijuana, and had decided they were all fascists. "You can't trust cops anyway! They won't do fuck all for those girls! Why put your neck on the line for something that won't work and will just cause problems? Ted Hughes and George Warren are both buddies of Hank's. Christ Abby!! You are crazy!"

"Oh, I don't know, Laura," Ken moved to calm her down. "The cops aren't all losers, you know. My folks got some help from Fedoruk one time when we had that problem with our fences getting cut."

"Yeah, they work out okay for people with property or some pull, like your folks are established ranch people, so the cops give them the benefit of the doubt. But anyone new...."

"Oh, babe, relax! Matt and Abby are getting known, too. Helping on the search party, sticking up for kids who need a place is all good stuff. Ted and George might expect them to do this kind of stuff, good neighbours, you know?"

Laura inhaled audibly as if to contain her irritation and groused, "Whatever…"

Over a quiet Sunday breakfast the next morning, Abby was still pondering the real mystery. "Matt, do you think Hank Talbot is still out there somewhere? I mean, skulking about waiting for…"

"I don't know, Abby. If so, where is he staying? Everybody says he's got enough bush craft to manage as long as the weather holds, and he isn't injured or sick. That's the point, though, isn't it? Chances are he's injured or running from something, or he would have shown up, to tend his stock at least. It doesn't make sense otherwise. Everybody says he's a miserable old coot but, when push comes to shove, he's reliable."

Something snapped for Abby when she heard "running from something". She decided it was about time Matt knew what Hank had done that night before the rodeo.

"What the FUCK, Abby!!!" Matt's face had drained of all colour, and his fists were clutching and unclutching as if seeking a target. Breakfast was forgotten. "And why in hell have you waited this long to tell me?"

"Well, nothing really happened, honey. I mean, he groped me is all that happened really, and I sure as hell didn't want you losing it!"

Matt, his eyebrow raised in a cynical arch, breathed, "What? You think I can't hold my own in a fight?" There was a dangerous edge in his voice.

"That's not the point and you damned well know it, Matt! I don't see any point in fighting, especially when there are kids caught in the middle. Besides, I figured if it wasn't serious enough for me to press charges, then you didn't need to know right away. I was always going to tell you. I was just waiting for a good time."

She rushed on, "The point is that now, I think we need to let the cops know everything we know. This guy's a dangerous man and an abusive father, and I don't think he cares who gets hurt. Those girls won't say anything, but I'm almost *positive* he has interfered sexually with them. That's a criminal offence. And now, he could be anywhere."

"So, I need to tell you that I am going to find Nora Macpherson Tuesday and tell her everything I know." These last words came out in a rush with a huge sigh to give them substance, and Matt considered her face for several breaths before responding.

He reached across the table to grab her hand, and cupped it in both of his for emphasis, "Sweetheart, we'll go together. Sometimes, the cops are the only answer. It makes me sick to think that creep touched you, and I have no problem with involving the cops. But don't you *ever* hold out on me again like that! Do you understand?"

Early the next morning, Thanksgiving Day, Matt got a call from Tim asking for an extension on his time off. He needed the whole next week so he could deal with the stock at the ranch. It was a short week because of Thanksgiving, so Matt felt he could cover Tim's shifts from the spare board. Tim would stay in the range cabin and check around for someone to take over so he could return to the mill. When asked about his sisters, all he would say was that they were being quiet, which was weird for them, he added.

# 32

# A House Fire Mystery

Nora was feeling out of sorts. Here it was Thanksgiving Monday, and she was bouncing along Antoinette Lake Road on the way to Bar T with Jed. There had been little news from the search party the previous day. When the last vehicle had reported back at six the night before, it became clear that Hank Talbot had either disappeared into the bush or lay dead somewhere. She had spent the day at the detachment office, coordinating the search through radiophones and the neighborhood telephone tree Abby and her friends had set up.

Today, as she drove with Jed Fedoruk out to the ranch to examine the burn site, she thought back to their near-visit the last day of the forest fire. If only they had made that stop before standing down! Who knows? They might have found Hank.

She reran the interview with Ellie on Saturday. Was she missing something there? Ellie had really reacted when Nora had asked how the house had caught fire. Could a forest fire jump across and hit the house without damaging the space between?

"Jed, do you know anything about forest fire burn patterns?"

"What do you mean? Burn patterns?"

"I mean, if an area is on fire, can it jump over a space to set something on fire that's a long ways off?"

"It all depends on the wind. It's the oxygen source. The fire needs it to grow, so wind can really kick it up a notch and spread it, too. So why do you ask? You're thinking about Ellie's statement?"

"Yes. She seemed pretty touchy when I asked how the house caught fire. Did you notice?"

"Yeah, she did spark up, eh? What do you think? That she knows how the house fire started?"

Nora stared straight ahead at the road. "I don't know, but I think we should try to find out."

"Well, once we've seen the site, we have the option of calling an arson team. They might be able to give us a scenario for the house fire."

"True." Nora remembered that the purpose of their visit was to assess the need for a more expert investigative team.

After arriving, they had spent about an hour around the house and yard when Jed observed, "My dad would have said that this is the kind of place you have to wipe your feet leaving!"

"Yes, it is a mess all right!"

They drove up as far as they could past the field behind the barn. Just as Ellie had said, there was remarkably little burn damage in that area of the ranch land. It was as if a protective hand had stayed the fire, confining it to the hollow where the house nestled near the creek. As Ellie had said, Hank's Ford truck was a blackened shell sitting in the driveway near the remains of the house.

"Well," Jed decided after another hour, "We definitely need an arson team for the site."

"And a tracker dog to try to get a handle on Hank's whereabouts," Nora added, "though after ten days, the chances are good that his trail has gone cold. Too bad that the kids didn't check sooner." Or that she and Jed hadn't checked during the bushfire evacuation. She shook her head. So much depended on timing. She prayed they hadn't been the ones to drop the ball!

Because the K-9 crew from Prince George was a priority, they sorted out that requisition first and radioed their request back to the Moose Forks Detachment. The crackle of the return message several moments later assured them that that an animal and its handler would be dispatched early the next morning.

The arson experts were another story. They would normally come from Glacier Lake and be available in a couple of days, but the forest fire had devastated several properties in the area south of that town as well, so the team was tied up for the next week at least.

In the meantime, while waiting for these radio messages to come through, Nora took several photographs of the burn site and surrounding debris. The house site was devastated. Even the stone foundations and chimney were blackened almost beyond recognition.

Together, she and Jed wandered about speculating, Nora taking photographs to document their investigation. The state of the yard was hard to describe. The litter of odds and ends from both the house and barn had been blackened beyond easy recognition. The place was a land-mine of safety hazards: spools of corroded barbed wire, charred wood with nails protruding, burnt skeletons of broken furniture.

"I know I'm just a townie," said Nora, kicking some charred barbed wire out of the way. She was struggling to be diplomatic. "I mean farm-ing is an organic, messy kind of business, but shouldn't it be safe?" Edg-ing a blackened rectangular can with her toe, Nora wondered out loud, "Do you think there's been some accelerant used?"

She picked her way out into what must have been a garden and poked about an old shed that had survived the blast of flames. She peeked inside and took some photos of the contents, thinking some of the canisters might contain something that could have been used to acceler-ate the fire.

Finally, she made her way to the barn and took several photos of the interior, now unoccupied as Tim and Tess had said. The remains of the herd and the horses had been set to pasture in the fields behind the barn.

On Tuesday morning, the K-9 team from Prince George arrived, and Jed Fedoruk drove them with Jack Wasniki out to Bar T. Nora had expected to go herself again, but had to concede to Wasniki as superior officer. However, she was puzzled by the sergeant's demeanour. He was worried about Hank, too. Of course, she knew they were friendly so that made sense. But why did he look so tense?

Nora spent part of the day developing her shots of the Bar T ranch fire for the arson team to examine. The K-9 team returned at five just as Nora was getting ready to hand over to the volunteer night shift. They told her the dog had had no luck finding Hank. Tim had volunteered an old coat of Hank's, but the scent must have been too faint. Also, the length of intervening time and the acrid condition of the burnt-over soil on the site had combined to obscure Hank's trail.

When he returned, Wasniki had said nothing as he entered the main office, but with his gaze focused straight ahead, just strode over to his private office and entered, shutting the door.

Nora couldn't help but feel he was a man who did not manage the unexplained very well. How could he manage as a cop if everything needed to be tidy to keep him happy?

# 33

# Abby and the Super

As she came into the main school office at the end of Tuesday's classes, Abby saw a note in her mail slot. George Warren wanted her to call him at the board office. Abby's chest tightened as she thought of the possible reasons why Warren would be contacting her directly. Usually, Tom, her principal, dealt with school board officials.

"Hello, Mr. Warren, Abby Clarke here."

"Yes, Abby. Thanks for getting back. I hope you had a good Thanksgiving?"

"Well, considering the search party and all, I guess it was okay." Somehow she didn't think he had called to inquire about her weekend.

"Abby, I understand that you might be able to help me get in touch with Eleanor Talbot. Tom Cooper told me you helped her find a place to live in town, and I need to talk to her. I think she should know that the police are considering arson charges for the fire out at the ranch."

Abby thoughts flashed back to her time with the search party on Saturday. They had not been assigned to the area around the Bar T so had not checked out the fire damage. Still, she wasn't stunned by the suggestion. She remembered from their September visit that the state of the yard around the house had been so chaotic that anyone could be forgiven for thinking the junk had been piled up for a bonfire.

She decided to play innocent. "Oh, why would that be, Mr. Warren? Who would want to set the house on fire?"

George Warren's voice grated across the phone line. "Mrs. Clarke, I know Hank Talbot well enough to be positive that he wouldn't be so careless. I understand from the search conducted yesterday that the house site is far enough removed from the nearest forest burn, that it likely

161

burned separately, meaning someone set it on fire, and as I said, Hank would never be that careless."

"But Ellie told me that the last time she saw her father, he was drinking whisky…"

"I don't care what he was drinking, young lady! Even when blind drunk, Hank would never be so inept that he'd set his own house on fire and not realize the fact!"

Abby had a vision of Hank's skillful handling of the axe that first day when she and Matt had dropped by when Ellie hurt her foot. He had been staggering drunk at the time.

"Yes, sir, I suppose you do have a point there…"

"So I need to talk to Eleanor and get her to come clean with the police. Surely, she can shed some light on this, and likely on her father's whereabouts too, I suspect."

The horror of this implication struck Nora like a blow. "You think she's responsible?"

"I didn't say that, Abby. I said she can shed some light on the events of that day. Jack Wasniki has already called to ask me to find Hank and talk to him about his other daughter, Tess. I had a different question to ask Sergeant Wasnicki which is what's being done about the fire and Hank's disappearance? He says there's an arson team on tap and an APB out, but in the meantime, we should follow up what we can locally. So, just to be clear, I want you to contact Eleanor and get her to report back to the RCMP. She'll be better off volunteering to come in than if they have to chase her. That's the last thing her father would want. I have already talked to Frank Hughes so Tim will know he needs to do the same."

Abby thought about telling Warren that she knew Tim wouldn't be at work for a few days, but decided not to say anything. Somehow, she felt she shouldn't volunteer George Warren any information that she didn't have to.

After Warren hung up, Abby was left wondering why the school superintendent had called instead of Wasniki? Was it just as he said, that voluntarily coming in would look better for Ellie? Why just her and Tim and not Tess as well? Or was Warren letting her know just how much influence he had in this small town? Did he know more than he was saying about Hank? How had that fire started? Could there have been a drifting flame from the Antoinette Lake burn? Did Hank accidently cause it himself chasing a cat skittering across the table? And then came a chilling thought: which kid had been the last inside the house?

In her mind, Abby turned over the motivations each might have had for starting a fire. Not Tim, surely, his father wants him to inherit the farm, Ellie says, but then Tim doesn't really want it. He'd rather live and work in town. But was he so protective of Tess that he might do something like that to punish Hank for hurting Tess? She couldn't be sure.

Tess, even though seething with anger over her father's mistreatment, would never do anything to endanger her horse and dog, but then she knew Blaze was out to pasture and that Mooch could go with her to town. Tess could have had both motive and opportunity. She had been left on her own all day that Saturday and much of Sunday. Also she had been so quiet that week after she came into town, and today, not in school again. What was she avoiding?

And Abby could remember Ellie's hatred of her father practically oozing from her pores on their first visit to the ranch. What would it have taken to kindle that hatred to arson? Abby felt nauseous thinking about the reality: not one of those kids was completely clear of suspicion.

# 34

# Tess's Secret

That night after supper, Abby dropped over to see Ellie and Tess in their basement suite. For now, she had decided not to tell Matt about George Warren's phone call. No need to worry him unnecessarily. Likely, the kids would be cleared.

Walking the short distance in the dark gave her time to plan her approach to the sensitive question of arson. She decided she would start with George Warren's suggestion, that things would go better for Ellie, and the others for that matter, if they went to see the police on their own.

As she cracked the door slightly ajar to Abby's quiet rap, Tess gaped in astonishment. She had not expected her teacher at their door. "Mrs. Clarke! What are you doing here?" The girl stood in suspended animation with the door mostly closed, as if awaiting an onslaught.

"Tess, I need to talk to Ellie and you. I have a message that needs some explaining. There's no phone so I had to come over."

The tension on Tess's face was relaxing by the time Ellie appeared at the door, and with a quick smile, she pulled it open.

"Sorry, Abby. Tess's a bit spooked still. I know she should be in school if that's why you're here. We'll try for tomorrow, honest. She's still pretty upset about, you know, about everything?"

"Actually, Ellie, I'm not really here about school, although it would be good if she came, of course. I have a message for you. Is this a bad time? Can I come in and talk to you for a moment?"

Ellie flushed in embarrassment, realizing she had neglected the most basic hospitality.

"Sure, come on in! You haven't seen our place yet, anyway, have you? It's kind of messy and simple, but it's home. Can I make you tea?"

"That would be lovely, Ellie, thanks." As she settled at the small dinette table and took off her jacket, Abby was aware that Tess was watching her with rapt attention. Turning to her, Abby smiled and patted the seat next to her. Without further hesitation, Tess slid into the seat. Apparently, the wordless invitation and her sister's offer of tea were all that were needed to allay Tess's anxiety.

With a steaming mug in hand, Abby broached the topic of Warren's phone call. "The thing is, Ellie, that the police who went out to the ranch today think there's a possibility of arson, and because you were the last people to see your dad, they want to have a clear statement from you about that day – when was it? A week ago last Sunday, right? So that would make it October third? Mr. Warren called me because he didn't know how to contact you, and he wanted you to see the police on your own before they have to pick you up for formal questioning." The alarm on Ellie's face at the suggestion of more questioning moved Abby to offer some reassurance. "It's a question of appearances, you see. If you volunteer to go in, they will be less likely to think you have something to hide."

"But I don't have anything to hide! For Crissakes, Mrs. Clarke! You know why we left like we did!"

"Yes, I know you were upset about Tess, but unfortunately, that means the police would think you might have a motive for doing something to get back at your dad, so I think it would be a good idea to tell them what you remember from that afternoon and evening, in particular where there was fire in the house, and what you remember from signs of fire outside."

Ellie sat for a minute, her eyes shut and hands cradling her chin. Then, she began to describe the scene in the kitchen that supper hour. "There was one kerosene lamp lit on the coffee table and another on the dining room table when we all left. There was also a fire going in the living room fireplace, and of course, I had the cook stove going because we were roasting a chicken in the oven."

"What about any sign of fire outside? Do you remember smelling smoke when you were by the lake? Weren't you and Tim riding around up there?"

"Yeah, well, Tim was riding a horse, but I was in his truck, on account of my foot." She kicked her walking cast in obvious displeasure. "But no, I don't really remember smelling any smoke up there. I mean, we would definitely watch for something like that, you know? Mind you, it was a tough day for herding. Yeah, I bet that's it. That's why the cattle were so restless. They could smell smoke even if we couldn't. Even Mooch was weird, remember, Tess?"

Tess, who had her head down on her arms as she listened, just nodded in agreement.

"So you're quite sure none of you smelled or saw any smoke when you were out in the upper range?"

Ellie shrugged and looked at Tess for confirmation. "Nobody said anything that I heard if they did, right Tess? Did you hear Dad or Tim mention smoke?"

Tess, as if roused from her memory of the day, slowly lifted her head. "Only Mooch was acting spooked all day, like he was antsy about something. You remember him whining and not settling even when we came to your place for dinner later that day, Mrs. Clarke?"

"Okay, so no smoke outside that any of you kids noticed or mentioned to each other, and you're pretty sure your dad would have said something if he had noticed?"

The two girls nodded in unison, their eyes following Abby's intently.

"Then what happened in the house before you left?" Abby sensed there was something here they hadn't been willing to talk about, certainly not on that Sunday night when they had all showed up unexpectedly.

"We were in the house getting ready for dinner together, and Dad had come in from the barn and was having a drink, but he was just relaxing because it had been a helluva day like we said. He wasn't drunk, at least not when we left."

"You say you were making dinner there. Did you sit down to eat?" Abby knew that busy ranch families often had to forego the niceties at round-up time. It might have been a meal eaten in shifts with Tim still out working while his dad took a break.

"No, we were planning on all sitting down together, but we couldn't get Tess to come in from the barn and sit down."

At this point in Ellie's story, Tess shrunk down in her chair so her chin was resting on the table edge. She took one brief look at Abby's face and then focused on her sister.

"Dad said to leave her be, but I insisted that she shouldn't stay out in the barn, that she was becoming even wilder with every day that passed. I said to him, 'Don't you know that girl has to learn to be social some-time?'"

"So what happened?" Abby was wondering whether the tension between Ellie and her dad had escalated beyond what she had noticed the first time she saw them clashing when Ellie had broken her foot.

"I just decided to go and bring her in." She looked over at Tess making herself as small as possible at the dinette table and spoke directly to her, "You want to tell Ms. Clarke what you said, Tess?"

Tess's voice was a whisper that Abby had to strain to hear. "I…said I did want supper, but I wanted Ellie to bring a plate out." She went on to explain, her eyes seeking out Abby's as if she was pleading to be understood. "Blaze was being restless, and I thought maybe because there was rutting moose around. This is the mating season for them, you know? Now, I guess maybe it was the fire she smelled, and I didn't wanna leave her. That's all …"

"No, that's not all!" Ellie broke in, "I moved over beside Tess and she moved away, like she didn't want me touching her. That seemed weird to me, and I moved quick to put my arms around her shoulders, and she let out an unholy screech like I've never heard her make!"

"I did not! I didn't screech, did I?" Ellie gave her the "Are-you-kid-ding-me?" look, and continued as if Tess had said nothing.

"So I lifted her jean jacket and t-shirt, and she had black and blue bruising from here," she indicated just below the back rib cage area, "all the way down her back to below the waistline here." Ellie patted her own butt to show the lumbar region. "I was so choked to see how bad she was beaten, I could hardly see straight! I asked Tess if she could sit down. When she said no, I knew that was it.

"I asked her what Dad had used to beat her up like that, and she told me he had started with his fists, but then switched to a belt and even whacked her with a piece of firewood at one point. She had a splinter in her back to prove it, too! This had all happened in the barn the night before when we all were supposedly sleeping. Tess had spent the whole day Sunday working around the corrals, too sore to sit. So I said to myself, that the bastard has gone too far this time!

"So I took hold of Tess by the arm, charged into the house, grabbed my purse and Tim's truck keys off the buffet, and threw both on the seat of Tim's truck. I was just making Tess get into the front seat when Tim came out to see why I took the keys. I told him to look at Tess's back and figure it out.

"So he said, 'Okay, we'll all go. Let's just go back in and do it up front, eat supper and then we'll go.'"

"I looked at Tess to see how she'd feel about that. I knew she wouldn't be up for handling a sit-down supper. So I said to Tim, 'You realize that's why she won't come in for supper? She's so beat up she can't sit! And I'm sick to my stomach with what he's done, and I *can't* eat. You go fill your face!'"

Ellie inhaled from far down if to find the air to finish her story. "So Tim says no. He'll come, but he said to take a minute to grab something to eat for the road. So I said, all right, if you have to eat! Are all men nothing but stomachs? But I said we'd make the chicken into sandwiches fast and get the hell out of there!"

"All the time we were making those sandwiches out in the kitchen, Tim was having a drink with the old man in front of the fire, you know, keeping him entertained so he wouldn't realize what was going on in the kitchen. I don't know what they talked about. You'll have to ask Tim."

Abby thought about telling her that the police would be talking to Tim too, but she decided to leave it for later. She looked over at Tess who had been silently listening all this time, her arms folded across to hide the bottom of her face. "I guess my biggest question is why your dad would want to beat you like that, Tess? Did you do something to make him angry?"

The whole time Ellie had been talking, Tess seemed to have been shrinking further into her seat so that now her face seemed barely to rise above the rim of the table. There was a long uncomfortable silence until Ellie reached across and rubbed her jean-jacket shoulder tenderly.

The girl erupted, "It ain't nothing I done, Mrs. Clarke. It's what I wouldn't do!" She peered in anguish at her sister as if to say, 'Do I have to?' and then continued. "He wanted me to … you know what I mean, but I ran out to the barn, and he got me there…"

Abby's throat was clenched so tight she felt choked by the effort to avoid retching. "It's okay Tess, I understand. You don't have to say anything else. Do you think you can talk to Constable Macpherson and tell her what you've told me? She can make sure it doesn't happen again."

The girl shrugged, her mouth clamped shut. She looked over at her sister, and seeing Ellie's smile, swallowed before nodding her head ever so slightly.

"I'm not afraid…I'm just…I don't know…like I hate talking to people! I don't know what to say!" Tess collapsed into sobs. The prospect of confessing her father's sexual abuse to the police was unbearable.

Ellie jumped in, "And I didn't do anything to start a fire! I mean, we had fires going, but when we left, they were under control. Maybe after we left, Pa got pissed and knocked over the lamp, or fell over and, I don't know, knocked stuff around. Anyway, after the sandwiches were made, we were gone within twenty minutes, and when we left, he was lying on the couch with the fireplace going and the lamps lit on the two tables. That's all I know. We got back to town and went right to your place to collect my stuff. Do you remember what time that was?"

"About 6:30 or so, just in time for supper."

Ellie reached across to her sister and mussed her hair affectionately. "Tess was happy to go when we did, maybe because Tim was on side too, and he had promised he'd go back to help Dad. I think maybe he said whatever Dad wanted just to keep him calm. Also, I think Tess was too sore and tired to fight back any more, right, Miss Muffin?"

"So you will see the police tomorrow?" Abby was sure they had to take that step. "See Constable Macpherson, okay?"

From behind the huddle of Tess in her arms, Ellie gave Abby a quick smile and raised her eyebrows as if to say, 'Who knows?' As Abby saw herself out, Tess kept her head buried in her sister's shoulder, sheltering from the demons that haunted her.

# 35

# Tim's Story

By the next Thursday morning, Nora Macpherson had heard back from Mike Horvath that the custody hearing for Tess had been arranged, and, given that Tess had also made a statement charging sexual assault against Hank, Nora had also decided it was time to tidy up their questions about Tim's conversation with his father that last evening. She and Jed were driving south on Antoinette Lake Road in the one of the detachment's pick-ups.

"This really is isolated out here, isn't it? I never realized how much further the ranch was from the place where we had to turn back that last day we were marshaling for the fire." Nora found Jed, who was driving the truck out to Bar T, an easy person to chat with. She was glad that Wasniki had decided on an office day to follow up paperwork from the K-9 visit and to pull strings to get the arson team on the Talbot case sooner. That had left her free to join Jed on the follow-up with Tim.

They were following Ellie's directions and, by taking a couple of runs at one steep incline, had managed to arrive within walking distance of the range cabin. There, when they rounded a corner, they could see the lime green flash of Tim's truck.

On the pullout, they parked the truck next to Tim's and began to hike westward through an uphill incline to the last few hundred yards of the upper range meadow. Below them, the Antoinette Creek valley spread out for miles to the north, and to the south, they could see the ultramarine expanse of Antoinette Lake. On the far side and to the west lay miles of once prime timberland, now blackened and in some few places, still smoking.

"Such a waste," Nora murmured. She wondered whether they would have to search this desolation for Hank. Where would they start?

Her mind drifted to the interview with Ellie and Tess the day before. They had come in after Ellie's workday and spent an hour filling in gaps for the last day with Hank. Their story about finding Tess's injuries and leaving in a hurry shortly afterwards needed to be corroborated by Tim. Privately, Nora was working out how she was going to present Tess's accusation of rape to Wasniki. Determined that Hank Talbot face charges of sexual assault and incest, Nora and Jed had prepared the paperwork. All that was needed was Wasniki's signature.

She could picture Jack exploding when he heard of this latest development! Privately, Nora was finding Wasniki creepier all the time. In her mind, she could still see Wasniki's beet-red face as it had loomed over her when she first broached the idea that Talbot might be beating his younger daughter. She wondered what he would do with the new, even more serious accusations.

The purpose of their trip today was to get Tim to corroborate his sisters' account of that last time they had all seen their father, and to tell the RCMP about the conversation Tim had privately shared with Hank that last afternoon.

Jed's voice broke into her thoughts. "There's the range cabin up ahead. There's no smoke coming from the chimney, but then it's mid-morning, and if Tim is up here, he's probably out tending to the herd they're going to winter over, the ones who scattered after the fire."

As they rounded a corner, the cabin came fully into view. Beside it was a small barn-like shed, probably for tackle and hay, and a corral containing a few head of cattle and a couple of horses that poked their heads up and eyeballed them as they made their way to the cabin site.

Nora noted that the cabin seemed unoccupied. No smoke emerged from its rough stone chimney, and no horse was tethered outside.

Jed nodded at the cabin, "Let's check it over before we alert Tim."

Nora nodded and trailed Jed along the path that led to the rear of a small log cabin where an enclosed lean-to extended at the back and a small shack, likely an outhouse, nestled behind it in the spruce forest

Circling back around to the front, they came again to the wide vista of grassy clearing, now mostly tawny and dehydrated. A few tongues of flame had licked at the edges, but for the most part, it seemed to have escaped the worst of the fire. Yet a few trees on both sides of the clearing had clearly suffered some fire damage.

"So here's a place where the fire seems to have jumped across a space and continued on," Nora observed. "Why couldn't that have happened with the Talbot house, too? It's on the opposite side of a clearing, the one where the corrals sit. The corral fencing is made of wood and it didn't get burnt."

Jed nodded, affirming the truth of what she had said. "We should check the cabin." His voice was non-committal, but she thought he saw the logic of what she was trying to say, that the Talbot house had not necessarily caught fire through arson.

Climbing up onto the broad-roofed front porch, they saw a table and an old cane rocking chair. A quick look inside the front window assured them the cabin was empty. After they tried the door and found it unlocked, Jed fired off three of rounds of his service revolver to alert Tim that he had company.

Within minutes, they could hear the sound of horse hoofs coming at a gallop, and then they saw the rider climbing up the incline of the front clearing.

"Hey, Tim," Jed extended his hand when the boy came forward and Tim, somewhat abashed, took it and shook. Tim looked at them both uneasily, his face a study in confusion about the how and why of their appearance at the range cabin.

Nora answered his unspoken question. "Ellie told us where we could find you when she came into the detachment to add to her statement about your last visit to the house, on October third. She came in with Tess yesterday, and we thought, since we were wondering if your dad's been around out here, that we could talk to you at the same time."

Jed, pointing to the cabin, asked, "Do you mind if we have a look inside?"

Tim flushed and said, "Yeah, okay, but it's a mess. Hope you don't mind. I don't spend much time here." As he made way for them to come inside, he took up the nameless tune he had been humming The hint of a shy smile playing across his boyish face made Nora ponder his character. Was he essentially easy-going? Or putting up a cool front to hide something?

The cabin was just one room with a Quebec heater in the middle. A rickety, wooden table and chairs occupied the space in front of the door, and two bunk beds were ranged against the walls on either side.

The heater was unlit, but a frying pan with congealed fat was testimony that it had been used recently. On the left, next to a window, one bunk had a rumpled sleeping bag. In the middle of the rear wall, there was door leading out into the lean-to they had seen when they had circled the cabin. The lean-to served as both coatroom and cold storage pantry for, through the glass panes of the door, they could see some skinned game suspended, a huge slab of side bacon, its fat glistening white in the darkness, and some plaid jackets and Stetsons hanging on hooks.

Nora wondered where the weapons were kept. She could see a .22 hanging next to the front door but nothing else. There had to be a more powerful firearm somewhere close by. The likelihood of major predators like grizzly and wolves would necessitate a serious weapon.

"When did you come up here to stay, Tim?" Jed took the lead on questioning while Nora wandered to peer through the glass windows into the dim space of the back lean-to.

"Last Saturday evening, I guess. After we came in and talked to you about the house being burnt down. Then we had dinner at Matt's and…Lady, I mean, Constable?" Tim's eyes had darted over to where Nora was about to open the backdoor. "He ain't here. I mean, you're looking for my dad, right? Haven't seen hide nor hair since I got here."

Jed followed up, "What about the cabin, Tim? Have you seen any sign that anyone's been up here since the last time you were?

"Nope, when I got here, there was nothing. I would of seen at least fresh wood chips out by the chopping block, or a new empty bean can in the burn barrel…

Jed interrupted, "Did you notice if anything was missing or had been disturbed inside the cabin?"

"Uh…not really… I ain't seen nothing…no sign of horse tracks or footprints that weren't mine. I seen some grizzly paw prints, though, over towards the lake side of the clearing."

Nora softly shut the door to the back room. She had found what she had been looking for. Leaning against the wall beside the outside door of the lean-to was a .338 Winchester magnum with a leather shoulder strap.

"You get many grizzly around here, Tim?" Nora was curious about how familiar the boy was with the formidable weapon she had seen in the back.

"Oh, they're out there. My dad and me have had to watch out for them a bit. Once a bear gets a taste for beef, you got to kill it, or they'll keep coming back. But I ain't never killed one. My dad had to when I was a kid. We've got a few big guns there to deal with them." He nodded in the direction of where Nora had just been looking.

Nora looked perplexed. "You say you have a few big guns here to deal with them? There's only one back there."

Tim blushed, "Of course, I got one in the saddle holster on Blaze outside, Miss." He said it as if any idiot would know that.

But before Nora could follow up, Jed asked, "Is there any other spot you think your dad might be, Tim?"

"Nope, can't think of none. I guess he could be over in another valley, like over Loon Lake way. Did you ask Mister Warren? He's got a spread out that way." He regarded the two uniformed officers briefly.

What was he thinking? Wondering whether they had really checked around with his dad's buddies? Nora had the distinct impression that Tim wasn't trying to hide anything, but that he was worried in his own way.

"You think he's out there hiding. Actually, I don't get why my dad would have to hide anyway. It just don't make sense, unless it's about being in shit, uh, sorry, in trouble with the coroner, but he paid that fine, so I figure that should be the end of that hassle. But then, the old man and me don't always see eye to eye, anyways. That stuff about beating Tess…" He cut himself off for a moment and then continued, "He does stuff that I don't get a-tall so I'm as buffaloed as you are." Tim's nervous chuckle at the end seemed to echo in the small cabin. It was the most he had said all at once in a long time. Nora got the impression that he was a decent kid with an old man who embarrassed him, but that he didn't want the whole world to know he felt that way. It was bad enough that he had to contend with the disgust.

After a pause, Nora spoke up. "You say he does stuff you don't get, Tim? Can you tell us about what kind of stuff? Actually, mostly we are wondering about what he said to you that last afternoon. Maybe you can help more than you think. You were with him more than anyone else those last two days up on the range. Can you tell us what he talked about? Or what happened that last time you saw him? Maybe he said something to you that you don't realize is important."

With his head cocked sideways, Tim regarded them for a moment from under lowered lashes. He paused so long that Nora wondered if he were afraid, or just at a loss for words.

Jed picked up the thread. "We have a team coming over to check into the cause of the house fire so we want statement on file before they get here. Do you mind sitting down with us here and answering a few questions?"

A couple of hours later they were on the road back to town. Tim had confirmed what Tess and Ellie had both separately said about the events on the late afternoon of October third, but one thing about his conversation with Hank had left them puzzled.

Hank and Tim had been taking a break from herding up top and talking about the ranch house yard, and Tim, trying to be helpful, had said he would come out some weekend after the round-up and cattle sale so he could take a few loads of the junk away to the dump, stuff that wouldn't easily burn. He had thought his dad would be happy at the offer, but in fact, Hank had exploded and said he didn't want anybody "coming around digging into his yard" – not even Tim. There was valuable stuff there, reclaimable stuff, and he wasn't so rich he could throw it all out! Tim had been a bit puzzled by his remarks, and had decided to let go of the idea.

Driving back to Moose Forks, Nora was quiet, mulling over this scrap of information. She was sure that Hank had a story, and it was certainly about more than just his daughter. She knew they needed to find him soon, if he was still out there, and Tim had said there were a few big guns in the lean-to, but she had seen only one, and Tim had just one in the saddle holster. That meant that if Hank was still alive, he was likely armed, and now she could say, definitely dangerous.

# 36

# A Surprising Discovery

The next morning when Nora opened the front door into the detachment office, her instincts alerted her to a different level of energy about the place. What was up?

Wasniki was prowling about the front detachment office, eyeing the road through the window facing Main Street. As Nora began trying to type up Tess's statement of Hank Talbot's abuse, she felt anxious lest he discover what she was working on. She needn't have worried. Wasniki was far too preoccupied with monitoring the traffic to worry about Nora. At one point Luke Gallagher wandered in from the coffee room with Eddie Braun to check the bulletins and stood chatting briefly.

Eddie, in his usual irrepressible fashion, broached the last topic she wanted discussed. "How's the Talbot case doing? Any word on the whereabouts of Hank Talbot?"

Nora shot him a warning glance, indicating Wasniki's presence as he circled between his office and the front window. Luke, aware of the tension, smiled at her and changed the subject; "I see you're set for field duty today." He was referring to the yellow-striped trouser and boot uniform that she had decided to wear again as she was hoping to follow up on the interview with Tim from the day before, and thought she might be going back out to the ranch.

"I find this uniform so much more practical." She smiled back, blushing slightly. Why did she find his presence disconcerting?

As she stood and bent down to retrieve a file from the bottom drawer of the cabinet behind her, he admired her supple, slim figure. "I would say it's way easier to work in something other than a skirt. Besides, those strides look good!" Nora looked up just in time to catch his playful wink, as he grabbed Eddie by the elbow and pulled on him to leave. At the door, after Eddie had moved into the coffee room, Luke turned back and whispered, "How about checking out the first hockey game of the season with me at the arena tomorrow night?"

Nora stole a quick peek at where Wasniki was looking, and seeing he was at his desk and out of her line of sight, she nodded, smiling her acceptance. She had a good feeling about Luke.

No sooner had Luke left than a constable she had never seen before flung open the front door and rang the buzzer. She pressed the release admitting him in from the foyer and looked up inquiringly.

The newcomer spoke, "Corporal Harris for Sergeant Wasniki."

Before she could turn to relay the message, Wasniki was out of his office and pulling on his jacket and hat. With barely a nod in her direction and a mumbled "Be back about four," he was out the door and climbing into the front seat of a black and white special units panel truck that had pulled up on the street.

It had all happened so fast that Nora had no chance to catch the lettering. It had been a RCMP vehicle for sure. Had Wasniki managed to get an arson team to go over the Bar T fire site?

Jed confirmed when he got into the office shortly after. "Wasniki has spent the last two days bending the ears of the brass at the North District office in Prince George. I'm glad he has some action for us. We can't do much of a search for evidence on Hank until we get the arson investigation specs on the books."

Later that afternoon around five, Wasniki paraded into the detachment office at the head of three other members in bright orange flak jackets. He gestured them into his office and beckoned Nora to follow.

"Yes, Constable Macpherson, ahem…these members," indicating the three rather tired-looking cops sitting crowded in his office, "Staff Sergeant Lavergne, Sergeant Holzer and Corporal Harris, are the arson team we have been expecting. We have a report to make about findings out at the Talbot ranch. I need you to make notes here so we can get the report actionable for Monday."

"Yes sir. Typed copy in triplicate for Monday."

The next half hour was taken up with the examination of routine investigation data to determine whether arson were the likely cause for the house fire. The search through ashes of the house and outbuildings had uncovered no solid evidence of any deliberate use of accelerant, but the existence of kerosene cans in the toolshed and traces of kerosene on the fireplace foundation made it impossible to rule out arson completely. However, there was a general consensus that arson would be difficult to prove given the proximity of a growing bush fire during the same time frame. Therefore, no charges were recommended.

However, the real kicker of the investigation had come with a discovery next to the toolshed on the far side of the garden. Some human remains had been buried there for some time. Forensic work was needed to determine the age and gender of the remains as there was little clothing beyond a few shreds of rotting denim and the remains of a cotton cowboy shirt associated with the corpse. There was no evidence of underwear or jewelry to help establish gender. The arson team couldn't be sure, but they also thought it possible that the site of the remains had been disturbed recently, perhaps even on the night of the fire, as there was some evidence of the cloth remnants being charred although the body itself had remained more or less buried.

Nora and Jed regarded each other in utter astonishment, each searching back in their memories to find any detail from the Talbot kids' testimony to help to identify the body. The death of Beth, Hank Talbot's wife, the previous May was too recent a corpse to be these remains.

The body had been left in the panel truck so Nora understood that no first-hand examination was possible. Wasniki, who seemed very preoccupied by the findings, had made arrangements for the contents of the body bag to be sent to Prince George for forensic examination. Results were expected back in about three weeks.

Out in the central office afterwards, Nora was the first to suggest a possible identity for the corpse. "Didn't Ellie say something about an old hired hand who had been working on the ranch?" A Jerry? Harvey? Casey? Anyway, I can't remember the name she used, but I think we might initially assume that the skeleton is that hired hand's."

Jed shook his head. "Here we go again. We need to connect with one of the Talbot kids to find out for sure. Do we have an address or phone number for Ellie and Tess yet? I don't much feel like driving all the way out to find Tim again."

Nora consulted her watch. "What time is it? After six. Ellie will be gone from the mill office. We could have caught her there. I guess we'll have to ask Abby Clarke to give us her address."

Nora phoned Abby at home and got no answer.

Well, it was Friday night after all! Where was she likely to find them? The bar. She wondered if she should leave it until the next day? Or even Monday? No chance.

Generally, Mounties didn't drink publicly. They might be found after shift at the Legion or the private back room at the Driftwood once in a while, but they never would stop into a public house of sale in uniform unless to make an arrest. Nora headed home to change.

The Eagles "Lyin' Eyes" was throbbing in the air as Nora pushed her way through the crowd and up to the bar at the Driftwood. Dressed in denim jacket, jeans and a pullover, Nora felt inconspicuous within the happy Friday night throng of loggers and mill workers. The mood was upbeat and friendly. Cigarette smoke hung like an acrid fog in the air, and the yeasty aroma of beer pervaded the roomful of terrycloth-covered tables. Standing in line to collect a glass of beer from the bartender, Nora caught the eyes of a variety of young men who clearly did not know who she was. She didn't feel out of place really, as she had been to lots of pubs in her civvie days, but it felt odd to be here without knowing anybody.

How to find Abby Clarke? Was she even there? Maybe just her husband? Matt? Yeah, that was his name. Before she could ask if anybody had seen him, Nora spotted Abby seated in the back chatting with a blonde pony-tailed woman. Forgoing the beer, she headed over to their table.

Minutes later, she was on her way to the Talbot girls' apartment. Abby had offered to come with Nora to show her the way. Knocking softly, Abby wondered if Ellie would be willing to talk to Nora like this, away from the detachment office or, it being Friday night, if she would even be home.

Opening the door, Ellie's eyes opened wide in alarm. Mooch nosed out the door and began to growl. Ellie nudged him back inside with her knee.

"Constable Macpherson? What are you doing here? Uh, hi, Abby…" Her voice drifted into nothingness if she were having trouble breathing. Then she called, "Tess, come get Mooch! I have to open the door!"

Nora didn't waste any time on casual chat. "Ellie, I'm sorry to bother you at home, but we don't have a phone number for you, and something happened today that we need to talk to you about. May I come in just for a few minutes?"

"Oh, yeah, sorry. We don't have a phone yet. Maybe next month. Sure, come in." She had opened the door, and they could see Tess hanging back uneasily watching them.

"Hi Tess! Hey, I'm glad you're here too. Maybe you can help." Tess, holding onto her dog on the couch, stared at the out-of-uniform police officer as if she were some kind of alien creature, but gave Abby a ghost of a smile in passing.

Within minutes, Nora was sitting next to Tess and had filled them in on the discovery of the body. However, she omitted any specific mention of its exact location except for the fact that it had been found quite close to the ranch house. Her news left both girls in confusion.

"So far as I remember, no one was ever buried at the ranch except for Mom." Ellie offered.

"Where is your mom buried, Ellie?"

"Oh, Dad picked a nice spot for her, up on a hill overlooking the lake, a little west of the range cabin."

"So if your mom's grave is up there, do you have any idea who that might be so near the house? Could it be Casey?"

Ellie stared at Nora, the expression in her eyes unreadable.

"I don't know about Casey. You know? It's weird. He disappeared right after Rosie quit coming around. Mom kind of wondered if they left together. But we never got any word. Mom always said it wasn't like Rosie to just take off without a goodbye, but Casey, well, he was a funny kind of guy, not too sociable, so him going off wasn't strange."

Nora was wrapped in conjecture. Had Hank and Casey had a falling out? Had Hank buried Casey behind the shed? Burying his wife would have been easy, especially if he'd done it before!

Abby recalled Ellie telling her about the Talbots' purchase of the ranch as an existing homestead with a barn and outbuildings. Ellie had been a toddler, and Tim not even born at the time. "Ellie, do you remember hearing much about the ranch before your family moved in, like what other buildings were already there?"

Nora picked up on the possibility. Was it possible this newfound body had been there from long before?

"Yeah, the barn was there and the old shed on the other side of the garden, but they built the house almost from scratch. Dad told me that there were some logs cut for the walls, but that was all. Him and Mom spent most of that first summer and fall building the house with some help once in a while from the Hitchcocks. I got tied to a tree nearby, Mom said."

Nora considered the possibility that the body could be from that era. If the garden shed dated from before the house was built, the body could have been there all along. Why did she think Hank had to be involved at all? Because her gut said so.

"Ellie, we're going to need you and Tess to come into the office and talk to Sergeant Wasniki. He's the one who found the body today. Can you do that tomorrow?"

Tess's eyes flew to Abby's face in a wordless plea.

"I'll bring them in, if that's okay," Abby offered. Tess's anxious expression relaxed slightly.

"And I guess we will have to find Tim again," Nora finished up, smiling. "That's okay, I like that ride out to the ranch!"

"Can I come, too?" Tess's voice was heard for the first time. "I can help you find him, and Ellie knows what to tell the sergeant, you know?"

"No, Tess," Nora replied as gently as she could. "This will be official police business, but there's no reason you can't drive out there with Abby as long as you don't go past the police tape. Oh, and one other thing, Ellie. Abby here says you have a photo of your Mom. We'd like to look at it, please. I'll make sure you get it back. I guess no one has a photo of Casey, eh? Do you know his full name?"

Ellie face was blank. "No, all I ever heard him called was Casey."

# 37

# More Mystery

The next day after lunch, the Saturday after Thanksgiving, Abby drove Ellie and Tess to talk to Sergeant Wasniki who wanted to hear once again their version of that Sunday evening when they had last seen their dad, and to ask what they knew about the newly-discovered body. Nora was out of the office and Tess, noticeably tense, was asked to come in first. She emerged a short time later. Abby, waiting in the outer office, took one look at the girl's face and opened her arms to give her a hug.

"I don't know why they keep asking the same questions Mrs. Clarke! I ain't got no more memories now than I did before! And...I don't know nothing about a dead body! Gives me the creeps!" Her voice was husky, choked with tears.

"Let's leave Ellie here and come back for her later. Why don't I drive you both out to the ranch when she's finished?" Tess didn't have to say anything in response. Her shining eyes spoke for her.

Shortly after Tess had left with Abby, Nora emerged briefly from the detachment darkroom. Seeing Ellie seated waiting to talk to Sergeant Wasniki, Nora opened the locked glass door, and smiled a welcome. She glanced in the direction of Wasniki's office and saw him just rising from his desk to come out, presumably to summon Ellie in.

Nora called to Wasniki, "Are you ready for Miss Talbot, Sergeant?"

Jack gaped at Nora briefly, as if trying to remember who she was, then at Ellie, who still stood somewhat confused. Sitting back in his armchair, he waved his arm to signal them in and then leaned back and swung around to stare out the window at the shrubbery behind the building.

Nora nodded at Ellie and pointed her head to follow her into the inner office. When Ellie was seated, Nora said, "I've got some photos for you to look at, Ellie." She turned to Wasniki, who continued to gaze fixedly out the window, and said, "Shall I just get the photos to show her, Sergeant?"

Wasniki, swinging in his chair from gazing outside, nodded curtly in Nora's direction and stretched his neck as if his collar were too tight. In the outer office, Nora was surprised to find Luke Gallagher by her desk, lounging up against the glass partition between the entryway and main office.

"Can I talk to you for a minute?" His hazel eyes sparkled with suppressed mirth.

"Oh, Luke, I can't right now! Sorry! Can I catch you later? We're in the middle of an interview, okay?"

"No sweat. Just a thought about Saturday night. It'll keep. So long. I'll check in with you later." With that, he heaved himself upright and leaned intimately against her to press the buzzer to let himself out the front door. She was left with the distraction of the woodsy aroma of his aftershave, something smoky and sexy.

She groaned inwardly, knowing intuitively that she needed to keep her emotions in check here. She couldn't afford a romance at work messing up her concentration, not with Wasniki already on her case. She collected her thoughts, gathered the photos from the dark room and hurried back to the interview.

In the meantime, Wasniki had rotated in his chair to regard Ellie evenly. "Hello, Miss Talbot, can I call you Ellie?"

She frowned at him but nodded.

"Okay then, Ellie. The thing is, we went out to your family's ranch the other day, and we saw the state of things there. That is, the yard and what's left of the house. I'm sorry about that, of course, especially because your father's a good hard-working man. We want to know what happened there and where he is now, of course. And I guess you have heard that we found some human remains and…"

Ellie cut in sharply, "I don't know who it is, if that's what you want to know."

"Well, not exactly. We'll get to that, Ellie. Just answer the questions I ask you." Wasniki was clearly struggling to maintain his composure. His face was becoming blotched, his nose an even more peculiar shade of red.

"About the appearance of the yard and house out there, first. I'm wondering why there were so many articles lying about the yard. Were you getting ready to haul them away…or burn them?"

"Articles? Oh, you mean garbage and stuff? You need to ask my dad that. He told us not to touch it, that he'd find a use for most of it. We've been so busy since Mom died just keeping up with the ranch that we haven't had much time for yard work."

"Yes, but there was so much that was, you know, dangerous. Surely, you must have thought so too?"

Ellie stared back impassively.

"For instance, Ellie, there was an empty kerosene can beside the greenhouse. Most people would wonder why it wasn't in the shed where the other canisters of gasoline were kept well away from the house – like you did with the diesel in the gravity-feed tank in the yard. Do you remember the last time that you, not your dad, filled the lamp, or how much was in the canister when you did?"

Ellie's face remained stony. "I don't remember, no. And that canister wasn't just garbage. Dad usually kept some kerosene handy for the house lamps. He filled it from that other big drum in that shed. You must have seen it if you saw the gasoline barrel. He must have left that kerosene can by the greenhouse the last time he filled the lamps."

At that point, Nora knocked on the door and edged her way into the office, taking a seat beside Ellie. In her hands, she held three eight-by-ten black and white photos, one an exterior shot of the shed taken that Thanksgiving Monday when she and Jed had driven out to do the preliminary investigation. In the background could be seen the remains of the house and where the greenhouse had been, as well as the fuel can Wasniki had mentioned. The second photo was an interior shot of the shed and the third, a shot of the body as it had lain when discovered that Wasnicki had taken with the detachment camera.

Jack took the first photo and held it up for Ellie to examine. "See this fuel can. That's the one…"

"Like I said, sir, my dad must have left it there because I sure didn't."

"Have a look at this photo, Ellie," Nora handed over a photo that showed the interior of the shed with a jumbled mess of fuel drums, tools, gardening implements and seed containers. Also flung about were rags once used for a scarecrow, poles for supporting garden plants and rolls of wire fencing.

Wasniki got out of his chair and came around to the front of his desk and hovered over Ellie. Taking the photo back, he asked, "Does the shed look the same as you remember it?"

"Hard to say, sir."

"Why is that?"

"I mean, I don't really know, because that was Dad's shed, and he didn't like anyone in there. He said it was too dangerous with the fuel especially."

"Is that all you know about that shed?"

"The only other thing is that he once kept blasting caps in there too, until Mom freaked out and told him to move them somewhere else."

"I don't see any padlock anywhere. How did he keep people from going in there?"

"Geez, Sir, my dad didn't need a padlock to keep us out! We all learned early not to go against him!"

Ellie asked to see the photo more closely and examined it carefully for a minute or so, then thoughtfully returned it to Nora without comment.

Wasniki turned to Nora to ask for the third photo in her hand. It showed a patch of ground with burnt debris scattered about. Barely discernible amongst the charred wood and rock was an arrangement of bones amongst shreds of cloth, the mere outline of a human skeleton with its face turned earthward.

Both Nora and Wasniki observed Ellie carefully as she processed what the photo contained. The sudden appearance of a grimace upon recognizing the human remains verified that she found the sight shocking. "Oh my God! Was this there in the yard somewhere? Uncovered like that? I…I don't know what to say! We never! I mean it was never there before…"

Nora interrupted, "No, Ellie, it's been uncovered a bit. You wouldn't have seen it like this. In fact, all you might have seen was some charred cloth. Our arson team almost missed it too. Even the K-9 team missed it."

Wasniki, taking a moment to review Ellie's statement from October ninth, slowly nodded his head. "Those human remains on the property were quite near the house, Ellie. I need to ask you about them, the ones in the third photo. The remains are from a person of medium height. We don't know the gender yet. How tall was Casey, the hired hand you mentioned before?"

"Oh, Crikey, I don't know. About the same as Dad maybe? Big people all looked tall back then!" Her nervous laugh clearly conveyed her uncertainty.

"So quite tall? About six foot like your father?" Wasniki watched Ellie as she nodded.

"And you have no idea who the person we discovered may have been?"

"No."

"And you don't remember seeing a grave near the house, some bones or anything like that?"

"What! You think I would have ignored something like that! Of course I never saw anything like that. Who do you think we are?" Ellie's voice had risen to a barely-controlled shriek, her whole body shaking in fury.

"All right, all right. We have to ask these things, you know." Wasniki regarded Ellie again speculatively. "So, is there anything else you can remember about that last time out at the ranch?"

"No. I've told you all I remember, but…I have some questions, please."

When Wasnicki said nothing, Ellie forged ahead. "First, what do we know about where my dad is? It's been a week now. I mean, since we said he was missing, you know? Doesn't anyone know anything? I feel a little nervous not knowing when he might show up! And second, you say the arson team has checked the ranch. Do they think anyone set the fire on purpose?"

Wasniki stretched his chin out again in what seemed to Nora like a nervous gesture and glanced over at her as if to ask what she had heard lately. Nora got the impression that he had had an earful from George Warren, and wondered if Jack knew more about Hank's whereabouts than he was letting on.

Finally, hearing nothing from Nora, Sergeant Wasniki arranged his face into a smile and addressed Ellie. "I'm sorry, young lady, we haven't been able to find anything yet, but we will keep looking, I promise. As for the arson, at this point, there's no evidence to warrant charging any-one. Thanks for coming in today. We'll let you know as soon as we have new information."

As Ellie got up to leave, she suddenly remembered something. "We want to go out to the ranch today. That's okay, I guess?"

Wasniki reacted, waving his finger at her. "Not you, nor your brother or sister either, is to touch anything around the house. It's a potential crime scene, and as such, may contain valuable evidence that must not be disturbed. Do you understand?"

"But Tim is out there tending the stock, so we just plan to visit and keep him company…"

Without looking up, Wasniki impatiently waved Ellie out of the office. When she had closed the front door, he got up from his desk and closed his office door. From her seat at the front desk, Nora could hear him phoning someone. After she saw Ellie leave, she rose and wan-dered across to Jed's office door, and knocked. Then she remembered Jed was off Saturdays. She would have to wait for Monday to fill him in. Hank Talbot's disappearance had put the charges against him on the back burner, but she was determined they wouldn't just get lost in the shuf-fle. Also, the question of the identity and whereabouts of the mysterious Casey was a new piece of the puzzle. The dimensions of the skeleton dis-covered on the ranch didn't seem to match Ellie's estimate of the hired hand's height. The likelihood was that the remains were someone else's.

# 38

# An Odd Disappearance

Ellie recounted the events of the interview to Abby, Matt and Tess as they all drove out to Bar T to connect with Tim around two that afternoon.

"Christ! What wasn't lying around that yard!" Ellie continued to grouse despite the silence of everyone else. "I don't remember seeing that kerosene can there, but then, I didn't go out to the greenhouse that weekend. There was nothing left in it after the frost we had the week before anyway. Even the herbs and stuff I showed you that day were all brown and burnt by the cold. I guess now, they're really burnt!"

Ellie snickered at her own feeble joke and then started to cry, tears streaming down her cheeks. Then as if tormented by the memory of Wasniki's questioning, she continued, "Why would I notice the kerosene can? Probably the old man tossed it out there, too lazy to take it out and refill it that night. Wouldn't be the first time! I mean, look at the junk in the yard! The thing is, that cop kept asking me when I had filled the lamp in the kitchen, and how much was left in the can when I did. And to say I'd ignore a body! That picture they showed me! Ewww! Gross! That's just disgusting! All that time it was there, and we didn't know!"

"It's gone now, right?" Tess's voice was a bare whisper.

"God, I've got a headache just thinking about that ass – I mean, jerk! Don't worry, Tess. We won't see anything today. They've taken it way."

Abby's thoughts were mixed. She saw Ellie's attitude as responsible and Wasniki's as callous. How could George Warren think she would commit arson? Abby hoped at least that Nora was moving ahead with the child abuse charges, but with Hank Talbot now a missing person, she wondered.

188

Matt's concerns were more immediate. "What happens with the other cattle, Ellie, the ones that are left after the market cattle are gone?"

"Oh, there's only a couple dozen breeding stock left right now. That last weekend we had with Dad, Tim and him got the market animals trucked to town. The breeders and ones too young for market were in the corral behind the barn. When the fire happened, they're the ones that spooked and wandered into the backfields. By now, Tim will have moved them for a few weeks back up top to what's left of the summer range. Once the weather turns, Tim will bring that herd down below for the winter, where the baled hay is. Right now, they can still feed up top so he'll stay there until the weather turns. Then, they'll manage down below all winter as long as they get water and feed twice a day. The barn's not off limits anyway, and there's a pump out there. It needs regular priming in the winter so it doesn't freeze up, so someone will have to come out daily."

Abby mused, "Imagine, in the old days, everyone used to either walk or ride all these distances…"

"Yeah, used to be Mom and Rosemary always…" Ellie stopped dead. "I just remembered, that picture Constable Macpherson had, of the inside of Dad's shed beside the garden? There was something in the upper corner on a shelf I wondered about. It looked like the flap from that backpack of Rosie's, you know, the one with the moose head beaded on it? It was sticking out from behind some old empty cans that Dad probably kept for pig slops. Why would that backpack be there? Rosie always kept it with her! Why would she leave it behind?"

Abby just shook her head in puzzlement. She had never looked inside that shed the one time she had been out to the ranch. Just then, the ranch yard came into view, and there was the astonishing collection of junk in the yard looking even more rotten and charred than when Abby and Matt had first seen it in September.

Abby, wrinkling her nose, decided she should have a chat with Nora about the state of the Talbot ranch as she remembered it when she had first seen it. At the very least, being one of the last non-family visitors out here, she could testify to the mess in both the house and yard. Then, it wouldn't just be a case of the kids saying so.

Matt had to slow down to drive close by the area where the house had burned down. The warning not to touch anything was reinforced by the perimeter of yellow crime scene tape strung around the house and smaller outbuildings. The barn was outside it, but the house and green-house foundations and the mysterious shed Wasniki had mentioned lay within.

Abby pointed to the shed. "Is that where you think the backpack might be, Ellie?"

"Damn," breathed Ellie. "I wanted to get into there to see if it really was Rosie's."

Abby nodded, her mind racing to account for the presence of the backpack in the shed in the first place. Was it connected to the body that had been found?

In the meantime, the trip up to the range cabin on the deeply rutted trail took another quarter hour, and then they had to holler a bit before Tim realized they were there.

As he rode up to the cabin from the far end of the range meadow, they could see the grin spreading across his face. "I've been here all week alone. Sure as hell is good to see faces again! Angus may be good beef, but they're still dumb-as-shit cattle!"

Climbing down from Blaze, he tipped his hat to Abby and then strode over to shake Matt's hand. "Hi, Matt, I got almost all of what's left of the breeding herd corralled up here, so before the weather turns, I just need to figure out a way to get them down to the barn corrals and then hire some help to feed and water them so I can get back to work. I'm real grateful you're holding my job at the mill for me."

Abby knew that Matt had entertained second thoughts about saving a spot for Tim, given the availability of dozens of young guys eager for work. But still, he had said that Tim was a solid worker, and it wasn't his fault his family was in such a bind.

Matt was gracious in his praise of Tim's efforts on behalf of his sisters. "I know ranching's not your thing. In fact, I think this whole mess has changed you a bit, eh, Tim?"

"Aw, I still don't like it much, Matt, if that's what you mean, but I can do the work, for sure. Someone's gotta!" He grinned at Ellie and Tess who were fussing over Blaze, stroking the mare and feeding her some carrots they had brought.

As Abby watched Tim interacting with his sisters, she was struck by the truth of Matt's observation. This experience had matured Tim. His new sense of self-assurance was evident in his direct gaze and upright posture. And he wasn't humming!

"Hey," Matt gave Tim a brotherly punch in the shoulder, "Tell you what! I'll ask Frank Hughes if Ken and I can get a couple of days leave to come out and help so you can get the winter herd back down, and then maybe we can figure some way to get help to tend to them until spring."

Tim grinned and nodded in appreciation.

"So, Tim, have you seen anything of the cops up here?" Ellie was curious if they had asked Tim the same kinds of questions as they had asked her.

"Hell, yes! I've seen enough of cops in the last week to last my whole life! What about you…." They wandered off together in the direction of the cabin and called back to say they would put the kettle on.

An hour or so later, they all wandered back down to where the truck had been parked and, as the Clarkes and Ellie were getting ready to drive back down to the house site, Tess hung back beside Tim.

"I want to ride Blaze, Tim, okay?"

"Sure Miss Muffin. Climb on in front."

At the bottom, she didn't want to get off. "I miss being here, Tim. Ellie, can't I stay out here when the herd is brought down below to winter? I can feed and water them. I can do that easy! Then Tim can go back to work."

Ellie stopped her cold. "No way! You know you're too young to quit school. We've already gone over this. Besides, there's really no place to stay here when winter comes. You'll die of cold. The range cabin's not insulated, and we didn't stockpile it with firewood this fall." Sheepishly, Tess cast a sidelong look at Abby to see if she was going to join in on the lecture, but Abby, seeing Ellie being so direct, kept quiet. She felt real compassion for Tess who was so torn, but admired that Ellie was hanging tough.

Before leaving, they took the time to wander around the cordoned-off house site. Staring balefully at the yellow crime-scene tape in front of the garden shed, Ellie muttered, "Shit! They would have this place blocked off!"

Tim scoffed, "Why not go on in? I do. I needed stuff outta there for the cabin. They never told me I couldn't go in!"

With that, he was over the yellow tape and off to the shed door, which he pulled open with a screech. Emboldened by her brother's flaunting of police security, Ellie was not far behind.

Peering into the dim light of the shed, he asked, "What did you want in here, sis?"

"That picture Constable Macpherson showed me, I think I saw something in here. You remember that moose hide backpack Rosie had? No? I guess you were too young. Anyway, I thought I saw the beaded flap of that backpack in that picture she showed me."

"I don't see anything like that, Ellie. Are you sure?" Ellie's shoulders edged past Tim so she could survey the interior, but what she had seen in the photo was no longer there.

Turning on her brother, Ellie demanded, "Did you take, Tim? Come on. Be honest. I know I saw that backpack in here. It has to be here, unless somebody else… Oh my God! Dad's got it! He must be alive and around here somewhere." She stopped to consider the options, "Or the cops maybe took it." Her words trailed off as she realized the myriad possibilities. Any number of people could have had access to the shed before the house site had been taped off.

Tim regarded her with disbelief. "Dad's nowhere 'round here, Ellie. Don't you think he would have come out to talk to me, if he was here? And why in hell would the cops want it?"

"I don't know, Tim. I just know what I saw in that picture, and it's not here now, and if you didn't move it, and the police didn't move it, then who? And an even better question is why! Why that backpack of all things? Who would want it? Actually, I do. I'd like it as a keepsake of Rosie. She was nice…"

In the big scheme of things, the backpack was a minor detail, but no one had any answers. The drive back to town was very quiet.

# 39

# Nora Has a Date

That Saturday evening, the air inside the hockey arena was so crisp their breath made wreaths of mist as Nora and Luke sat in the small glassed-in viewers' gallery to watch the Moose Forks Furies take on the Glacier Lake Grizzlies. The echo of sticks slapping at the puck and the shouts of other viewers made conversation impossible, but Nora felt convivial warmth in Luke's company. Several townspeople attending the game were quick to recognize that Constables Gallagher and Macpherson were out for a social evening and had smiled a welcome. Luke seemed well-accepted, even appreciated as someone who came out to coach the younger boys. Several fathers came over to shake hands and mention their sons' involvement. Nora could see how being a part of the community paid off in good will.

At the end of first period, Luke led her to the heated cafeteria concession where they sat close on a bench sipping hot chocolate.

"What do you think?"

Luke's smiling eyes gave no clue what he wanted her to be thinking about, so she played it safe. "The hockey is fun to watch. The teams seem pretty evenly matched."

"Oh yeah, Glacier Lake is the big rival here. We just love to whomp them. We always end up pitched against them for the regional finals. "

"How big's the region?"

"Oh, let me see, as far as Prince Rupert, I think."

"Rupert? So that's, what? A day's drive? And you go with the team all that way to play other teams in the league?"

"Oh, no. I don't get to travel with them. Not usually anyway."

Nora was enjoying their conversation. There was something comforting about being out on a date, shoulder-to-shoulder sitting on the bench talking about just hockey. She could feel the warmth of Luke's body pressed close against hers, and the realization produced a wrench in her gut. How long had it been since Erik? No, she mustn't! He was history, probably already engaged to some other girl back home. This man, here and now, was sincere and interesting. Nora felt a sudden urge to run her fingers though that mop of thick, dark hair and caress those broad, muscular shoulders. How wise was that? Not very, she realized.

The detachment was a small place, and an office romance could be dicey. But he was appealing in all the right ways: warm, open, generous, smart, good-looking, sexy…

She realized he was gazing at her intently with those twinkling hazel eyes, and that she was overdue to say something back. Her blush betrayed her, and she laughed, "Sorry, Luke! I was thinking about our grass hockey trips when I was in school." Her fib was so lame, she doubted that he believed her.

"Why? Did you do anything you shouldn't have? All those teenaged girls away from home, must have been fun, eh? But guys don't play grass hockey, do they? So what did you do for fun on those trips?" His lop-sided smile and eyebrows raised in teasing speculation said he was sure she hadn't been any kind of an angel.

"No, really, I…" She couldn't contain her annoyance. "You seem to think a group of girls doesn't know how to have fun without boys around! We played hard, on and off the field! When there were no games, we played cards or crokinole in the hotel rooms or went for sprints outside. Our coach even had some hacky-sacks she had brought back from Oregon so we could keep limber on the road trips. We were an awesome team!"

He was grinning ear-to-ear listening to her. "Hey, I never said girls didn't know how to have fun. I just always assumed it was easier if there were guys around." The look in his eyes was earnest, and she felt some regret for her outburst, but then she saw the stern line of his lips crumple into a sheepish grin.

She leaned into him and whispered, "Well, this girl's having fun right now. Is that good enough?" She smiled into his eyes and was beginning to draw away, when he reached out to wrap his arm around her shoulders. Just then, the buzzer sounded to signal the start of the second period, and he pulled her close for a quick hug. "That's great. Me, too. Let's go."

Back in the stands, they watched as the second period ended with the teams tied. Emotions were running high in the arena even though the season was just starting. Nora commented on the energy of the team as they wound their way back for another hot drink.

"Yeah, they're already keyed up for a good season," Luke acknowledged. I'm looking forward to seeing how they develop. They're Double A Adults officially, but they're really pretty young, mostly nineteen and twenty year-olds. I think the oldest is twenty-three. I usually work with the Midget Minor team, the younger high school boys. But once in a while this bunch needs an extra supervisor to travel with them. It's fun, hanging out with them on the road, even though they don't have any hacky-sacks." He nudged her elbow and checked to see if she was appreciating his teasing banter.

"Where have you been with them?"

"Hazelton, Quesnel, Kitimat. One time I had to go to Terrace anyway, so I caught the game later when work was finished."

When he caught her quizzical look, Luke filled in. "I had to go to check on a body found around there, and the team was playing there that weekend."

"Really! The one from last year, the local girl?" They were back being cops again.

"Exactly, that sixteen year-old, Monica, whose surname escapes me, but her body was found in a ditch near Terrace. You maybe saw the Missing Person Poster when you were in Regina? She had been a resident here the year before, so Sarge thought we should have some boots on the ground for the prelim. I stayed just a couple of days to get the scoop and then came back to file a report. We've never heard anything more since, although we issued a reminder last month at the high school, mostly to alert the kids to the dangers of hitchhiking.

The reminder of this cold case cast a shadow over the moment, but then the buzzer sounded for the final period, and for the next half hour Nora was absorbed as the local team lost by one goal during the final minute of play.

As they emerged from the arena, Luke grabbed her hand and pointed to his vehicle. "Let's go for a quick cold one at the Driftwood."

"The Driftwood? Isn't that a bit too public? I mean, we won't have much quiet there." She was remembering her stay there during the first few days when she had first arrived, and how noisy the pub behind the lounge had been.

"Oh hell, there's a private room in back that Jimmy Jaworski makes available to us, along with a few other well-known customers." He grinned at her astonishment as he escorted her to the passenger side of his khaki-coloured Jeep. "It's okay, Constable Macpherson, nobody expects us to be teetotalers, and I promise I'll get you home by curfew!"

She could feel the heat of her blush as Luke pulled away from the arena. Curfew? Did he think she was that wet behind the ears? Later, after he had driven her home, carefully, because they had had more than one "cold one", she let him know she wasn't really too concerned about a curfew, or about whether there might be talk around the office.

In the dark of her apartment, their lovemaking was sweet and somehow anonymous. Luke was a considerate and accomplished lover, and she gave herself to the pleasure of the moment. Afterwards, admiring the long, golden leanness of him as he sprawled next to her in the narrow single bed, Nora realized she felt serene, somehow complete. She had forgotten how fulfilling a lover's touch could be.

But the next morning, she was shaking her head at her own stupidity. It had been fun, and he was a great guy, but she knew being romantically involved and working out of the same detachment was a bad idea. She'd have to find the right time to tell him.

# 40

# Nora and Abby Do Coffee

On Monday, Abby dropped into the detachment office after school and, after being buzzed in, leaned over Constable Macpherson's desk to ask, "Are you up for coffee later, *Nora*?"

Catching the emphatic use of her given name, Nora grinned her cockeyed best and whispered back, "Sure thing! How about at 5:15 at The Hideaway Motel Coffee Shop? It's got some privacy. I need to go home and change first."

Dressed in blue jeans and a fuzzy pink sweater, Nora opened the front door to the café, and Abby waved her over to where she sat in a secluded corner at the back.

"Hey! Abby, this is a nice surprise! I was hoping we could do this. I hate to admit that I don't get much social life, so just plain coffee with you is a treat! I don't have to mind my English grammar, do I?"

Abby chuckled, "Hell, no, if I corrected everybody's English, I wouldn't have any friends either! Oh sorry, I didn't mean to suggest you had no friends Nora, I meant..."

"No sweat! You're right, I don't. One of the worst things about this job is how socially isolating it can be. They mentioned the possibility at Depot, but I think it's even worse for women officers in small towns. I'll manage though, because I won't be here that long. Maybe one or two years, and then I can try for a bigger place." She wondered if she'd last even that long.

"What about the other officers?" Abby was trying to remember who else besides Jack Wasniki was in the detachment.

"Oh, they're nice enough guys, but I really can't see myself getting serious with any of them. I was at the hockey game last night with one of the other constables, but you know," she peered at Abby to see if she could understand the problem of fraternizing within a detachment, "I just think I need to be single for a bit. For one thing, most of them are married, or engaged, and for another, I'm kind of on the mend myself, romantically. "When she saw Abby's raised eyebrows, she added, "He dumped me when I said I was becoming a cop."

"Nice guy! Why? He didn't want a woman with better moves than he had?"

Nora blushed and laughed out loud. "Something like that. I thought he was a keeper, but I was wrong. It won't be the last time!"

"Don't worry, I won't say anything!" Abby was enjoying her chat with Nora. She felt a level of companionship she hadn't really expected. However, realizing she had to broach the topic of Hank Talbot, she broke in when a natural pause occurred in the conversation.

"Nora, I need to talk to you about the Talbots."

"No problem. I just need you to know that's it's on the record, whatever it is."

"Oh, that's cool. It's not about me. It's about Tess and her father. First of all, do you know if he's turned up anywhere? The kids are hanging in there. They have each other, and the two oldest are watching out for Tess, but the not knowing is so hard.

"Secondly, Ellie thinks he may, in fact, be around here." She filled her in briefly on their visit to the ranch, the mess in the yard and their peek into the shed.

Nora frowned slightly when she heard they had crossed the police tape cordon, but she didn't interrupt.

"So Ellie is sure she saw that backpack in a photo you showed her, so I was wondering if you should follow up on that, because I can testify that the kids didn't touch it, at least I am sure neither Tess nor Ellie did. Tim did say he'd been into the shed, but honestly he seemed as surprised as anyone when…"

Nora was looking perplexed. "What backpack are you talking about?"

"Oh, of course, you don't know! In the photo of the inside of the shed that you showed Ellie, she recognized a part of a backpack that her mother's friend used to carry everywhere. It had a silhouette of a moose head beaded on it, a pretty distinctive decoration. At least I've never seen another like it around here."

"And why is this backpack important? I'm not sure I understand…"

"It was owned by Rosemary Joseph who disappeared about thirteen years ago, in the spring of 1963. At least, she suddenly wasn't around anymore. Ellie remembers her quite well because Rosemary was a good friend of Beth Talbot's, a mid-wife for her when she had Tim and Tess, and a helper around the ranch, that sort of thing. Then one spring, Ellie remembers just before her mom got sick the first time, Rosemary wasn't there for Easter when she was expected. Rosemary is the other woman in that photo Ellie gave you of her mom, and she's carrying the bag.

"The thing is Ellie said this bag was really important to Rosemary, that she never went anywhere without it. So seeing it in that shed was a shock. The other thing is, I never mentioned it, but the night I was in the truck at the fairgrounds with Hank, you know…" At this point she looked Nora right in the eye to remind her of what had happened. "Anyway, he suggested that he had had sex with Rosie, and that even though she had seemed to accept it at first, that after a while, she didn't, and she told Beth."

"So what do you make of all this?" Nora was now alert, rummaging in her bag for a pen and paper.

"Well, don't you think it's odd that the bag was there, and now it's not? And what about that body found right next to the shed? Isn't it possible there's a connection?"

Nora paused to collect her thoughts before answering. "I agree there is something here, but until we know for sure Tim didn't take the bag, I can't very well buy the theory that Hank Talbot, or whoever, must have done so.

"Also, a woman missing for thirteen years…well, we'll have to dig into the missing persons' files to check that out. She's in that photo you say? Where was she from? Did any family ever show up? So many unanswered questions here. We need to find Hank to answer for his actions before we go off on a tangent."

"Oh, I realize Hank would be the logical person to ask, but Ellie knows a bit about her, too." Abby related Rosemary's story as Ellie had told it to her.

"And Hank paid her back by stealing her bag and what else?" As Nora said it, she realized how important a clue this bag might be. She was still lost in thought when, after a quick look at her watch, Abby jumped up and started to put on her coat.

"I'm sorry Nora, I have to go. I promised Matt I'd be only an hour or so."

"Sure, Abby, this has been great. I don't know what to say. I'll start looking into this Rosemary person for you as soon as I can. About Hank Talbot, I don't know what to say. If anybody knows where he is, they aren't talking! That's all I know. And you, Mrs. Clarke," Nora smiled as she uses the formal address, "You, please, will not cross any more security barriers, and you will stay away from anywhere Hank Talbot is likely to be. That means the Bar T especially. I think we can assume he's one nasty customer who needs to be apprehended, but don't quote me, all right?"

When Abby filled Matt in on her conversation with the constable, he reacted with exasperation to the idea that the whole Bar T ranch was off limits. He and Ken had just made arrangements to take Thursday and Friday off to help Tim.

"Matt, honey, she just said I should stay away from Bar T. She didn't mention anyone else. Actually, I want you to take a peek inside Tim's range cabin for me just to be sure he didn't take that backpack. You know, he acted pretty believable yesterday, but you never know. Brothers have been known to lie to their sisters when they thought it didn't matter."

"Really? Now you want me to spy on Tim? Isn't that asking a bit much? Well, I guess he's still my employee… Okay, whatever. You, Miss Smarty-Pants Teacher, are such a pain in the ass sometimes!"

# 41

# Nora Lowers the Boom

The next morning at nine sharp, Nora was standing in Wasnicki's office doorway with a file folder clasped to her chest. "Sergeant, I need to talk to you about following up on the Talbot case." Wasniki eyed the folder briefly and nodded his head for her to come in.

"And what precisely do you think needs 'following up' as you put it, Constable? I thought things were settled well enough with the young-sters. Isn't that so? Their father's not bothering them anymore, if he ever was. The arson team has decided there isn't enough evidence to justify a charge against anyone. I told Eleanor that."

"Well, there is still the matter of Hank Talbot's being a missing per-son, and in fact, I think we should consider making him a person of inter-est in the matter of the body that was found last Friday. I believe he may be avoiding arrest, and not really be 'missing' at all. Also, we need to lay charges for child abuse."

"What evidence do you have to back up such action, Constable? There isn't any record of his ever being charged with an offense or even questioned. A man's got a right to be on his own if he wants. Those youngsters left him. Young Tess chose to join her sister in town. I say leave well enough alone! He's got no record of complaints or charges against him that I can find!" His eyes dared her to contradict, his voice steadily gathering intensity and volume as he glared at her. His eyes darted momentarily to the file in her hands. "What have you got there in that file, Constable?"

"Actually, Sergeant, there is a record of past problems." Here was the showdown. Back in September, she had taken photos of all the paper-work in Hank Talbot's file and saved the prints for just this moment. Before knocking on Wasniki's door this morning, she had shown the whole file to Jed Fedoruk, who had whistled and shaken his head in disbelief. Even he, second in command, had never seen the contents of Hank's official police file. Now, added to it were the statements and evidence collected since she had started to work on it, all of which she had also photographed. By showing the whole file to Jed, Nora calculated that at least if she did get in shit with Wasniki, someone else would know the real reason why!

Wasniki's face was a study in crimson. "What do you mean? Hand over that file!" Getting up, he reached behind her to slam his office door and turning back, ripped the file from her grasp. Flipping through the contents only served to raise his temper further. In it were photographic copies of the previous records of Hank's run-ins with Public Health and Social Services, two separate diagrams of Tess's bruised back and buttocks both witnessed by Abigail Clarke and Margaret Vermeer, as well as the paper statement of abuse made by Tess and confirmed by Ellie. His face contorted in fury as he shook the file in her face, spitting his venom in a hoarse whisper that could not be heard outside the room, "You stupid, interfering *cow*! How dare you rifle through my desk? Where and when did you collect all this other crap?"

Nora kept her voice low, but firm. "I am the officer tasked with community liaison, Sergeant. That includes investigations of domestic abuse. I needed evidence to protect the Talbot daughters. It's common knowledge in town that there were complaints lodged against Hank Talbot. I didn't need a file to know that. All I had to do was ask around. In locating those files, I was just doing my job."

"I don't give a rat's ass what you think your job is! These are confidential files, in my office for a good reason! Those do-gooders at Social Service and Public Health wouldn't know criminal behaviour if it jumped up and kicked them in the ass. I'll keep this file, and you'll keep your mouth shut! Hank Talbot's a good man!"

"Hank Talbot's a child beater, a sexual predator and possibly a murderer! You can't protect him anymore. There's something else you need to know, Sergeant. Not only have I shown this file to Corporal Fedoruk, but also, I have sent the negatives and duplicate prints by special courier to the Crown Council's office in Prince George. If anyone there asks about them, and why they've arrived as photographs instead of a paper version, I can tell them the truth, that you were attempting to suppress evidence, or I can say that the originals were mistakenly destroyed. It's up to you, and before you ask, here is my request for transfer."

Wasniki looked as if he were about to explode. He put the file down on his desk to devote his full attention to shaking his fist inches from her chin. "I will have you…"

He never got to complete his threat. A knock at the door left him with his mouth slack-jawed like a fat fish on a hook.

"Sarge?" It was Jed Fedoruk, who as he peered in, captured both Jack's beet-red face and gaping mouth and Nora's look of fierce determination.

"Prince George HQ on the phone, Sergeant. Do you want me to tell them you'll call back? It's about the body from Bar T. They are wondering if there's any paperwork to indicate the possibility that it's a homicide. They have some photographic files, they say, but wonder if there's any paper on the way too." Jed's glance strayed to the file lying open on Jack's desk.

Neither Jed nor Nora had ever seen Jack so disconcerted. "Oh, yes. Yes, the body at Bar T." He cleared his throat, "Ahem, yes, I'll have to call back, Corporal. Tell them I am tied up just now." With that, Nora deftly retrieved the file and deposited her request for transfer on his desk. She managed to exit just as he slammed the door shut.

Jed peered down at her stony face. "So, that went okay?"

"Yeah, like hell. I'm out of here, probably. I can't work with him, Jed. But I did show him the file, so he can't say we went behind his back when we file child molestation charges against Talbot. You'll authorize, right?"

Fedoruk nodded his head. "You got that right. Give me Talbot's file. I'll start the charge sheet myself."

Nora spent much of the next morning sorting through dusty old files in the back office. Wasniki was off somewhere at a meeting with Jed. Luke, Eddie, and the rest of the highway crew for a change were not hanging out between shifts in the coffee room, so she had the place more or less to herself.

Finally, after an hour and a quarter, she located the missing person's report.

"April 19, 1963 – Joseph, Rosemary Angeline, aged 28, DOB April __ 1935?"

Hmmm. The blank is interesting. Whoever filled out this form wasn't sure of Rosemary's date of birth.

She looked at the signature but could not make out the name. The water-based ink had faded, and the person's writing was nearly illegible anyway. Fortunately, someone had printed a name clearly underneath: Angus Peter. But the contact address space was empty.

She wondered who he was. Someone from Moose Forks? She'd have to ask around. She made a note of the particulars and closed the file, marking it so she could find it again when necessary.

# 42

# The Search for Rosemary

Mike Horvath of the Community Resources Board surveyed the group gathered before him. It was the usual Wednesday time slot for the resolution of custody or other ongoing cases. As Tess Talbot's caseworker, he had called the meeting to decide where Tess would stay until Hank Talbot's missing person case was resolved. Now that the Chairman of the School Board, George Warren, had arrived to join Abby Clarke, Public Health Nurse Liz Lundstrom, Constable Nora Macpherson, Ellie, and Tess, the meeting could begin.

Abby's presence was required only to report on Tess's academic progress and to give some particulars about attendance and behaviour. Abby reported that Tess was trying well enough and just needed a stable environment to make progress. Abby added that the girl still needed to adjust to being around people other than her family. Liz reported her involvement in helping the late Mrs. Talbot and in getting Tess enrolled in school. Then, both Liz and Abby were asked to wait outside in case they could provide further information. Shortly afterwards, both Ellie and Tess joined them to sit next to Abby on the bench seating of the lobby. All sat in suspense until finally Ellie and Tess were called back in, and Abby and Liz, not being included, sat back down again in the waiting room.

Afterwards in the hallway, Abby stood close enough to listen in when George Warren emerged from the meeting and took Ellie and Tess aside. "I advise you to contact the insurance agency to begin a claim for compensation as soon as possible, Eleanor. In light of your father's disappearance, no doubt the insurance company will hold off before writing any cheques, but it never hurts to get them informed as soon as convenient. No doubt he'll show up, I'm sure, but better to be on the safe side.

Oh, and tell Tim I can lend him one of my stock hands to help up there until things get sorted out. I know he can't do it all himself. I'll cover the wages."

Ellie expressed a quick 'thank you' and was moving to follow up with even more when, with a pat on the back for Tess and a nod to Abby, Warren was gone.

Catching Ellie's eye, Abby raised her eyebrows in question. Ellie looked ecstatic with relief. "I'll have to get Tim to call him and give a proper thank you. That was so nice of him! Oh, and guess what! I've been awarded interim custody of Tess, but I guess only until they figure out what happened to Dad, you know, the missing person's investigation. The Community Resource Board has authorized a monthly support cheque for me to keep Tess in town. It's not much, but with my pay from the mill and help from Tim, we can manage." Abby could see that Ellie felt both relieved to have the situation clarified, and proud that the Board had found her to be a suitable guardian for Tess. So much rested on Tess being settled somewhere safe.

Abby recalled her impression that George Warren's attitude had seemed paternalistic and insincere as he spoke to the girls. She wondered whether he expected them to just hang around living on handouts until their father turned up. Ellie and Tim had some money, but not enough to see through the complicated legal channels they might now have to negotiate to get an insurance settlement and to get the ranch back in working order.

Ellie, though, was still ecstatic about George Warren's offer. "But you know what, Abby? Mr. Warren has offered to lend us one of his stock hands for the winter so Tim can get back to the mill. Tim'll be pumped!" Abby wondered if Warren had accepted that there would be no arson charges.

Before they left, Nora Macpherson approached Ellie. Drawing her away from the others, she inquired, "How's it going? You know, I just realized in there that we have almost the same first name!"

Ellie looked at her in confusion. "I don't understand…"

"Nora is my nickname. Eleanora is my given name."

Ellie's face glowed with her sudden smile. "Oh, that's weird! I never would have connected…" A casual conversation ensued about the state of Ellie's foot and how long she would be in a cast, and about whether she was enjoying her job in the mill office.

Ellie was feeling much more relaxed when Nora finally got around to asking, "Can you stop by the office again tomorrow? I have some questions about Rosemary Joseph that maybe you might be able to answer."

"Does this have anything to do with the fire or Dad's disappearance?" Her anxiety about the prospect of more police interrogation was obvious.

Nora, picking up on Ellie's agitation, moved to lessen her fears, "No, no, nothing like that. There's no problem for you, and we don't need much time. In fact, we could just have a quick chat here. Would that be all right?"

Visibly relieved, Ellie flashed a quick smile to Abby who was talking to Tess, and then turned back to Nora. "Sure, Constable, coming into the detachment is a hassle." She pointed to her foot in its cast. "I'm still hobbling around, you know?"

"Okay, Ellie, what I was wondering is if the name Angus Peter means anything to you."

"Angus Peter? Um, no. Should it?" She stared at Nora in confusion.

"It's the signature on the missing person's report for Rosemary Joseph. Angus Peter is the person who filed the report.

"Angus…I don't know Constable, I don't remember, I'm sorry. Are you trying to find out what happened to Rosie?"

"Just a routine inquiry right now. But you're sure you don't remember ever hearing that name?"

"No, I don't think so. I remember hearing in town, let's see, I was in Grade Nine, the first year I came into town for school, that Rosie's family had come into town asking about her. I never talked to them myself, but I remember someone saying they were told to go see the Mounties."

By this point, Abby had noticed that Nora was engaged in some kind of conversation with Ellie and, with Tess in tow, came over to see if there was any problem. She was relieved to hear that Nora was just trying to discover the identity of someone.

Nora was looking puzzled. "That's odd. I'll have to check that file again. I didn't see any record of her family making inquiries. But about this Mr. Peter, you're sure you don't know the name? Would Tim be a better person for us to ask? The point is, Mr. Peter could have heard something about Rosemary since then and just forgotten to notify us."

When no one offered any further information, Nora smiled,"Well, that's too bad. I thought we might be on to a lead there for a bit. I found the missing person report, but it might be a dead end. But you say you heard her family came looking for her? I'll do some more digging the first chance I get."

With a quick wave good-bye, she headed back to the office and relocated Rosemary Joseph's missing person file again. Sure enough, she had missed something. Lying flat on the bottom of the file drawer where it had landed after slipping from the file folder was a note to the effect that Stanley Earl Joseph and Verna Gladys Joseph had inquired about whether there had been any word of their daughter, Rosemary, in the Moose Forks area. The note was dated September 19, 1969. She had disappeared in 1963 and had last been seen in Hazelton. There were references to similar inquiries made as far as Terrace, Prince Rupert, Prince George, Quesnel and Kamloops.

Nora was at first puzzled about why they had waited so long to check into Moose Forks, but then she reasoned that they had been looking systematically, checking and eliminating the bigger centers first before moving on to the small places. How tragic! She wondered if they were still looking. There was an address in the Babine Landing area she could check, but there was no phone number. The lack was just another detail she would have to somehow find some spare time to follow up.

# 43

# Coping with Bar T

The fall day was clear, cold and windy, the overhead canopy a deep sky blue. Along the winding Antoinette Lake Road, the leaves of poplars and cottonwoods, now turned a rusty bronze, were drifting to the forest floor with every fitful gust. Matt and Ken, on leave from work, were driving out to Bar T to spend the day helping Tim.

Once they arrived, Tim filled them in, "We ain't got no more hay up at the upper range so the herd has to be brought down to feed them. Besides, there are wolves and grizzlies in these parts. We don't need them spooking the cattle. Generally, the cows can run off any predators when they're in a herd, but when the calves come in the spring, we need them somewhere we can keep an eye out for trouble. So Ken, you can ride herd with me? I've saddled a pinto for you, and Matt, can you drive the truck?"

Riding range was too hazardous for Matt who had no experience, so he drove Tim's truck that served as chuck wagon and equipment storage. He also helped with the corral gates and feeding and watering the steers once they were contained. The day was exhausting; the physical effort of driving up and down the mountainside, running around to open and close gates, and fetching food and drink meant Matt had no chance to check into the range cabin to see if the moose hide backpack was there.

The next day, a Friday, played out much like Thursday, except there was even less time spent up top looking for the last few strays of breeding stock and getting them into the corral by the range cabin. Then the rest of the day was spent driving the thirty or so head down from the upper area on the track Tim normally used for riding Blaze. By then, the weather had turned windy. There was an icy chill in the air. On the mountaintops there was a new frosting of snow that had not been there the day before. Winter was coming.

At mid-day when Tim had been gone with Ken to round up the last of the strays, Matt, on the pretext of needing some extra coffee from the cabin, drove up to take a quick peek inside. As he reported later to Abby, there was a god-awful mess of stuff there – sleeping bags, outdoor wear and camping gear – but he didn't see anything like the beaded backpack she had described.

The next day, Abby made a point of phoning Nora to tell her it looked as if Tim was in the clear.

"Thanks for following up on that. That's good to know." Nora sounded thoughtful. "How's Tess doing? I was just wondering if she's more settled now that she's staying in town with Ellie."

"I can't say she's 'more settled' really." Abby paused, trying to decide how to frame what she wanted to say. "She's not a town person, really. She's putting up a good front, showing up for school and at least going through the motions, but I can tell her heart's not in it. She really wants to be back at the ranch looking after her animals."

"So what will happen out there now?"

"You mean at the ranch? Oh, I suppose Tim will try to find some help to tend the herd. Either that, or he will have to truck out there morning and night, even if only to keep the water line in the barn from freezing up. I can't see him being able to keep that up for long. I think Matt said last night that Tim was going to take George Warren up on his offer of a loan of one of his cowhands for a little while. He's even offered to cover the salary for a month to help the Talbots. I guess Warren's place is a fair size and some of his stockmen will be looking for winter work. They usually get part time at the mill or go on Pogey, you know, join the UI ski-team!"

Nora snorted scornfully. The federal government's Unemployment Insurance process was a source of irritation for both those with and without jobs. "Well, if Tim can give someone work instead, why not? Better than a handout, no?"

"The problem is that whoever it is will have to board with a neighbor, and have a vehicle. Hired hands around here always work with room and board included and get mileage. Tim will have to have more than his mill hand's salary to keep someone on after Warren's money runs out. By the time Tim pays for gas and lodgings, he might as well do it himself."

Hanging up, Abby wondered if the kids could get some help from the insurance people. The easy way out, of course, was to sell all the stock, but legally, the cattle still belonged to Hank Talbot, so that wasn't an option.

# 44

# The Beaded Backpack

"Anything else new on this file, Nora?" The following Monday morning, Jed Fedoruk was looking through the Talbot file and scanning the photos taken at the property as Nora worked on typing up the sexual assault charge against Hank Talbot.

"Just a notice from the Great Northern Life Insurance adjusters that they want to interview the Talbot kids. Just standard procedure, so I phoned up to the school to let them know." Nora cast a speculative eye as she saw Jed absorbed by the ranch site photos in the Talbot file.

"Surprising that Talbot has insurance, don't you think? It doesn't seem to fit."

Jed shrugged, "Probably got talked into it by one of his more sensible buddies!"

Looking over Jed's shoulder, Nora commented on the contents of the photo showing the ranch yard. "Sure a lot of crap lying around, eh? I'd forgotten how much." There was shot after shot of the house and yard from various angles, all of them detailing the debris littering the area. "Nobody has said anything to me about the negatives sent to District HQ in Prince George. No sign of Talbot either. Has Sarge talked to you again, about your request for transfer, I mean?"

"No, I think he must wonder how fast he can make it all happen, to tell the truth. He can't wait to see the back of me! What a way to finish my very first posting! Awww …Crap!" She tore the form out of the typewriter and crumpled it into the wastepaper basket.

Jed paused to consider his junior colleague. "Nora, I know he's been tough on you. I just want you to know that as your partner, I have some input into the report that he'll send forward. I'll see that it's fair." That lop-sided grin of his was reassuring.

"Gee, thanks Jed. I know it hasn't been all bad. I just really want to put this Talbot case to bed, and I doubt I'll get the chance."

"Actually, I was wondering about something. You know that beaded backpack you said was missing from the shed out at the ranch?"

"Yeah?"

"I was over at Jack's for drinks last Friday. You know downstairs where he has all that indigenous stuff? He had a bag that could have been a backpack, but it had no straps anymore, but here's the thing, it had a beaded moose silhouette on the flap! What colour was the beading?"

"I don't know. I never really looked at the bag. I took the picture of the shed not knowing it was there, but even the Polaroid of Rosemary Joseph is black and white. Maybe one of the Talbot kids will remember what colour. Do you think that bag at Jack's is the one? How did he get it then?"

"Hold on. I never said it was the one. It looks similar to this." He shuffled through the photos in the file to find the one showing the flap of the bag peeking out from behind the empty cans in the shed.

"I didn't say anything to Jack, but he saw me looking at it." He leaned over to look more closely at the bag flap in the photo. "Yeah, it was just lying on the counter of his bar, not mounted on the wall or anything like the rest of his art stuff."

"And?"

"I didn't want to ask him outright where he got it. Don't worry. I was cool. I just said he had some interesting stuff, and then Wagner from the highway patrol crew came over, and we didn't talk about it again. The thing is, Nora, when I next looked, the bag was nowhere to be seen."

"What can we do?" Nora's was aghast. Would Wasniki go this far to protect Hank? Steal evidence?

"The problem is we have never made any official reference to that backpack. In fact, there's nothing written down linking Rosemary Joseph to anything at that ranch, so in Jack's mind, why should anyone think the bag matters? He didn't notice the pack flap in the shed photo, or he would have known better than to take it."

"You mean he took it because he wanted it for his collection?"

"If it's the same one, I think if we ask about it, that he might say he's always had it, and just never displayed it before." Jed's tone of voice seemed to suggest he doubted Jack would say anything of the sort, but he had to admit the possibility, however remote.

"But if it is the one, and we can ask Ellie to identify it, then that means Jack is complicit!" Nora was working herself up to some right-eous anger. "I mean, how did he get it? Did Hank give it to him? Or did Jack himself remove it from the shed that day he was there with the arson team? If so, why? Somehow, it must be important. That's why we have to get Ellie to identify it!"

"But it will be his word against a young girl's. Tess or Tim won't be any help. If Tim was only four or five at the time, chances are he won't remember this backpack, and Tess was just a baby. No, I'm afraid we can't move on this yet. At least we can't accuse Jack of anything. We'll ask Ellie to give us a detailed description of the backpack for the record though. And once we find Hank, we can ask him about the bag."

"If we ever find Hank! Jed, there is suddenly much more to this case than a mysterious fire and child molestation. I think we have a murder here."

Jed regarded her thoughtfully, nodding his head. "He was cleared by the coroner for Beth Talbot's death. But you're right, this second body is a problem."

# 45

## Tess Gives an Interview

Tom Cooper shut the door to his office and found his way to his desk. He motioned Abby to sit. It was Friday afternoon, and what he was about to broach with her was the last thing he had energy for.

"Abby, today I need you to sit in on an interview. Some insurance adjusters are coming in to talk to Tess Talbot and, for propriety's sake, we need to have someone in the room with her."

She moved to speak, but he cut her off and continued. "I don't want you to say anything at all during this. The adjusters have the police's okay. It's on the up and up. No need to be concerned."

"I was just about to say that she might not understand the consequences of…"

"I said I don't want any hassle about this. Just sit in while she talks to them. I don't even need to hear how it went."

"Have you told Tess already that they want to talk to her? Does she know what for?"

"No, you can do that. They're waiting with Margaret at the front desk. You have a spare block, so find Tess and ask her to join you in the counseling office. Thanks." The last word seemed an afterthought. Tom's thoughts were already elsewhere.

Walking along the hallway towards the math classroom where Tess was working, Abby felt circumspect, still vaguely astonished to discover that Hank even had insurance. Somehow, it didn't sound like the kind of thing he'd ever worry about. Deep down, she was appalled that Tom Cooper didn't see how compromising such an interview could be for Tess, who wouldn't have any notion of how her words might be construed, nor would the insurance adjusters have any idea about how stirring up these memories might be a problem for Tess. While mulling over these misgivings, Abby made arrangements for the two dark-suited strangers from the insurance company to take seats in the small counseling office, and then went to find Tess.

Abby wondered why they wanted to talk to Tess. She wanted to call Nora to clear it, but Tom had said the police had already given the okay, so what point was there? She'd only get herself in trouble with her principal if she kept the adjusters waiting too long. Maybe they wanted to ask Tess about the way the fire got started, to corroborate whatever Tim and Ellie had given them as testimony? She didn't even know if Ellie and Tim had spoken to them.

Of even more concern was whether Tess would want to cooperate. If not, Abby decided she would find some excuse for her. To hell with what Tom thought! He was just too eager to please the big shots. On the other hand, maybe if this interview went well, the kids could get some money to live on. They could use some financial security what with the extra burden of tending to the ranch as well as keeping their town jobs. No, she really should try to help Tess through it.

When Tess emerged from her class, Abby was struck by how tired she appeared, and by how the girl drooped against the doorframe as she spoke to her. "Hey Tess, how's it going?" The girl seemed almost comatose. Abby pulled her aside out of the doorway and shut the door so their conversation would not disturb the class. "Did you have a late night?"

Tess stood up straighter and smiled, "Yeah, Ellie got us a TV! We've been watching stuff every night this week! "Happy Days" and "All in the Family", even "Sidestreet" and "Gunsmoke". I quit when that old guy who talks all the time comes on. Peter Guzow somebody. Yeah, I'm kinda tired."

"You do look like you could use more sleep, and maybe less TV?" Abby suspected her suggestion would fall flat. The television must be an amazing option for someone like Tess.

"Besides, I'm worried about Dad! Mostly, that's why we haven't been sleeping too good, wondering where he is and all." She yawned and her head drooped as she slowed her pace.

"How are you doing with your school stuff, Tess? Report cards are coming soon…"

"Uh…okay, I guess." Looking up at Abby, she stopped. "Why do you want to see me?"

"There are a couple of men from your dad's insurance company who want to talk to you…about the fire." She saw Tess's face fall.

"What do they want to know? I told the cops everything already, and they said there wouldn't be any charges, for – what do you call it – arson?" Abby could see this was not going to be easy. Tess seemed on the point of turning around and going back to class. Abby reached out to encircle the girl's shoulders and kept walking so that Tess fell in beside her.

"Tess, I will understand if you don't want to talk to them right now, but the truth is, you need to get this sorted out so you can get some money to help you live. So, at some point, you need to talk to them and help them understand that you didn't have anything to do with the fire. Do you want me to ask them to come back? I really don't mind doing that. But you need to give them a time when you're ready to talk to them." The girl looked so tired and lost-looking that Abby thought it might be better to postpone.

"No, might as well get it over with."

"Are you sure?"

They stopped outside the counseling office, and at Tess's almost imperceptible nod, Abby bent down to look her in the eye. Her face was pale and drawn, with great dark smudges beneath the blue eyes.

Softly, so the men inside would not hear, she said, "Tess, we can wait if you want."

"Are you going to be here, too Mrs. Clarke?" Those beautiful eyes were so tired and resigned.

"Of course I will." But Abby felt uneasy as they entered the room.

Inside, Peter MacIntosh and Jerry Butler were waiting patiently. Abby introduced herself and Tess and then took a seat beside her. The interview proceeded smoothly with all the questions about the day of the fire ones that Tess had answered before.

Peter MacIntosh, the lead district investigator for Great Northern Insurance, told Tess that she, Ellie and Tim were the beneficiaries of her dad's farm insurance policy. A claim would be filed on their behalf as soon as the inquiries were complete. However, the question of their dad's whereabouts had to be sorted out first.

"Do you understand what I have explained so far?" MacIntosh's voice was gruff but not unkindly. Tess nodded, her face ashen.

Watching Tess during the interview, Abby was struck by how much in shock the girl still seemed to be. Holding herself tight, arms wrapped defensively across her front, she answered in monosyllables: "yes" or "no". Mostly, her responses were a shrug or a "don't remember". The fatigue on her face was clear to everyone. She was wishing she were anywhere but there, stuck in a windowless room answering impossible questions.

In hindsight, Abby was particularly struck by Tess's response to a couple of questions, one about the area behind the shed in the back garden where the unidentified body had been discovered. Tess was asked if there were any solvents or gasoline ever kept in that shed and she replied that she was used to going wherever she wanted on the ranch, but knew her dad didn't want her going into the shed.

"I wouldn't go in anyways. Being round it was enough to make me throw up." After a pause, she added with what appeared to be an afterthought, "It smelled bad, you know? Oil fumes 'n stuff."

The investigators didn't follow up, and Abby had no chance to ask Tess anything herself, since at the end of the interview, she had to rush off to class.

For the rest of that afternoon and evening, something niggled away in the back of her mind. Had Tess suspected there was a body buried right next to the shed? Or was her aversion more about her father sexually assaulting her out there? Was it really just the smell?

She made a mental note to ask Tess first thing when she saw her Monday morning.

The second question was one that Abby recalled often in the next few days. MacIntosh had asked Tess if she thought her sister Ellie, or anyone else, might have had any reason to want to burn the house down. Tess's response was to wrap her arms even more closely around her body and stare at the ceiling instead of straight ahead as she had for all the other questions. When at last she had whispered, "Don't know," it seemed as if the words had been wrenched from her by torture. The interview ended shortly afterwards.

The most painful point for Abby came just as Tess was leaving.

Looking straight in her eyes, Tess had muttered, her eyes cloudy with rage, "Was that what you wanted?"

Abby knew Tess felt betrayed by someone she had been trusting to keep her safe.

# 46

# Tess on the Run

Abby was dreaming. There was some enormous creature crashing against the walls of the small cabin where she crouched terrified. She could feel the walls shaking. The wood of the door was splintering…

"Babe! Wake up! Someone's…" Matt's voice was muffled as he buried himself in his pillows again. After a Friday night late shift, he had hit the sack only four hours before and wouldn't be stirring for another three.

Abby for the first time heard the pounding and urgent shouting at their front door. Opening the door in her dressing gown, Abby beheld a frantic Ellie who looked as disheveled as Abby felt.

"Hey! What's up? Are you okay?" Ellie was panting; she clearly had run all the way from her place, her jacket thrown over her pajamas.

"It's Tess! She's gone!"

"Where? What do you mean…gone?" Abby, recalling that last devastated look on the girl's face after the interview with the insurance adjusters, felt her chest tighten. Guiding Ellie to the kitchen table, she busied herself with coffee while Ellie filled her in.

"I spent some time with her after work last night. She seemed a bit down, so I got her to take a bubble bath and fed her some supper. Then, you know, I went out with someone from work."

"So she was gone when you got back?"

"No, she was sleeping when I got in about two. I crashed right away, and then, when I got up about fifteen minutes ago, she wasn't there." Her voice was thick with tears.

"Would she be over at a friend's?" Even as she said it, Abby knew it was unlikely Tess would be with anyone from school. She didn't have any friends at school that Abby could recall. Tess was such a loner.

"No," Ellie responded, "she's upset about something. She didn't say what. Did something happen at school?"

"She had an interview with some insurance adjusters who came to the school. I was there the whole time. They asked some stuff she didn't want to deal with, you know, about why anyone, they mentioned you, or anyone else, would want to burn the house down, but they weren't rough on her, really."

Ellie's face was stony. "Aw, shit! That did it then. She's run 'cause she's afraid they'll pin the fire on one of us. Christ!" Meeting Abby's confused gaze, she continued, "I swear, none of us started that fire. But the question wasn't 'did one of us do it', but 'did one of us *want* to do it' wasn't it? You would think the cops' not laying charges would be enough to satisfy them, wouldn't you?"

"Have the adjusters spoken to you yet?" Abby was sure they wouldn't confine their inquiries to just Tess.

"No, they called the office yesterday, and I told them I'd see them today later, but I can't now. We have to find Tess!"

"The question Peter MacIntosh asked was whether you, or anyone else, might have had any reason to want to burn the house down."

"Well, Tess would have had trouble answering that honestly, because she would have known how I felt, and for that matter, how she felt about Dad at that point."

"Well, this isn't helping us find her. I think we better notify the police." Abby reached for the phone. "In the meantime, you think about what she took with her."

"Mooch is gone with her. I didn't notice what else."

"The police will want to know what she's wearing, and what she took with her. I'll just call to let them know we're coming in. Matt has to sleep a bit yet anyway, so I'll come over to your place and we'll make a list."

On the way to the detachment from Ellie's, a new complication became apparent. The weather had just turned wintery. In the half hour they had been at the girls' apartment, snow had already dusted the landscape white. Turning on the car radio, they heard the forecast was for steady snow all day with no end in sight until Sunday midday.

Nora met them at the door and ushered them over to her desk right away. "We'll make out a missing person report to get this rolling right now. Ellie, what can you tell me about when she might have left and what she was wearing? I understand she has her dog with her? What breed is it? A black Lab?" Nora remembered seeing Mooch that time she had visited the girls' apartment.

Ellie answered the questions carefully. Mooch was a black Lab. Tess had been there when she had got home from the bar at two in the morning, but was gone when she got up at seven. She had taken some meat and cheese from the fridge and made some peanut butter sandwiches. She likely was wearing the knee-high black rubber snow-packs and the khaki-coloured, full-length goose down parka Tim had lent her. Ellie suspected Tess was on her way to the ranch.

Nora cut in, "So at least, she's somewhat prepared for the trek, but it's about forty miles by road to Bar T, thirty along Marcel River Road and Antoinette Lake Road and another ten into the ranch site, if that's where she's going."

"I can't imagine Tess opting for anywhere else, but who knows? She will have to go non-stop to make it to the range cabin, but, if she took off onto the trails, as she's likely to do, she has less than twenty-five miles because the trails cut off a lot of distance by going cross-country. But she has no snowshoes, no weapon, not enough food." Ellie slumped over onto the desk and held her head in her hands as the tears finally began to stream. "This is grizzly country, you know? Even if they aren't at their most ornery this time of year, still, they're unpredictable at the best of times." Then, her head shot up. "Jesus Murphy! First Dad and now Tess! He's been gone almost a month now! We have to find her!"

Abby and Nora exchanged brief, knowing looks as Abby tried to comfort the distraught young woman. Nora reached for the phone, "We'll get a search party organized ASAP. Why don't you try to get some friends to help?"

Relieved to have something to do take their minds off Tess, Ellie and Abby drove back to Abby's to wake Matt up and get some of the mill hands to help.

"I guess we can't reach Tim, eh?" Abby remembered Matt saying Tim would be back for Monday's evening shift, but she didn't know where he was for this morning.

Ellie snorted, "Nah, he's in town somewhere. At least he was at the bar with me last night, likely crashed out at his place. We'll get his sorry ass outta bed."

"So how are things at the ranch?" Abby knew there was still some stock that needed watering and feeding.

"Oh, Tim said he got it all squared away. One of Warren's stock hands has a place a few miles closer to town from Bar T. He's going to see to the stock during the week, and Tim and I will take over on weekends. So we had to go out there today anyway. Now we'll make the trip and look for Tess at the same time."

"Do you really think that's where she'll go? Won't she maybe head for the highway and hitchhike out of town? " Abby was remembering the story of the girl who had gone missing the year before, and her chest felt heavy with apprehension.

"Naw, she'll go back to Bar T, I'm betting. The range cabin is there and her horse. She won't want to go anywhere else."

Later, at the detachment, Jed disagreed. "I don't think she'll head back to the ranch." Jed was looking at a map of the area to plan the search strategy. "She's probably afraid of meeting up with her dad after what he's done to her. Remember you mentioned the missing bag as a clue that Hank may still be around."

"Tim and Ellie are sure she'll be on the way to the ranch," Nora didn't know how much Tess feared Hank compared to how much she missed being at the ranch, but she suspected that it was a toss-up.

"Well, no point in all of us heading out there to start. The cruisers are going to do the highway east and west. Every young person, male or female, who's ever gone missing in this country has at some point been on Highway 16. Likely this runaway's no different." Jed jabbed his map into his parka and headed for the door. "You coming, Constable? Or do you need to stay and monitor the radio phones?"

"I'll stay and coordinate the search plan for the private vehicles. We've contacted the volunteer search and rescue coordinator, and they will mobilize right away. The Clarkes have offered to get some friends to drive along the local back roads."

"That's a good idea. Okay, I'll see you back here by 6:00 p.m., and we'll keep in touch by radio."

Once Matt heard the news, he was up and on the phone to rouse as many of his crew as he could find. First was Tim, of course, whom he located at the place he shared with three other mill hands. Once he heard his little sister was missing, Tim moved like a man with his tail on fire. Like Ellie, the first place he thought Tess would go was the ranch. By 10:45 a.m., he and Ellie had left in Tim's four-wheel drive. Shortly afterwards, Ken and Matt headed out to check Little Bear Creek Road and Loon Lake Road. Both had hot soup and coffee in their thermoses to last the day, which was steadily becoming colder and snowier.

Abby stayed behind to answer phones. If there were any sightings or tracks to report, she would pass the word along to Nora. In any case, they all planned to meet at 6:00 pm. at the detachment to report out.

The two highway search parties radioed back at noon with a nil report. No one along the highway has seen a hitchhiker. The people at the gas stations between Moose Forks and Simon Lake had no recollection of a passenger in any vehicle matching Tess's description. The search team relayed that they would continue on to Brandenhoff before turning back so they could be sure of being in Moose Forks by 6:00 pm.

In the other direction, the road to Prince Rupert was closed so the search party radioed that they had gone only as far as Terrace with no better luck. They had thought of making the cut down to Kitimat, but had run out of time. In any case, the weather was becoming more extreme by the hour. With blowing snow and icy roads, they would be lucky to be back on time.

Only the two Highway 16 search teams reported back by 6:00 p.m. Abby, Matt and their friends who had volunteered gathered for the update meeting in the detachment main office. Sergeant Wasnicki was off for the weekend, so Jed took the lead. Neither the police teams nor the civilians who had taken the back roads had anything further to report, except that weather conditions appeared to be worsening. The first major storm of the season was transforming the country from a picturesque backdrop to a treacherous terrain. On hearing the lack of news, Abby, who had spent the day puttering half-heartedly around her house, felt disheartened, and Nora, who had been stuck in the office all day on her day off, disgruntled. She had favoured everyone focusing on the search out towards the Bar T, but her input had been ignored.

They were just about to end the meeting when Ellie and Tim, tromped in to say that, after tending to the cattle at Bar T and doing a cursory search for Tess around the property, they had driven back along

Marcel River Road to a point where the horse-trail intersected at a bridge across the river. It was a distance from Moose Forks that they thought Tess could have walked. As Ellie drove, Tim had got out of the car and started walking southward for a mile or two on the trail that cut through the bush roughly parallel to the road. He wasn't sure, but he thought he had seen depressions in the snow that could have been footprints. He had also seen another looping pattern, one left by an animal like a dog as it ploughed through the deeper stuff.

Earlier that week, there had been significant snowfall up in those higher elevations, so some drifts were at least three feet high. It was hard to say if what Tim had seen were really tracks because the snow was so deep, but he thought it was worth checking at first light. These might have been Tess and Mooch's tracks – it was an outside chance – but the dog-like tracks could just have easily been made by a wolf.

"So what is the plan for tomorrow?" Nora directed the question to Jed who was in charge since Wasnicki was off for the weekend.

"Well, I guess we better check out the road out to the ranch, and plan to get up to the range cabin, because if she's headed up there, that's the only place she'll likely go. What do you think, Tim? Ellie? Would she go anyplace else, some place we don't know about?"

Ellie, exhausted from the tension of the day, took a moment to collect her thoughts. "There's no other building where she could stay and be warm. I mean, the barn is there and she does love that damn horse, but chances are she'd get Blaze and ride her up to the range cabin and stable her in the lean-to. Tim, you were just up there. What do you think?"

"Oh hell, yeah, that's where she'll be if she's anywheres. There's no place else. She couldn't a made it there by this morning when we was there, or I woulda said we shoulda waited for the little pipsqueak to show up! Then I would of tanned her ass myself!"

The group erupted in laughter at the thought of Tim's unlikely paternal streak.

Ellie cut in, "We would have gone back up to the ranch later this afternoon, but by the time Tim finished checking out the trail, it was getting dark. You need daylight to get up to that cabin."

"Well, that's what we'll do then," Jed confirmed. "Tomorrow, I'll head up in the detachment four-by-four with…" his hesitation gave Nora the opportunity to volunteer.

"I'm not staying behind tomorrow, too." Nora looked over at Abby who was about to insist on a spot in Matt's truck when Jed continued on.

"And Tim, you and Matt can take your trucks up and take whoever wants to go along. For a search party, the more eyes the better."

Matt spoke up for the first time, "We can make it up there with chains. Tim, you'll take Ellie as an extra pair of eyes, and I'll take…"

"Me!" Abby blurted out.

Matt looked unsure, " Uh, Honey, I don't know. It could be pretty dangerous. I mean, Hank's got some crazy idea about you. I was thinking maybe Ken could go with me."

Nora spoke up. "Abby, I know I said you had to stay away from the ranch, but since it's a search party, the more eyes the better, but you must stay well behind us with Matt, Tim and Ellie."

Abby nodded her agreement.

# 47

# Into the Snow

The next day, it was a snowy Halloween Sunday. They left town in a convoy just after sunrise. Jed Fedoruk and Nora Macpherson rode together in the detachment four-by-four, Tim and Ellie in Tim's truck and Abby with Matt in theirs. All vehicles were equipped with chains and bags of sand.

Abby was mesmerized by the cocoon effect of travelling through the snowstorm encased in the warm cab of the truck. The snow swirling in coils into the windscreen had an eerie, almost hypnotic effect. She thought of the little kids planning to go out trick or treating that night, and about how they would manage their costumes if they had to wear snow gear. Thoughts of children brought Tess to mind. How was that delicate slip of a girl managing? Was she warm or safe?

"Matt, do you think Tess could walk all this way to the ranch? This weather is miserable! Shouldn't somebody be looking for her on the trail along the way?"

"Ken and Laura have promised to snowshoe the trail once we get to the ranch and find she's not there. The cops can radio back to get word for them to start. Otherwise, it's just wasted manpower, and you're right, the weather is bad! All the more reason not to send people out into it for no reason."

"Did you bring our snowshoes?" Abby hadn't really expected they would ever use the ones Matt had bought from Pete Furtado's Gitxsan wife.

"Hell, yeah! The dump of snow down here is already building up, so it's bound to be pretty deep up in the mountains. We'll need those to get up to the range cabin."

Ahead of them, both Jed Fedoruk and Nora Macpherson were

equipped for winter trekking: felt boot packs, regulation down parkas with hoods and snowshoes. Each carried a brand new mobile radio unit. Jed carried a Winchester Magnum and his sidearm in his Sam Browne belt. Nora had her .38 Special Smith and Wesson tucked into an inside breast pocket holster specially designed for it, but Jed had also insisted she carry a Winchester.

Tim carried his dad's pump action 12-gauge shotgun, having left his dad's .338 behind in the range cabin, but Matt was armed only with a hunting knife. Ellie and Abby were unarmed.

When they set out, the weather was snowy with visibility limited to less than one hundred yards. The unplowed road slowed them down. The trip that usually took forty-five minutes at most had stretched to an hour and a half. Once at the ranch house site, where the house now truly looked haunted with the charred remnants looming out from the swirl of snow, they parked the trucks to reconnoiter. Jed asked Nora to radio in their position and connect with other patrols who were still keeping a lookout for Tess.

Tim pointed off past the ruined house site towards the little valley by the creek where Abby had encountered Tess playing with her dog on that memorable first visit to the ranch. Tim pointed, "There's the back-country trail Tess would take, I reckon, so we won't likely see none of her tracks here in the yard off the road. As he veered off toward the barn, he called back to them, "Look around the yard, while Ellie and me do the stock, okay?"

While Tim and Ellie disappeared to feed and water the cattle in the corral and barn, the others checked the ranch yard but found no evidence of human footprints.

After they finished with the cattle, Tim put on snowshoes and tromped through the snow to the creek running behind the house to see if Tess might have used that leg of the trail. He came slogging back, puffing and waving his arms.

"No sign of Tess, but a grizzly's been at the creek in the last few hours!"

Jed signaled to everyone except Tim to stay back, and the two trekked back to check the tracks out.

The distinctive pie-sized tracks were clear in the shallow snow next to the creek, which had not yet frozen over. "I thought I seen a bear the first day or so when I was tending the steer back a week or so," Tim offered. "I for sure seen a print in the soft soil at the creek bed. I wanted to check it out to see where it was feeding, so I kept my eyes peeled, but it never showed itself again the rest of the time I was up here, so I figured it had gone off somewheres else."

"Where do you think it would go?" Jed, considering all the civilians he had on the search party, was starting to feel a little nervous about a grizzly bear sighting.

"There'll still be a few spawning salmon this time of year further up Antoinette Creek," Tim nodded back in the direction they had just come from town, "so that would be a likely direction."

Nodding, Jed turned back toward the group waiting by the corral. Trudging along, he spoke so only Tim could hear, "Do me a favour, Tim. When we get to the cabin, I'd like you to get your dad's Winchester and load it, just in case, okay? That shotgun you're carrying won't do much if we meet a grizzly."

"It's okay, corporal, I got slugs I can use…that'll do the job."

Upon joining the group, Jed informed everyone about Tim's finding. "The prints suggest a big grizzly, an adult of maybe five to six hundred pounds, and at that size, likely a male. He's just getting ready to sleep, so maybe not too energetic. Sometimes by now, ones in this region are hibernating, but grizzly are different than black bears because they don't sleep as deeply and can be woken up fairly easy. Anyway, we need to keep our eyes open, because Tim here says he has seen one around in the last couple of weeks, and for sure there's been one here since the snow fell yesterday. Everybody just rest for five while I radio in that we've got a grizzly around. We might need a Conservation Officer to give us some back up. "

Abby felt vaguely sick to her stomach. She was wondering if maybe she shouldn't have asked to come.

News of a nearby grizzly had electrified the whole group, as now they had to reconsider their plan to hike on snowshoes from the house site up to the range cabin. The less time they spent exposed out-of-doors, the better.

"What do you think Tim? Ellie? Can we make it up to the clearing below the cabin in our trucks? You know the terrain better than anyone else here."

Ellie spoke up, "We can do it with the chains, but we'd best stick with two vehicles, leaving Matt's behind. There's not much room up there for parking." Tim nodded agreement and added, "I'll take a different route up to the spot where we park, more over to the west. That way I can check that way for any sign of the bear."

They chained up and divided the group into two search parties comprised of Jed as lead, going with Ellie and Matt, and Nora, taking Tim and Abby. This arrangement gave each team an officer with a weapon, someone with a long gun, and someone who knew the terrain.

Tim drove his truck for Nora's team. The bush was still just lightly dusted with snow under the big timber, but there was three feet or more in the clearings. They took a wide tractor trail that wound back around the barn and corrals and up a rise to a plateau where they could see the ranch land spread out below.

At about 9:30 a.m., Tim stopped the truck further along the plateau and got out. The weather was now starting to clear with the cloud ceiling lifting so visibility had improved to several hundred yards. To the south and west lay the land singed black by the bush fire. It poked dismal spears of dead conifers against the wintry sky. He pointed ahead over the rise where they were standing, to a thread of smoke that could be seen drifting skyward above the ledge of pine. There the fire had not reached, and the bush was still a grey-green fringe against the slate-grey clouds.

"That's about where the range cabin is," he said. With a grin, he added, "I think someone's home! But I also think we need to be careful not to spook her."

Nora examined the thread of smoke thoughtfully, "I guess we might assume the smoke means Tess is in the cabin, but it could be your dad too, couldn't it?"

He continued, "Could be, maybe. Now the weather's turned, he can't live rough anymore. He'll know nobody would stay here in the cabin over the winter. But if we both drive up, either him or Tess could cut and run again. I don't know about you, but I don't much feel like chasing anybody with a grizzly stalking about!"

Looking at Nora, he added, "Maybe you should radio to the other guys what we've seen here, and they can park the RCMP truck somewhere outta sight? If Tess sees this truck, she won't panic so bad, I don't think, but the other one would scare her."

Hearing that Tim thought Hank could also be at the cabin left Abby feeling even queasier. The last thing they needed was for Hank to take Tess and make a run for it!

Nora radioed Jed to leave the truck further down below the cabin site than they had planned and to proceed on foot. After Jed agreed to the change in plans, Nora handed the radio receiver over to Tim so he could consult Ellie about the best place to meet. Nora's team drove along the tractor trail for another ten minutes before pulling over into a roadside clearing where they met Jed's team who had snow-shoed up from below along the trail. Jed's team had nothing new to report. Tim advised all the others to gather their gear for the last leg up to the cabin.

The route he led them on was a game trail, though there was no evidence of tracks this morning. It first wound up and around a steep cliff to the east of the cabin, close to the road leading farther south to Antoinette Lake. There they had to find their footing carefully and use the sparse lodge pole pines for handholds. The going was slow since, as well as the radio equipment and rifles, they were all now carrying their snowshoes for when the terrain opened up further ahead into deeper drifts of snow.

Once on the top, they put on snowshoes and trudged silently, skirting the edge of Bar T's wide alpine range, on the other side of which sat the cabin snugly nestled among a copse of poplars, their yellow leaves now replaced by snow tracery. An even more solid smudge of smoke now rose from the cabin's chimney.

# 48

## Tess Has Company

On approaching the cabin, they heard the slap of a door closing but saw no one exit at the front. Tim offered an explanation, "There's a path from the cabin's back door to the outhouse. She's likely just got up. I think I can see Blaze in the hay shed over to the left."

As they finally neared the front door, Jed motioned Ellie and Tim ahead, "You go in to check on who's inside. Signal us when you've connected with Tess."

Ellie took off her snowshoes and went first, calling out as she ascended the porch steps in front of the door. There was no response from inside, so she entered with Tim following close behind. In the meantime, Jed took Matt and headed around to the back of the cabin where they could check the outhouse before entering from the rear. Abby and Nora took their snowshoes off and waited on the porch. A moment later, Ellie and Tim signaled them to come inside.

When Nora entered and saw Tess sound asleep on the bunk bed near the woodstove Quebec heater, she quietly posed the obvious question, "Then who just left from the back door?" Those words were still hanging in the air when Jed and Matt, having checked that the outhouse was empty, entered the cabin from the rear. Their arrival at last awakened Tess who, in sleepy-eyed amazement, could say nothing as she surveyed the group in front of her. At her feet, Mooch yawned himself awake. Both appeared lethargic, no doubt so exhausted from their trek the day before that they had not awakened to Ellie's calls, Nora's question or even the opening of the cabin door.

Tess avoided eye contact and looked around behind the group as if trying to spot someone in the background.

Nora asked, "Who just left by the back door, Tess?"

"Um…my Dad? Isn't he still here?"

Nora had guessed that Hank would manage "living rough" until the snows came. It made total sense that he had only now showed up at the range cabin, and that Tim had seen nothing of him while he was here tending the stock. His son had chosen to side with Ellie that night he had left, and in Hank Talbot's world, such disloyalty was unforgivable.

Jed nodded to the women, "You stay inside to talk to Tess, while the rest of us see if we can find Hank's tracks. The snow has been pretty steady up until about a half hour ago, so there should be something we can follow."

He signaled Tim and Matt to come behind him out the back, and then after checking for tracks in that direction, they turned onto the snow path that led to the front of the cabin. There Jed stopped to radio back the news that Tess and Hank Talbot had been located. The squawk of the radio briefly echoed in the clearing. They heard that a Conservation Officer was being dispatched to help monitor the grizzly. Then, they stood reconnoitering on the porch for a few minutes before heading south and then east along the edge of the alpine meadow.

Ellie sat down beside her sister. "Why did you leave, Muffin?"

"I just wanted to come home, Ellie! It wasn't that I didn't like being with you in town, but I just like being here more…" Her voice drifted low as her eyes swam with tears.

"Tess, weren't you worried to come back here, knowing maybe your dad was around? You told us he had done things he shouldn't have." Nora was well aware that the children of abusers would sometimes still side with the abusive parent if they were confronted with too much pressure, so she was trying to frame her questions with as much tact as possible.

"Oh, he's okay, now. He hasn't got any whisky here. I was all right with him here. He had a fire going and everything. I didn't get in 'till it was almost dark."

Nora glanced quickly at Abby and Ellie to see if they felt comfortable with Tess's acceptance of her dad. Their faces were somber masks, as if they felt hard-pressed to accept that Hank could take care of a daughter he had beaten so savagely not that long before.

"Can you tell us about what your dad did the night of the fire?" Nora broke in with what was at the top of her mind, "And where he has been up until now?"

"Dad said he had drank a lot after we all left that night and passed out. I felt bad, 'cause usually he can hold his liquor, you know? He never passes out. He must of been some busted up with us all leaving to drink like that." She reached over past Ellie to where Mooch was lying at the foot of the bed and ruffled his fur. "He didn't even have Mooch to keep him company."

"How did the house fire start, Tess? Did he say?" Nora wanted to clear up this issue before anything else.

"He said he waked up when he smelled smoke, and he saw the coffee table lamp turned over on the floor. The kerosene was running across to the fireplace, and then he said he tried to stop it, but fire crawled up the curtain beside the fireplace. Then, the whole wall caught. I figure he freaked then. He said he hardly got out himself."

"So we were right in thinking that the fire wasn't deliberately set." Nora nodded. "Did he say anything else, Tess?"

"He said when he realized the truck keys was still inside the house, he seen he was stuck there. So he got the horses out of the barn and opened the corral so the cattle could move into the pasture behind the barn. Then he led the horses away from where the fire was, and when he seen the barn wasn't catching, he went back to see if he could do anything to save the house. He got a couple of pails of water from the pump, but he said he could tell it wouldn't help any. He poured water around the outside of the house fence line hoping the other buildings like the garden shed and tool shed wouldn't catch too. He doused everything as much as he could. By then he was pretty done in, he said, so he just fell into one of the stalls in the barn. He crashed out there and didn't wake up 'til late the next day."

Tess had never before said so much all at once and seemed exhausted by her own talkativeness.

"Did he say how the lamp got turned over? It must be what started the fire." Nora was trying to picture the room. "Where was it compared to everything else? Why would it tip over?"

Abby broke in, " I remember when we were there in September, that a kerosene lamp stood on that coffee table, and there were some kittens playing on the kitchen table when we first got inside. They got shooed off right away, but if they got used to going up on tables, they would maybe have kept on doing it, especially if no one was around, and there was food left out."

"Oh, hell, you're right," Ellie groaned, "At the last minute, Tim did grab a chicken sandwich for Dad and left it on the coffee table. Those cats were big by then too. They could have knocked the lamp over and then taken off scared."

Now Tess's face was awash with tears, "He shouldn't of let me take Mooch! He would of waked Dad up with his barking when he smelled smoke! The house might of been saved! I feel so bad…." Ellie moved to hug her again, "You couldn't have known, honey. Mooch is your dog after all. It's only natural he should be with you."

"What did your dad do when he woke up?" Nora hoped Tess would want to keep talking so she should get as much of this statement witnessed as possible.

"He said he spent that day gathering up what he could find from the yard and rode Ebony off into the bush, taking a packhorse for his gear. He headed east away from the Antoinette Lake fire and found someplace south by Loon Lake by Little Bear Creek, I think. After that, I guess he stayed the last month camping and living off the land. He had a canvas-covered goose down bag to keep warm at night and food from the range cabin, and a rifle I guess."

"So when you got here, when was it?" Nora wanted to establish Hank's movements from last night onwards.

"About dark last night…"

"And was he here this morning?"

"I guess so. I was sleeping until you came."

Nora took a quick peek out the front to see if she could figure out where the men had gone. All she could see was a trail of blurry snowshoe tracks leading off to the right to the edge of the alpine meadow. There was no sound except for the occasional throaty call of a raven.

Turning back inside, she saw that Tess was up, and that she and Ellie were making coffee. Abby watched as Tess winced with every step. "Are you okay? That was a long walk in the cold! Are you feeling sore or sick?"

"I'm okay. Yeah, my legs are sore. I ain't done much trekking for a while! I sure could have used some snowshoes! That's why my leg muscles are hurting, I guess, lifting them through the snowdrifts. I came along the trail we use for the horses, so it isn't as long as the road because it can cut some corners, about twenty miles maybe, but where the trail's open to the sky there were some big drifts, up to my knees anyway."

Nora regarded the girl thoughtfully. She was young and wiry, but it was hard to imagine her all that way on her own, and with a grizzly in the area! She wondered if Tess even realized how much she had risked.

A knock on the front door heralded Jed who popped his head inside to ask Nora to come out. As she gathered up her gear to go, Mooch nosed his way out the door and ran off barking. Tess rushed to the door and called for Mooch. "He smells that grizzly! I don't want him outside! Can't somebody get him?"

Nora noted that Tess did know about the bear even though none of them had said anything. She thought Hank must have told her, which meant he was also out there also knowing it was close by.

Matt came in looking a bit sheepish. He explained that, not having a firearm, he had been sent inside when the grizzly had been sighted foraging for rosehips in the shallow drifts of snow on a nearby hillside to the east of the cabin. Jed told Matt to stay with the women while he, Nora and Tim took the firearms to keep an eye on the animal. They hadn't caught sight of Hank, but thought they had heard some twigs breaking a little way up the hillside.

Next, Tim strode in, walking through quickly to the back lean-to, then left again abruptly, his face grim. He still had the shotgun in his hand. Tess pleaded with him to find Mooch, but he just barreled outside again without answering.

Abby looked at Ellie, her eyebrows raised in a question. What was that about? What's up with Tim? The tension was thick, time somehow suspended as if they were all wading in some thick fluid.

Ellie shrugged, " I guess he hoped to see the .338 still here, but I'm thinking Dad took it."

Stillness descended on the cabin. Hank was well-armed.

Abby, whose stomach was feeling funny, broke the silence, "Matt, maybe we should take Ellie and Tess and head back to town?"  Like Tess, she really just wanted to be home.

Amongst Tess's loud protestations that she wasn't going anywhere without her dog, Abby caught Matt's sensible reminder, "Our truck is down at the house site, so we are more or less dependent on Tim or the cops to get us back to it. Besides," he added, "they told us to stay put. You want them pissed off at you, too?"

Tess wandered over to her sister and whispered in her ear. Ellie shook her head, "Tess, let's wait a while to see what happens, okay? You will have to go back to town eventually, even if Dad's back, because you can't live up here all winter. It's got no firewood, and there's no insulation. You'll have to come with us today when we leave." She looked meaningfully at Nora and continued, "Dad has his own problems to deal with, as usual, but if I have any say, you will do as I ask!"

Tess flounced off to throw herself on the bed, her arms wrapped around and her face obscured by a tangle of hair. Silent little sobs shook her body.

Abby felt helpless to do anything to ease her unhappiness. Clearly, Tess couldn't stay out here by herself, and given that Hank faced charges and questioning by the police, he was unlikely to be staying on at the cabin either.

# 49

# Abby Goes for a Walk

Ellie, followed by Matt and Nora, headed out the front to watch what was happening from the porch. The sun was high overhead in the south. It was pushing towards midday.

Inside the cabin, Abby was still feeling a bit odd. Her stomach was in knots and doing flip-flops all at the same time. She decided a trip to the outhouse would take very little time and pose no danger, so she slipped out the back. Maybe her stomach would settle if she just attended to the call of nature.

As she was exiting the outhouse minutes afterwards, she heard the crack of a breaking twig behind its door.

"Matt? Is that you? I'm finished."

"Why no, Missus, it ain't Matt…"

Abby's stomach did a kamikaze nosedive. There was no mistaking the low rumble of Hank Talbot's voice. Crouching low behind the outhouse, he had his .338 aimed not three feet from her head.

"Come on round very slowly, Abby, and don't you make a sound, or this here gun might go off."

Abby froze. She heard her heart thumping and tried to swallow. She couldn't summon the breath to say anything.

"Atta girl. Now come back this way, and you won't get hurt."

Inside her head, a voice was hammering, "Oh my God, Oh my God! I have no choice! I'm alone! Everyone else is on the other side of the cabin or out on the meadow."

"That's it. Turn this way. Go in front. You got no snowshoes, so we'll head over to the bluff where the pack is still thin." Poking her in the ribs with the rifle slung on its strap over his shoulder, and holding one arm behind her back in a vice-like grip, he forced her ahead of him uphill along a barely discernible game trail. He shuffled his feet to obscure their tracks as he followed behind. Soon they were on the bluff where the trees stood tall and thick. Underfoot was a bare drift of snow dusting a thick carpet of evergreen needles. Abby was shivering as much from the cold as from fear.

Their path led them southward and upward, towards where the Talbot land ended in a bluff overlooking Antoinette Lake. Abby could see that here there was some fire damage from the burn that had destroyed the forest on the south shore of the lake, but that it hadn't been extensive enough to ruin their cover. They were about a quarter mile from the cabin.

"I want to show you something here, Missus School Teacher Woman." He pulled her over to the edge of the bluff where she could fathom the five hundred foot drop to the rim of the lake below. "This here's…"

Abby was mesmerized by the dizzying height of the bluff. She could make out the deep blue of the lake not yet frozen over, its rocky shoreline fringed by a lacery of white ice where the water edge was just starting to solidify. She imagined herself helpless, hurtling downward, her head bashed against the rocks, her body submerged in those cold depths. In her terror, she was sure he was about to heave her over.

"Hey, what you so tense for? This here's Beth's resting place, you know, my wife…here's where I buried her, see? What did you think I was going to show you?"

Then, when he followed her gaze fixated on the edge not three feet from where they stood, he laughed a hoarse croak, "You scared of heights, Abby? Don't worry none. You got more value to me alive than dead just now. Who's at the cabin?"

The abrupt shift in topic left her gaping for words. "I…uh…Tess?"

Hank shook her so hard her teeth rattled. The growl of his voice seemed to vibrate the very air she breathed. "Course I know Tess is there, you stupid bitch! Who else? You're not alone!"

She wondered if he had seen or heard the police. She decided she would assume he hadn't, because they had mostly kept to the front of the cabin, and he had been in the bush out back. She was praying he had not heard the squawk of the radio.

"Uh…Matt, my husband, and Ellie and Tim…" She was hoping he had not seen the RCMP truck parked below.

"So you all came all the way out here because…?"

"Because Tess went missing, and we were worried about her, of course!" She had finally found her voice, her indignation spilling over in a spate of explosive fury. "We had no idea where she had gone. She could have easily been killed! You know there's a grizzly around here somewhere?"

"Yeah, woman, and you better keep your voice down, or likely that bear'll get you right up close! Why do you think I'm out here with this gun? I saw the bear out the front window at first light this morning." He continued on, as if to himself, "Stupid bitch! Fucking city slicker don't know her arse from her elbow in the bush! And I'm nice enough to show you Beth's grave to prove I ain't got nothing to hide where she's concerned. I don't think you understand missus…"

His mood swung again, his face assuming a crafty appearance, his eyes narrowed on her in speculation. "You been nosing around the burnt-out house, ain't you? That's where you been before here, right?"

"We had to come by it to get here, and we stopped to look for Tess's tracks in the snow."

Her answer did not seem to satisfy him, for he shook her again and breathed into her face, "Tell me who's been digging around there." He had pulled her back from the brink of the cliff and now forced her to sit down with her back against the trunk of a tree while he prowled around her. She tried to control her chattering teeth.

"D-D-Digging? There was a f-fire, and there's b-been an investigation to f-find out how it started, you know. Tess told us you g-got out. We're…uh…very…glad you're okay, Hank." She finished up with a watery smile she hoped he would see as genuine.

"Out by the shed next to the garden. The digging there. I told those kids not to go there! But I ain't sure now that it wasn't a bear nosing in there. I took a shot at the one I seen there yesterday, and I think I got it in the haunch, so now it's real pissed off."

"What was there, Hank, where the b-bear was d-digging?" She was trying to keep her tone light and conversational, but the chattering of her teeth made the effort almost comical. Still, she was feeling a new confidence now, knowing he was off balance, vulnerable even, but just as she knew he would like to talk about the body, she also knew it was a tightrope she walked in pursuing that subject.

"There was a woman. I might of told you about her before maybe? Rosie Joseph? She was one helluva a woods woman, I tell you. Nobody, but nobody could match her skill in the bush. I had a lotta respect for that squaw!"

Catching Abby's shocked reaction to the last words made him come over and poke her with the rifle again. "Never you mind what I call her! She was a squaw, a female Injun, wasn't she? That don't mean she was something less than a white woman!"

Abby, sensing he wanted to keep talking, nodded, "Of course, you clearly had a close connection with her."

"Oh it was close all right! We was pretty tight, you know what I mean? She was a right lusty one! She knew where to fish for a trouser trout!"

Abby could barely control her impulse to retch. "Really, Hank, I didn't realize. I guess…uh…Mrs. Talbot didn't mind?"

"Oh, she didn't know. This was when Tess was on the way you know. We couldn't. Anyways, Beth was a different sort altogether, but Rosie. Now she was something else, sort of like you might be, I'm thinking." He knelt down on one knee to come to her level. His eyes travelled up and down her seated body. "Why don't you open your top a little, Abby? It's not real cold here now."

Abby thought that now she was definitely going to puke. Jesus!

"Now Hank, really, that's no way to talk right next to you wife's grave. You need to be more respectful, don't you think?" Her shivering had stopped, but now she felt a cold dread seeping through her innards.

"Shit no! She's dead, and you're not."

"Uh, back to Rosie, Hank. Tell me what happened to her. Did she just go away after a while?"

"Yeah, she went away all right. She had a little accident. " His head was down, but he raised his eyes and peered past his eyebrows to see Abby's reaction. "We was playing around in the shed. It was a good spot to keep an eye on the house from there, and outta nowhere, that Casey showed up. He'd heard us arguing. The stupid bitch was telling me she had to tell Beth what was going on with us, and I couldn't let her do that! Beth didn't need to know! Rosie said she had to tell Beth and leave."

Silence fell with his last words. Abby waited for him to continue. "And?" she prompted carefully.

"Casey heard her and realized her and me had a thing going. I guess he didn't like that much. I figure old Casey had took to Rosie himself, but anyways, he was some disgusted with her being with me, and pushed me aside to slap her around a bit. It happened so fast I couldn't do nothing to stop him. She fell and hit her head. Then, I took a poke at him and next thing I know, he punched me up good and knocked me out. Must of been a boxer!

"When I woke up, Casey was gone and Rosie was dead. So I buried her quick. I couldn't have any questions about how she died. I always meant to do it proper, because I only put her in a shallow grave, but I never did. And now something has disturbed her, probably that bear after the fire. Fuck! I took a shot at it a while back when I saw it nosing around. I clipped it in the rear, and now it's still out there, pissed right off." He paused. "I don't know where Casey went. Never seen him again."

"Can you prove Casey did it? Why are you telling me all this, Hank?"

"Cause I gotta come clean about it, if the body's come up. Besides, I'm thinking actually, Abby, you like me, don't you? I could tell by the way you looked at me that first day you come out to the ranch with your man. You had that look in your eyes. I can tell when a woman likes me. You're just that uppity type that likes to play hard to get. But you don't really think I'm a bad guy, do you?"

"I don't know…that's right…you should let the cops know…she's on record as a missing person…" She knew now that he was delusional, that life for him was something lived apart from the reality of what normal people experienced. His fixation on her just now was evidence for her that he was becoming unhinged, that he lived in some fantasy world, maybe some holdover from some wartime-related mental breakdown where he was the irresistible hero no woman could resist. Perhaps, if she could just keep him believing long enough that she was on his side, he would let down his guard, and she could get away somehow.

Just then, they heard what sounded like a shotgun blast way off on the other side of the cabin clearing. Grabbing Abby's arm, Hank began shoving her recklessly in front of him through the bush in the direction of the distant gunshot. "C'mon, move your ass, woman! I gotta know what's going on! Who's got the gun?" He hauled on her arm, twisting it painfully to pull her close to him, his face close enough that she could feel the stubble on his cheek. "I said, who's using the rifle?"

Her voice faltered, her mouth so dry she felt it was full of sawdust. "Tim has a shotgun. Maybe the bear…"

"Don't you make a sound…you hear?" He punctuated his demand with another poke of the rifle just as another blast sounded from the same direction.

Abby, her arm wrenched at an impossible angle, just nodded in terror as she floundered along.

# 50

# Fur Flies

Back in the cabin, Matt shouted, "Where's Abby?" The panic in his voice aroused Tess from her crying jag on the bunk bed and brought Ellie inside from the front porch.

"I don't know…wasn't she with you on the porch?" Tess was fully alert now and jumped up to check the back door. "Maybe she went to the outhouse?" Ellie stood in the back doorway following Tess's steps as she ducked out the back to check the privy.

When Tess came back in, Matt was pacing, his panic focused on Abby's disappearance. "She's not there? I don't even have any way of getting word to the cops that she's gone! Why in hell would she leave?" Flinging his arm in the direction of the bush behind the cabin, he exploded, "How stupid! She must be out there somewhere!"

In the meantime, through the front window they could see Tim heading for the cabin, shushing as fast as he could go on show-shoes across the open expanse in front, the shotgun waggling wildly on its strap over his shoulder. Behind him by fifty or so yards, lumbering along at a respectable pace given its size, was the grizzly, its golden brown fur raised along the hump at the top of its back. Clearly, it was enraged as it vocalized its growl, a deep, breathy rasping that boomed across the clearing like the sound of countless rusty saw blades being scraped across barbed wire. The bear was heading straight for Tim, whose eyes were bulging in terror as he swung across the meadow, his back hunched over and his arms swinging wide to provide momentum.

Far in the distance, they could just make out the figures of Nora and Jed following up on the bear. They were also themselves shushing steadily on their snowshoes, though at not so frantic a pace as Tim. Matt and Ellie could see Jed had the rifle off the shoulder harness and was holding it ready to shoot. They couldn't quite make out what Nora was doing, as her figure was obscured behind Jed's, but they suspected she had her rifle loaded as well.

Suddenly, from an angle high on the hillside, there was the blast of a rifle. It brought everyone in the cabin out onto the porch. The drama had become suddenly much more complex, as there could be no doubt that the source of that shot had been Hank.

Ellie whispered, "Dad just shot in the direction of the bear. From up there, he can see the field and where the bear is. He's trying to distract it, probably just hoping to scare or daze it to give Tim enough time to get to the cabin. We've had grizzly trouble before. Dad knows bears."

"But does your dad realize that there are other people beside Tim down there, possibly coming into his range of fire? He could hit the cops if a shot ricochets. Now that would be a stupid move!" Matt was still wildly alternating between searching the right hillside to see if he could spot Abby, and at the front, keeping track of the bear's progress as it trundled across the clearing towards Tim's figure, now much closer.

"Let's hope Dad *doesn't* know there are cops out there," Ellie breathed, her voice grim. "Everyone inside!"

Backing towards the door, she held it open as Tim scrambled up to the porch and flung off his snowshoes in a wild arc against the house. He staggered to the cabin door right after all the others had gone through and, after leaping through and landing on his knees, banged it shut just as the grizzly, no more than twenty feet behind, rumbled across the cabin clearing, its mouth frothing as it snuffled up the rise, its throat continuing to emit horrific, rasping snarls as it neared the porch.

It halted on all fours near a solitary, tall, wide-spreading spruce. It stood on its hind legs to sniff the air. The audience inside the cabin observed Nora and Jed stop as well. They were watching where the bear had risen in all its majestic fury.

"Why don't they shoot?" Matt had opened a side window, still trying to catch sight of where Hank was hiding with his rifle.

"He ain't got a clear shot yet. It's too far. " Tim breathed the words, "and the hayshed and tree are in the way. That bear is touchy as hell. All I did was look at it the wrong way, and it took after me. I shot upwards to warn the others off, but you can see where it's injured. Look. I didn't do that." The animal was close enough that they could make out the matted fur around a wound in its haunch.

Time hung in the balance. The grizzly was sniffing to determine what had happened to its quarry, and Nora and Jed were frozen in their tracks until the bear made its move. The wild cards in the drama, though, were Hank and the fact that Jed and Nora could not know that Abby was out there as well.

"Abby!!" Matt's voice was a strangled cry across the clearing. As much to himself as to the others, he added, "Maybe the cops will hear me and know she's not in here with us! They won't shoot if she's in the middle, will they?"

Hank's next shot, which appeared to come from just behind a bluff south of the cabin and to the rear of the spruce tree, acted like a key to unlock the action. The bullet hit close enough to the grizzly to send it bellowing up the wooded bluff.

Ellie spoke again, "Most folks around here know that shooting at a grizzly will attract it because they might think there's some kill. Dad's trying to draw it away from us."

Tim, by now having reloaded the shotgun with slugs in the cabin, raced back out onto the porch.

Matt watched him go and turned to Ellie asked, "He's going with just a shotgun?"

"Yeah, but he's loaded it with slugs. That'll take down a grizzly if he can get close enough, a hundred yards or so. He shouldn't go, though. It's too risky. His chances of getting a clear shot in this bush are zip. A shotgun with slugs is what you use if the bear's facing you close, advancing, or in a stand-off."

Tim had been hoping to catch the grizzly before it disappeared from sight, but he was too late. With astonishing speed, the beast crashed up the hillside disappearing into the brush beyond their line of sight. Not fifty yards farther along the same hillside, they could see the movement of somebody hurtling down the incline towards the clearing.

"Oh my God! Abby?" Matt called from the porch.

A sharp snarl erupted from beneath the porch, and Mooch exploded out from where he had been watching the action. Tess raced out onto the porch in a futile effort to call Mooch back. By now, they could hear the grizzly thrashing through the underbrush of the incline and could follow its route as the ripple of brush movement progressed up the hill. It would have to change direction to intercept whoever was coming down. Somewhere, in all that rustling of snow-covered brush, Mooch was barking a frenetic tattoo. Then, they heard the shrill howl of a dog in pain, and the corresponding deep growl of the bear on the attack.

Fifty yards below, Abby shot out of the underbrush, running to escape Hank who, while aiming at the bear, had lost his grip on her. Now, she was floundering wildly through the deep snow across the clearing towards the cabin, her face beet-red with exertion. In the distance, they could hear the reunion of Mooch and Hank who could be heard shouting, "Get down, dammit!" The dog must have managed to elude the bear.

By this time, Nora and Jed were almost at the point where Hank had first aimed at the bear. They veered off in the direction they had seen it go, first stopping to unstrap their snowshoes at the perimeter. Then, they disappeared, the hillside swallowing them up just as it had done Mooch and the bear.

Tim was still standing on the porch watching as Abby neared the cabin, but Matt had moved down to help her up the last incline. Then, Tim turned to Ellie, "I'm going out."

"Why, Tim? There's enough firepower out there now."

"I ain't planning on shooting. I can't see good enough in the bush to be sure of a target, but I don't plan to set back and do nothing."

"Why do you have to go do something? You know the chances of killing that bear with a slug are zero unless you're close enough to put yourself in danger too!"

"All I know is the old man's out there, and he has a bear after him. I know he's been a bastard, but it don't seem right somehow to just leave him to that bear. He'd do something for us if we was out there."

"And you can check to see if Mooch is okay, too…" Tess interjected.

Matt stepped up. "None of us is going anywhere. There are two cops out there armed with heavy-duty rifles. Hank's got his Magnum. They don't need any of us getting in the way. We need to stay inside where it's safe. In fact, we should stay away from the windows. There's no telling where a stray shot might go." Now that Abby was safe, he had recovered his composure. His eyes swept the group standing like statues on the porch, and he moved to wrap his arms around Abby who still stood traumatized. "Abby, you look done in. It's damned cold out there and you have no jacket. Let's all get inside and get some heat and coffee."

Out on the hillside, Nora and Jed were carefully tracking Hank and the grizzly. Both had their rifles loaded. They had already radioed the Moose Forks detachment to notify the duty clerk of the most recent developments. They were expecting to hear back from Wasniki.

Speaking softly, Nora asked Jed, "What charge do we cite for arrest, Jed?"

"Let's see how this grizzly thing plays out first." Jed stamped his feet to improve his circulation. Standing around in the snow had its downside. "We just may have to take it out. You cover Hank, and I'll deal with the bear." He nodded towards his rifle. "It's important that Talbot doesn't get away. We'll figure out what charge to use once we have him in custody, but the imperative right now is taking down the bear."

They had at one point caught sight of the grizzly's golden brown pelt and were gauging what direction to take to track it through the underbrush. They could hear it grunting up the hill to their right.

Just then, nearby, they heard gunshot, the yelp of a dog and a furious roar.

Frantically clamouring in the direction of the commotion, they cleared the crest of the hill to catch a brief glimpse of Mooch scampering in and out barking furiously at the grizzly as it advanced towards Hank, who was trying to take cover behind a couple of lodge pole pines. He appeared to be holding his wrist as if it were injured.

"Where's his rifle?" Nora looking through her binoculars could see that Hank was now on his knees reaching around with his left arm feeling the ground for something. "He must have dropped the rifle, Jed." It seemed unlikely that Hank could have been so careless, yet he clearly seemed to be favouring his right hand, and his rifle was gone.

Jed shook his head and glanced briefly at Nora who echoed his thoughts, "I think likely the bear knocked it out of his hand. That would have been a close call. We have to hope we can stop its attack."

In response, Jed just nodded grimly and tilted his head for her to follow him closer to where the grizzly was still advancing. Hank had retreated farther along and now was crouching at the foot of a rocky outcropping, backed up against a crevasse in the bluff. In front of him was a clump of low spreading fir that had divided into two trunks early in its life. The density of its lower limbs obscured a clear view of Hank. They could just make out the blue check of his padded lumberjack shirt. Nora stepped back to let Jed take the lead, wondering at the same time whether Hank had managed to recover his rifle.

She used the pause to take another look at the situation through her binoculars. In horror, she realized that Hank had moved to a place where he could be trapped if the bear kept advancing, and they were still too far from the bear to get a good shot at it. At least from her position, an outcropping of rock and several good-sized trees obstructed the view through her rifle's scope. The bullet might ricochet.

Jed's prospects were no better, "We've got to get closer! Listen to that racket!" Their ears were being assaulted with the uproar of the bear lunging and growling at Mooch as the snarling dog fought to defend itself and its master. Creeping closer up the hillside, they could see that the Lab was lunging and snapping at the bear, thus far with such speed that it had eluded those enormous claws. It couldn't go on for long, though. The dog was tiring, and the bear getting angrier, its fur rising in a giant ruff on the back of its neck as it swung its paws to lash the dog. In behind, no more than twenty feet away, Hank stood agape, reaching with his empty hands up into the tree as if trying to get a handhold.

"Look, Hank may be a dead man…" In horror they watched as the bear swiped the dog off its feet with a sickening crack. Mooch landed in a pitiful heap to one side, and the action paused briefly as the grizzly lumbered over to inspect its kill. In the interval, Hank made a dash to get away from the crevasse, but was stopped when the bear swung back in his direction.

"Hank!" Jed yelled, "We'll try to get a shot at it. Get down!" Turning to Nora, he pointed her over to the right, so he could take the left. From about ten yards distance, the bear turned and plunged towards the sound of Jed's voice, but seemed to change its mind to focus on Hank once again, gnashing its jaws and swinging its massive head from side to side. The unearthly rasping growls seemed to be intensifying. Nora was awestruck by the magnitude and ferocity of the huge creature as it momentarily raised itself on its hind legs and swayed back and forth.

Nora positioned herself to set up a shot. She sighted the skull of the bear in her scope and was about to pull the trigger when the grizzly moved behind one trunk of the twin fir tree. On the far left side, she thought she could see where Jed was arranging himself to fire.

When the explosion split the air, it seemed to spur the bear to even greater rage as it rose on its rear legs to a full seven feet and lunged forward. With a mighty swing of its front paw, it swatted a powerful jolt at Hank's head as he cowered, trapped in the crevasse. Nora had by now scrambled close enough to see Hank crumpled lifeless on the ground, and to catch a horrifying glimpse of the bear batting and sniffing at the body, and trying to drag it away. Nora's first thought was that Hank might be just unconscious. She took aim again, this time a clear shot to the bear's skull, right behind the ear. It was a near miss.

Jed shouldered the Winchester and yelled over to her, "Better from here!" His shot also went wide. The bear, distracted from its prey by the shots, was now flashing its great yellow teeth and swinging its head from one side to the other as if trying to decide which one of them to attack first. It still stood over Hank's body on all fours behind the double fir tree.

Nora took two shots in rapid succession. All her Depot training on the firing range had suddenly kicked in. The shots seemed to bounce off the massive skull, the bear swatting at them as if chasing off irksome gnats. With astonishing speed, it wheeled around the base of the tree and launched itself in her direction, a heaving mass of ursine fury, foaming at the mouth. Nora's third shot hit the tree just above its head, and she began to doubt they could ever stop it. But the fourth connected in one last deadly shot, piercing the bear's amber eye. The animal stood wavering, its head half-raised for a moment as if questioning its fate, then collapsed into the snow with a thud.

"Stand back! We don't know if he's done yet!" Jed's voice was calm, but Nora could hear that edge in it, that clear, crisp sharpness that killing created, as if one had stood on the rim and looked over the edge into the abyss.

After waiting a moment to be sure the grizzly would not rise again, Jed trudged over and put another round into its head just behind the ear. The shot echoed hollow in the now silent bush. Nora followed over for a closer look. The mass of the body emitted a vaguely fishy aroma mixed with the scent of wet grass. She moved to where Hank lay crumpled at the base of the twin fir.

The dead stare of Hank's one undamaged eye amid the shredded flesh of his face and neck told them all they needed to know. The bear had broken Hank's neck with that one powerful swing. He had not felt the subsequent assaults as claws and teeth had done their bloody work. The body seemed so much smaller now that he was gone. Between them, Nora and Jed lifted it and carried it haltingly down the hill to lay it on the cabin porch.

No one needed to break the news to the Talbot children. Before anyone could stop them, they had rushed out to the porch to see the gruesome evidence for themselves. With tremendous difficulty, Nora kept her own feelings in check as she tried to frame her words carefully, "Ellie… Tess…Tim, I'm so sorry! We really tried to get to him in time. The bear must have knocked his rifle off into the bush somewhere, and he couldn't get to it. He couldn't defend himself, and we couldn't get a clear shot." She opened the door of the cabin to lead them back inside where they would not have to face the reality of their father's grisly end.

Nora felt quite helpless in the face of the girls' grief. They collapsed shrieking and sobbing on the floor of the cabin. As she watched them, Nora was struck by how the death of even a cruelly abusive father could be mourned. Abby encircled them protectively, her own face streaming.

Outside, Matt led Tim to sit on the porch while Jed found a sleeping bag to wrap around Hank's body. Then, Jed trudged back up the hill to retrieve the body of Tess's Mooch to lay it beside Hank. Afterwards, with his characteristic calm, he radioed in to inform the detachment of the latest developments, and to notify the Conservation Service that the RCMP had been forced to kill one of its grizzlies.

# 51

## Nora Has a Late Night Visitor

Nora closed the door into her apartment with a purposeful bum thrust. McNab, the cat, meandered over purring his welcome. She picked him up and strummed his ears, and he responded with a head butt to her chin. It had been a long day since she had first set out for the ranch with the search party that morning. Now, after several more weary hours of filing the paperwork on the Talbot case, she realized how grateful she was to be home with only the cat for company.

Abby's statement had clarified Hank Talbot's role in the death of Rosemary Joseph, but had raised the likelihood that Casey, whoever he was, should be charged with culpable homicide. She still had to follow-up on contacting Rosemary's family to notify them of the discovery of her body, but thought she would wait until the forensic report came back.

Thinking over the day, she smiled to remember Jed's thoughtful retrieval of Mooch, Tess's dog. The girl had been distraught enough over the death of her father, but the added shock of realizing that Mooch had died defending him had unhinged her. Ellie had stepped up though, quickly offering to find her a pup to replace Mooch, and though Tess had denied wanting one, by the time they were on the road back to town, Ellie said she was inquiring shyly about what kind of pup they should look for. The essential resilience of youth was heartening.

Nora turned on the television and collapsed on the sofa, ready to wind down until the sign-off. She had had no supper but didn't feel hungry. She just felt somehow empty, as if the death of Hank had drained her of some elemental energy.

The knock on the door roused her from half sleep. Nora looked around as if unsure of her surroundings and then grimaced. Who the hell would that be? It was almost ten o'clock, too late for impromptu social visits.

"Trick or treat!" Luke stood there in a cowboy hat and simulated cowhide mask holding a six-pack. In her fog, she dimly recalled it was still Halloween.

Luke saw her consternation and raised his hands in surrender, "Hey, I know it's late, but I just stopped by the detachment to see how the Talbot thing was going, and they said you had gone home. Thought you might like to celebrate a little, but that's okay. I can see you're pretty done in."

She smiled in gratitude. Luke was so sweet that she hated to be such a sorry ass. She opened the door and gestured him in. "Just for a bit, okay? I'm all in. It's been a long day." They sat down on the little couch and opened two beers.

"No sweat, I've got a shift at seven tomorrow morning, anyway. I just want you to feel proud. You pushed this thing and got it done! Jack tried to stonewall you, and he lost. That's worth something."

"Yeah, it's worth a trip out of Moose Forks, Luke. You realize I've asked for a transfer? I'm pretty sure Wasniki can hardly wait to get that rolling."

Luke's face fell. "No, I didn't. Are you serious? Why would he want to lose you? You just helped close a case! I've been wondering if Casey was involved in the Terrace case, you know that young girl found last year? Maybe we can get some details to compare. Was this girl, Rosemary Joseph, was she strangled? Monica in Terrace was strangled, and dumped in a ditch. But Rosemary was buried wasn't she?"

"Whoa, Luke, I'm not sure we can make connections. Maybe. First of all, we haven't had the forensic report yet. It's probably Rosemary, but we can't know for sure how she died until we get that. I suspect the body is too far-gone to determine soft tissue injuries for one thing. And Talbot, in his confession, specifically didn't tell Abby Clarke that Casey killed her, just that Casey hit her and she fell. Talbot's dead, so we can't know for certain now how much he was responsible, or whether he was just blaming this Casey. Also, Casey, whoever he is, could still be around so we should look for him to clear up the case.

"As for Sergeant Wasniki valuing my contribution here, I'm not so sure. My guess is that I showed him up so his pride is hurt, not to mention that I compromised his reputation within the Force by letting it be known all the way to Prince George that I think he's incompetent. Sending those photos cooked my goose, I suspect. I doubt he sees me as an asset!"

Luke sat speechless. There was little he could say to counter her arguments. "I did hear about the photos. In fact, Eddie and I had a quiet little chuckle about that! But I have to admit, my interest here is a tad personal." His eyes sought hers, but she avoided them. Now was the right moment to tell him. Being romantically involved when they worked in the same space was too complicated. He ruined her concentration, and she was still thinking about Erik too often.

"Luke, I think it might be for the best if I do move on. I do like you, and don't want this to be some big break-up thing, you know? It's just, I don't know, I need some time before…"

"Oh, I get it, Nora, you don't have to spell it out. You just want to be friends, right?"

'Yes, but not how you mean 'just friends', Luke. I am attracted to you, I really am. Actually, that's part of why I know I should move. At work, it's hard for me to keep my feelings separate from…I mean I react when you're there, and that's not a good thing. I think that I need at least some time to grow into the job, maybe."

She wasn't quite sure how to gauge the look in his eyes. Was it puzzlement or disbelief? There was a severity about the mouth she had never noticed before. Then his face crumpled into a grin, and he reached out to hug her.

With his arms wrapped around her, he nuzzled her ear and murmured, "Nora, honey, I'm just glad you explained the 'friends' bit." His lips sought her mouth, and she felt the crush of his chin against her cheek, and the darting tip of his tongue as he thrust it to meet hers. It was a dizzying kiss that left her a bit shocked and breathless. She hadn't expected such a display of desire. "This doesn't feel like 'just friends' to me, anyway." There was a touch of mockery in his voice.

He released her so that he could look at her directly and continued, "That line is almost always the kiss of death for a guy. I get that you want some space and time. I just hope you don't get a posting so far away that we can't keep in touch, you know?" He reached out to massage her shoulders gently.

"So do I." She did want to stay connected, she had decided. Since her split with Erik, there had been no one else except Luke who had kindled those dormant feelings. "There's always the phone, Luke. And maybe we can get together during time off?"

"Yeah, maybe we can." His smile lit up his face, and the hazel eyes flashed a wicked twinkle. "I hear there's a new hotel in Prince George with a huge indoor tropical garden and spa attached. Maybe we can check it out sometime."

"Well, I don't know about a hotel stay…"

"Oh, come on, Nora. Lighten up. I just meant for lunch and a swim."

"Sure you did…" she nodded, laughing. Somehow, Luke always managed to salvage her most naïve reactions from seeming immature.

"Well, you need your sleep after today, so I better go, much as I'd like to ask to stay."

Nora chose to ignore his last words. She smiled, stifling a yawn as she got up to see him to the door. "Thanks for stopping by. It means a lot to me that you did." After a last lingering kiss, she shut the door, and reflected that she did feel exhausted, but somehow exhilarated too.

# 52

# Rosemary's People

"What's the follow-up to the Talbot case, Jed? Have you asked Wasniki about that beaded backpack?"

Nora and Jed were alone in the office, Wasniki being away at his monthly district meeting in Glacier Lake. Nora was finishing up the paperwork in Hank Talbot's file. Tess's statement about the fire and Abby's about Rosemary's death had cleared all pending charges. Abby had come in to make a statement about her last conversation with Hank Talbot so the circumstances of Casey's disappearance had been clarified. A search had started to determine his identity and next of kin. No results thus far. All that remained unfinished was the identity of the human remains found next to the garden.

"We're waiting on that forensic report to give us a lead on the identity. If it's female and aboriginal, we can make a case for its being Rosemary Joseph. Hank's confession to Abby Clarke would fit in with the facts, too."

"But the backpack being right there in the shed should solidify that case, shouldn't it? It was seen in Rosemary's possession in the Polaroid, and it was in the shot of the interior of the garden shed taken during our first look after the fire. As for Wasniki's part in all this, I say removing associative evidence from a crime scene and taking it home contravenes chain of custody. He must have known better. There's also the question of whether he was trying to protect Hank Talbot somehow, in which case, that's obstruction of justice."

Fedoruk's face was a study in conflict. "You may be right, but in order to prove Sergeant Wasniki's culpability, we have to prove the backpack is the same one that Rosemary carried. Unfortunately, the photos we have are black and white and the actual image of the bag is incomplete, so we can't use it. The beading might not be the same colour, for instance."

"Do we have probable cause to ask for a search warrant for his place? Then we can show the actual bag to Ellie…"

"I'd rather go the route of asking him to surrender any artifact he might think would be helpful in the investigation. Once he realizes the bag is a critical piece of evidence, I suspect he'll cooperate. He's already embarrassed that he's been championing Hank Talbot. I don't think it'll take much for him to see reason. He loves the Force. He won't want to sully it."

"Do you think he didn't realize the importance of that bag? He looked through the file while we were interviewing Ellie. That photo was there."

"Then maybe he missed the bag. It's hard to say. He should have known not to take it from the shed, of course. But I don't think we can prove any deliberate obstruction of justice."

"That's the way it works, I guess? It's a stressful job with few perks so we give each other the benefit of the doubt?" Nora wanted a cigarette. "And I shouldn't bitch, because I may need the same consideration one day?"

Jed considered her, his face a mask. "We're all human, Nora. That's all. He's a veteran officer with a clean record." He noticed her astonishment, and quickly continued, "Yes, I have checked his record. I have at least some pull at HQ. And I say we wait for the forensic report, and then I'll show him what we have, the Polaroid, and the crime scene shot of the shed, and I'll ask him for the bag back. Okay?"

Nora hesitated. Was this complicity? Or just reasonable compassion for a fellow officer? Oh hell, she had requested a transfer anyways. She nodded, avoiding Jed's eyes.

Two days later, the forensic report came back from Prince George. The remains found in the garden were deemed to be female, and the length of the skeleton was consistent with what they estimated from the Polaroid to have been the height of Rosemary Joseph. A forensic anthropologist from UBC had confirmed that the remains were indigenous. They had been in the ground for between ten and fifteen years. The cause of death was uncertain, but the neck vertebrae did appear to have suffered some trauma. There could be little doubt of the identity now.

Nora followed up with a phone call to the RCMP Detachment in Babine Landing, requesting that contact be made with Stanley and Verna Joseph, on record as Rosemary's parents, to notify them that there was news of their daughter, and that they should contact the Moose Forks Detachment as soon as possible.

The next day, a bright sunny November morning, Nora was sitting at the front desk checking out some traffic stats when Jed dropped a brown paper bag on top of her paperwork.

"What's this? I'm trying to get this tally done!"

"Just look…you'll like it…" His eyes were smiling.

Looking into the bag, she saw the rough, tawny leather of a moose hide article. Pulling it out, she was assailed by a sweet, pungent aroma. Unfolded on her lap, the bag revealed the intricate black, white and brown beadwork of a standing bull moose, the blue line of beading at its knees the mere suggestion of the pond water where it would graze. It was an artful and original rendering, not reminiscent of anything Nora had ever seen.

"What did he say?" Nora was touched by Jed's effort. She knew he must have had to call in some favours with Wasniki to retrieve the bag.

"Not much. He just reminded me that you had requested a transfer, as if to see if I would object, or maybe to figure out if you had changed your mind. But there was no hassle about the bag. He knew he was wrong to have it."

"Did he say how he came by it?"

"Yeah, the day the arson team showed up, he said he saw it and waited until they were busy before tucking it into his personal bag. He even said he thought about putting it back, but when he saw it in the file photos, he knew it was too late, so my guess is he just decided to pretend he had always owned it."

"Humph! Just another knickknack for his rec room!" Her indignation rose as she recalled his pride in the indigenous artifact collection. "Was it empty?"

"He said there was nothing inside when he took it."

"So you're satisfied he wasn't trying to protect Hank Talbot?"

"I don't think he was. He would have hidden it better, I think, or destroyed it if he really thought it would make a difference to our case against Hank. Anyway, Nora, we have it now to give back to her family, if that helps."

"Yes, we have notified the family. They will want it, I'm sure."

"What about the Talbot kids?" It was Jed's turn to ask questions. "Have you seen them this last week?"

"I talked with Ellie when we released her father's body to them for burial. I guess their plan was to bury him beside their mother. Ellie said Tess still wanted to stay out there, but she knows she can't manage on her own, and she can't miss school. Ellie was very clear about that."

"Yeah, she should be in school." Jed had developed an almost paternal bond with the kids during that fateful afternoon. "At least until she's sixteen."

"Yes, Ellie says she'll do her best. The Clarkes are on side too. Tim can get a leave to keep the ranch going until the girls decide what to do. No doubt Tess will want to keep it, and Ellie will help now that Hank's gone, so they'll be okay, I think. They're pretty tight, those three."

"Well, they've been through a lot together. They've had to grow up fast. And you, Nora? Are you going to retract that request for transfer?"

Nora regarded Jed solemnly. "Oh, I don't think so. I think I would find it hard to work with the sergeant the way things are. I just hope he doesn't give me a negative report to drag along to my next posting."

"Don't worry on that score. I got more than the bag when I bargained with him today."

Nora's smile lit up her face. "Hey, I'll miss working with you, buddy!"

"Ditto, Constable!"

A few days later, the parents of Rosemary Joseph from Old Fort Babine came down to Moose Forks. Arriving with them were at least a dozen soft-spoken, kind-faced matrons and dignified elders, all relatives of the Joseph family. When they asked to see the remains, they also wanted to hear the story of their discovery.

Nora and Jed spent an afternoon with them recounting the story of the unexpected discovery of Rosemary's body and of the hunt for Henry Martin Talbot, deceased, who was involved but not directly responsible for her death. They stressed that there was an ongoing investigation into the identity of the cowhand, Casey, who could be charged if he were ever located. Rosemary's parents did not speak English very well, so everything had to be translated into Wetsuwit'en, the language of the Lake Babine people.

Chief Angus Peter, speaking for the band, thanked the RCMP for their efforts and for helping them to find their missing sister. "It's only fitting that she had been a member of the Grizzly Clan because, in the end, "Cas" – that's the Wetsuwit'en word for grizzly – has exacted some revenge for the loss of her life. She lived her life following the ways of our people. Cas did not forget her."

Afterwards, Nora asked, "How long have you been looking for Rosemary?"

Chief Peter reflected a moment, and replied in a voice so soft that Nora had to cock her ear to catch it all. "She left home as a youngster, about fourteen maybe, and went to live with an aunt in the woods. She didn't want to go back to that school, the church one, anymore. It had hurt her spirit to be there she said. She suffered at that school, I think. The nuns and priests were not kind to her. When she ran away the last time, she was about fourteen or fifteen. She came home to tell us she had to go away because she didn't want to go back. So she left to live on the land.

"Over the years, she came back to the village regular. But she wouldn't stay. She learned to hunt and fish as a girl and knew the ways of the woods good. Her aunt, Sophie Maurice, was a healer and taught Rose everything she needed to know, so she could live without help from us. Most of her time she was looking for healing herbs and food to feed herself and Sophie. She was doing good work in her life because whenever she came home, we saw her tending to our sick and helping with birthing. She was a true healer."

"And the last time you saw her was when?" Nora was curious about how long Rosemary had been in the Moose Forks area.

"I don't know the year for sure." He turned to Verna and Stanley and posed the question to them in Wetsuwit'en. They whispered back and forth a moment or two before looking back to Nora and waiting for Chief Peter to translate. "They say she came back for the last time the same year the salmon came back in a big run on the Skeena, I think, 1962."

"Do you remember where she had been before coming home?" Nora wanted to get a sense of how wide an area Rosemary had travelled.

After a brief question to the parents, Chief Peter responded, "Her last place was in the Kispiox Valley, north of Hazelton."

"Did they ever hear from any of the police in those other towns you contacted? Any word of Rosemary being spotted in other places besides Moose Forks?"

Chief Peter seemed to avoid her eyes, and she had to stoop even further to catch his reply. "None of them ever talked to us very much, even when we went there. And they couldn't get word easy to Stan and Verna because they've never had no phone. I said they could call the band office, but we never got no messages. You Moose Forks cops have been all right, though. Too bad it's too late."

Nora nodded and thanked them for talking to her. Once again, she expressed her condolences for their loss.

Chief Peter raised his hands almost in a benediction, "Healers cannot be caged; they must be free to go where the healing takes them. They must be brave to face the world. Our sister had courage."

Nora could only admire the old chief's faith in "the world". She had already seen quite a bit of evidence to the contrary.

She watched in silence as the elders wrapped the cotton package containing Rosemary's remains in a moose hide shroud and arranged the beaded backpack on top of it. She wondered how many others were out there. How many daughters, sisters, mothers? How many other Rosies? Generous, loving, trusting, but doomed? How many missing women or girls were lying waiting to be uncovered? She decided she wanted to find out. She would ask for a transfer to keep her in northern BC, somewhere along Highway 16 so she could stay close to the heart of the puzzle.

When Nora's transfer came through in January, she and McNab, the cat, were off to Brandenhoff, a community larger than Moose Forks that lay a couple of hours along Highway 16 to the east. Somehow, she felt upbeat.

Made in the USA
Charleston, SC
20 October 2016